Microsoft Azure
Networking:
The Definitive Guide

Avinash Valiramani

Microsoft Azure Networking: The Definitive Guide

Published with the authorization of Microsoft Corporation by:
Pearson Education, Inc.

ISBN-13: 978-0-13-756989-2
ISBN-10: 0-13-756989-0

Library of Congress Control Number: 2022938822

1 2022

TRADEMARKS

WARNING AND DISCLAIMER

SPECIAL SALES

For information about buying this title in bulk quantities, or for special sales opportunities (which may include electronic versions; custom cover designs; and content particular to your business, training goals, marketing focus, or branding interests), please contact our corporate sales department at corpsales@pearsoned.com or (800) 382-3419.

For government sales inquiries, please contact: governmentsales@pearsoned.com.
For questions about sales outside the U.S., please contact: intlcs@pearson.com.

EDITOR-IN-CHIEF
Brett Bartow

EXECUTIVE EDITOR
Loretta Yates

SPONSORING EDITOR
Charvi Arora

DEVELOPMENT EDITOR
Kate Shoup

MANAGING EDITOR
Sandra Schroeder

SENIOR PROJECT EDITOR
Tracey Croom

COPY EDITOR
Sarah Kearns

INDEXER
Timothy Wright

PROOFREADER
Donna E. Mulder

TECHNICAL EDITOR
Thomas Palathra

EDITORIAL ASSISTANT
Cindy Teeters

COVER DESIGNER
Twist Creative, Seattle

COMPOSITOR
codeMantra

GRAPHICS
codeMantra

Pearson's Commitment to Diversity, Equity, and Inclusion

Pearson is dedicated to creating bias-free content that reflects the diversity of all learners. We embrace the many dimensions of diversity, including but not limited to race, ethnicity, gender, socioeconomic status, ability, age, sexual orientation, and religious or political beliefs.

Education is a powerful force for equity and change in our world. It has the potential to deliver opportunities that improve lives and enable economic mobility. As we work with authors to create content for every product and service, we acknowledge our responsibility to demonstrate inclusivity and incorporate diverse scholarship so that everyone can achieve their potential through learning. As the world's leading learning company, we have a duty to help drive change and live up to our purpose to help more people create a better life for themselves and to create a better world.

Our ambition is to purposefully contribute to a world where:

- Everyone has an equitable and lifelong opportunity to succeed through learning.
- Our educational products and services are inclusive and represent the rich diversity of learners.
- Our educational content accurately reflects the histories and experiences of the learners we serve.
- Our educational content prompts deeper discussions with learners and motivates them to expand their own learning (and worldview).

While we work hard to present unbiased content, we want to hear from you about any concerns or needs with this Pearson product so that we can investigate and address them.

- Please contact us with concerns about any potential bias at https://www.pearson.com/report-bias.html.

Contents at a Glance

Contents

About the Author

Avinash Valiramani is an IT Infrastructure and Cloud Architect with more than 15 years of expertise in areas of Microsoft Technologies such as Microsoft Azure, Microsoft 365, Office365, Windows Server, Microsoft Exchange, SCCM, Intune, Hyper-V, and others. He is a certified Architect on Azure and Microsoft365 and primarily helps enterprises globally in their Cloud Roadmap Architecture and Onboarding/Migration Strategies & Implementation. Avinash is publishing four books on Microsoft Azure Best Practices series including this current one, collating real-world experiences to deliver a comprehensive and concise experience for new and budding technologists. Avinash also holds certifications in Barracuda, AWS, Citrix, VMware, and many other IT/Security industry certifications to complement his Microsoft expertise. He has authored a course of Azure Virtual Desktop for Oreilly Media and is planning many others in the coming months. You can follow Avinash on Twitter at @avaliramani.

Acknowledgments

I would like to thank Loretta Yates for trusting me with this huge responsibility. These books would not have been possible without your confidence in me and I will be forever grateful for that. I would like to thank Charvi Arora and the entire Microsoft Press/Pearson team for their constant support and guidance on this project. I would especially like to thank Kate Shoup for editing and reviewing this book and for all her guidance and attention to detail throughout these series of books. Kate, it has been a wonderful experience writing these four books with you and I could not have asked for a better collaborator. Thanks to Thomas Palathra for his thoughtful technical edits, Sarah Kearns for the amazing copy editing and Tracey Croom for adding the final touches to bring this to fruition. This book is the fruit of all our labor, and I am extremely happy we worked together on it.

I would also like to thank my family with gratitude, especially my brother Junaid and uncle Chandru on this effort. Your assistance in helping me organize my life and ensuring I could stay on track while wearing multiple hats was invaluable. This has been the biggest reason I managed to get this mammoth series of books out and it would not have been possible without all your support during this process. I would like to thank my mom for all her strength and belief throughout the years even when things were not going well and for believing in me throughout. Love you all.

Introduction to Azure networking services

Welcome to *Microsoft Azure Networking: The Definitive Guide*. This book was developed to convey in-depth information about various Azure services that provide networking capabilities, as well as best practices based on real-life experiences using the product in different environments. The book is largely based on the versions of Azure networking services available during 2021 and early 2022, and takes into account the development work done on these services over the years. At that time, there were a few features and functionalities under preview. Because these features could change before becoming available to the general public, the most notable ones will be covered in subsequent iterations of this book, as they become available globally.

Who is this book for?

Microsoft Azure Networking: The Definitive Guide is for anyone interested in Azure infrastructure solutions—not just IT and cloud administrators, network professionals, security professionals, developers, and engineers, but the entire spectrum of Azure users. Whether you have basic experience using Azure or other on-premises or cloud virtualization technologies or you are an expert, you can still derive value from this book. It provides introductory, intermediate, and advanced coverage of each networking service.

The book especially targets those who work in medium to large enterprise organizations and have at least one year of experience in designing, administering, deploying, managing, monitoring, and migrating network infrastructure to services such as Azure virtual networks, Azure Firewall, Azure Web Application Firewall, and others that comprise the Azure network stack.

How is this book organized?

This book is organized into ten chapters:

- Chapter 1: Azure virtual networks
- Chapter 2: Azure Application Gateway

- Chapter 3: Azure VPN gateway
- Chapter 4: Azure Load Balancer
- Chapter 5: Azure Firewall
- Chapter 6: Azure DNS
- Chapter 7: Azure Traffic Manager
- Chapter 8: Azure Front Door
- Chapter 9: Azure Bastion
- Chapter 10: Azure Private Link

Each chapter focuses on a specific Azure networking service, covering the inner workings of each one in depth, walking you through how to build and test the service, and offering real-world best practices to help you maximize your Azure investment.

The approach adopted for this book is a unique mix of didactic, narrative, and experiential instruction:

- Didactic instruction covers the core introductions to the services.
- Narrative instruction leverages what you already understand to help you bridge that knowledge with new concepts introduced in the book.
- Experiential instruction takes into account real-world experiences and challenges facing small and large environments, as well as what factors to consider when designing and implementing workloads. Guided step-by-step walkthroughs show you how to configure each Azure networking service and its related features and options to gain all the benefits each service has to offer.

System requirements

This book is designed to be tested using an Azure subscription. Microsoft offers a 30-day, $200 USD trial subscription that you can use to test most services covered in this book. However, some services, such as dedicated hosts, cannot be used with a trial subscription. Testing and validating these services requires a paid subscription.

The following list details the minimum system requirements needed to use the content provided on the book's companion website:

- Windows 10/11 with the latest updates from Microsoft Update Service
- Azure PowerShell (https://docs.microsoft.com/en-us/powershell/azure/install-az-ps)

- Azure CLI (https://docs.microsoft.com/en-us/cli/azure/install-azure-cli)
- Display monitor capable of 1024 x 768 resolution
- Microsoft mouse or compatible pointing device

About the companion content

The companion content for this book can be downloaded from the following pages:

MicrosoftPressStore.com/AzureNetworkingTDG/downloads

or

https://github.com/avinashvaliramani/AzureNetworkingTDG

Errata, updates, & book support

We've made every effort to ensure the accuracy of this book and its companion content. You can access updates to this book—in the form of a list of submitted errata and their related corrections—at:

MicrosoftPressStore.com/AzureNetworkingTDG/errata

If you discover an error that is not already listed, please submit it to us at the same page.

For additional book support and information, please visit *MicrosoftPressStore.com/Support*.

Please note that product support for Microsoft software and hardware is not offered through the previous addresses. For help with Microsoft software or hardware, go to *http://support.microsoft.com*.

Stay in touch

Let's keep the conversation going! We're on Twitter: *http://twitter.com/MicrosoftPress*.

Overview

Over the years, Microsoft has introduced various services related to the Azure networking stack alongside the Azure compute services designed to leverage them. Microsoft has enhanced these services on a regular basis, making them more robust and resilient as well as easier to deploy and manage. The first of these services was Azure virtual machines (VMs). After that came additional platform as a service (PaaS) solutions like Azure App Service, Azure Container Service, Azure Functions, and Azure Virtual Desktop.

Following is a brief timeline of the announcement of each of these services in public preview:

- **Azure Traffic Manager**   Nov 2013
- **Azure VPN Gateways**   Dec 2014
- **Azure Load Balancer**   Sept 2015
- **Azure Firewall**   Nov 2015
- **Azure Application Gateway**   Sept 2016
- **Azure DNS**   Sept 2016
- **Azure Front Door**   April 2019
- **Azure Bastion**   Nov 2019
- **Azure Private Link**   Feb 2020

Over the years, each service has added new capabilities to Azure's networking stack. These have provided customers with various networking-service options for use based on their application and security requirements.

Each service helps address different requirements in an organization's application design and architecture as well as overall security requirement. Each chapter of this book covers a single service, enabling you to dive into each one to better understand how it works and includes the associated best practices.

Each chapter initially focuses on factors to consider when selecting a particular networking service. Thereafter, it conveys in-depth concepts related to each service and the components that make up that service. This enables you to better understand how each service works. Once you have gained this understanding, you will focus on deployment considerations and strategies, with step-by-step walkthroughs of deployment methods, followed by best practices.

Cloud service categories

As in other books in this series, let us start by first presenting the various cloud-service categories. Currently, cloud services are broken down into four main categories: infrastructure as a service (IaaS), platform as a service (PaaS), function as a service (FaaS), and software as a service (SaaS). SaaS is not relevant to the content covered in this book series, so the following explanations relate to the first three categories:

- **Infrastructure as a service (IaaS)**   Using VMs with storage and networking is generally referred to as IaaS. This is a traditional approach to using cloud services in line with on-premises workloads. Most on-premises environments use virtualization technologies such as Hyper-V to virtualize Windows and Linux workloads. Migrating to IaaS from such an environment is a much easier first step than migrating to PaaS or FaaS. Over time, as an organization's understanding of various other types of cloud services grows, it can migrate to PaaS or FaaS.

- **Platform as a service (PaaS)**   One of the biggest benefits of using a cloud service is the capability to offload the management of back-end infrastructure to the service provider. This model is called platform as a service (PaaS). Examples of back-end infrastructure include the various layers of an application, such as the compute layer, storage layer, networking layer, security layer, and monitoring layer. Organizations can use PaaS to free up their IT staff to focus on higher-level tasks and core organizational needs instead of on routine infrastructure monitoring, upgrade, and maintenance activities. Azure App Service and Azure Container Service are examples of Azure PaaS offerings.

- **Function as a service (FaaS)**   These offerings go one step beyond PaaS to enable organizations to focus only on their application code, leaving the entire back-end infrastructure deployment and management to the cloud service provider. This enables developers to deploy their code without worrying about back-end infrastructure deployment, scaling, and management. It also enables the use of microservices architectures for applications. An example of an Azure FaaS offering is Azure Functions.

In the Azure networking stack, the services largely fall under the PaaS category. For example:

- Azure Firewall is a PaaS service that allows you to deploy a native firewall in Azure to protect both IaaS and PaaS workloads.

- Azure Bastion is a PaaS service that gives you the ability to securely access IaaS VM workloads in Azure using a browser without exposing them directly to the internet.

Each of these cloud service categories has various features and limitations. Limitations might relate to the application, technological know-how, and costs for redevelopment, among others. As a result, most organizations use some combination of various types of cloud services to maximize their cloud investments.

Each service provides a different level of control and ease of management. For example:

- IaaS provides maximum control and flexibility in migration and use.
- FaaS provides maximum automation for workload deployment, management, and use.
- PaaS provides a mix of both at varying levels, depending on the PaaS service used.

Each service also offers varying levels of scalability. For example:

- IaaS requires the use of additional services to achieve true scalability and load balancing—for example, using Azure Load Balancer, a PaaS service, to balance requests across multiple Azure IaaS VMs.
- PaaS and FaaS services are generally designed with built-in scalability and load-balancing features.

Cost-wise, each service provides varying levels of efficiency. For example:

- FaaS offerings charge for compute based only on the usage hours for compute services, making it extremely cost-effective.
- IaaS products charge for compute services regardless of usage once the compute service (for example, a VM) is online.
- PaaS offerings are a mixed bag depending on how the service is configured. Some PaaS products charge for the service regardless of usage, while others, if configured correctly, charge based on usage. For example, Azure Bastion has a fixed monthly cost for the service whereas Azure DNS is charged based on number of domains and number of queries per month.

Service selection factors and strategies

There are certain factors to consider when selecting which Azure networking service would be ideal for a given environment based on the application architecture, connectivity requirements, application security requirements, application delivery requirements, and other business needs. Some of these key factors, and the Azure networking services that best addresses them, are as follows:

- **Deliver applications securely**   The networking stack provides multiple services that you can leverage to securely deliver applications to your end users. These include Azure Front Door, Azure Traffic Manager, and Azure Load Balancer.

- **Protect application connectivity**   You can protect connectivity to the applications using services such as Azure Firewall, Azure Private Link, Azure Web Application Firewall, and Azure Load Balancer. You can use these services individually or in combination to provide higher levels of protection.

- **Provide connectivity to Azure and on-premise resources**   Services such as Azure virtual networks, Azure VPN Gateway, Azure vNET Peering, ExpressRoute, Azure Bastion, and Azure DNS provide you with different connectivity options to securely connect your Azure services to each other and to on-premise hosted services.

As you can see, there are multiple services for each factor. As you get more clarity on your requirements and a better understanding of each of these services, it will become clearer to you when each of these services should be used in your environment, as each one provides distinct capabilities.

Selecting the right load-balancing service

Certain network load-balancing services provide functionality that is similar or overlapping in nature, such as Azure Front Door, Azure Traffic Manager, Azure Load Balancer, and Azure Web Application Gateway. Let us take a moment to narrow down which of these load-balancing services might be best suited for your application. Figure I-1 offers a good starting point for identifying which service might best serve your requirements. While the diagram shown in the figure is not exhaustive, it can help you narrow down which services to focus on before making your final decision.

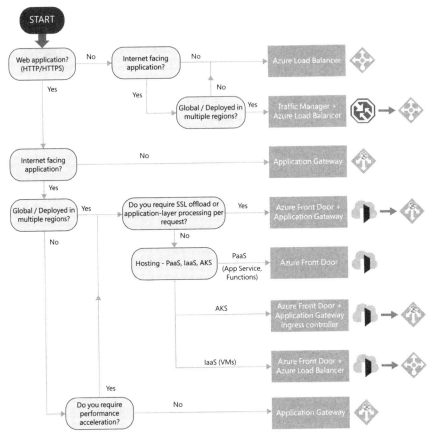

FIGURE I-1 Load-balancing service selection considerations.

Let us examine the flowchart shown in Figure I-1 in more detail.

- **Non-web application workloads** The first factor you should consider is whether your workload is web application–published using HTTP/HTTPS. If not, then the Azure Load Balancer service might be best suited to handle your needs. If your application is hosted in multiple Azure regions with local redundancy in each region, a combination of Azure Traffic Manager and the Azure Load Balancer might be best suited to meet those needs.

- **Web application workloads** When it comes to web application workloads, you need to consider a few factors before you can identify the appropriate service:

- **Will the web app be accessible only internally?** If it will only be accessible internally, then you can use the Azure Application Gateway service. If, however, the web app will be publicly accessible, then you'll need to consider the following factors as well.

- **Will the web application be hosted in multiple Azure regions?** If you plan to host the application in a single Azure region, then Azure Application Gateway might suffice (unless you need to accelerate application performance). If you will be hosting the web app in multiple Azure regions, then there are multiple Azure networking services that you can choose from, including Azure Front Door, Azure Application Gateway, Azure Load Balancer, or a combination of these. To better narrow down the appropriate option, let us continue further down the chain.

- **Will the multi-region public web application require SSL offloading or application request processing?** If this is a requirement, then the Azure Front Door service might be most appropriate for your needs. If, however, you do not require SSL offloading or application request processing, then depending on the application hosting model (such as Azure Kubernetes Service, Azure App Service, Azure Functions, or Azure VMs), you can work with a combination of the Azure Front Door, Azure Application Gateway, and Azure Load Balancer services.

As you can see, different factors can affect your decision-making process. Moreover, these may evolve over time, as your application requirements evolve. You might start with an application hosted in a single region and over time move it to multiple regions for global scalability.

As you read this book, you will better understand how you can leverage these networking services as needed over time to meet your ongoing needs and business demands.

Conclusion

Now that you have an overview of the various Azure networking cloud offerings, let us dive deeper into each of the networking services. We'll start with the network service that forms the backbone of most Azure deployments: Azure virtual networks.

## Chapter 1

Azure virtual networks

Overview

In traditional, on-premises datacenters, virtual networks (vNETs) help connect devices, virtual machines, and datacenters to make services accessible in different locations and across geographic boundaries. A vNET emulates a physical network in that it is a combination of hardware and software resources working together to provide networking capabilities for virtual infrastructure resources. In Azure, a vNET provides the base layer for a private network to host Azure resources, such as Azure virtual machines (VMs), Azure virtual machine scale sets (VMSS), virtual private network (VPN) gateways, firewalls, and so on, to securely connect and communicate with each other and other resources hosted on on-premises networks or on the internet.

Azure virtual networks features

An Azure vNET has a number of unique features to take advantage of the Azure cloud's extensibility, scaling, and global availability. These features help address different types of vNET requirements or scenarios, such as the following:

- **Communication with on-premises resources and services**   Various options are available to communicate with on-premises resources and services such as Azure ExpressRoute, Site-to-Site (S2S) VPN, and Point-to-Site (P2S) VPN. An Azure vNET helps support Azure-based connectivity services, Azure resources, and on-premises resources and services.

- **Communication between Azure resources in the same and different Azure regions**   Azure vNET enables resources within the same vNET, as well as resources in different vNETs in the same or different Azure region using vNET peering, to securely communicate with each other.

- **Communication between Azure and internet-based resources and services**   Inbound connectivity to resources in a vNET requires the use of either a public IP address or public-facing load balancer that can route traffic to internal resources. However, all resources in a vNET can communicate externally by default.

- **Network traffic management**   Azure vNET supports the use of network security groups (NSGs) and network virtual appliances (NVAs) to filter traffic between subnets in the same vNET and between vNETs. Azure vNET also supports using route tables and Border Gateway Protocol (BGP) routes to route traffic between different subnets or networks on-premises or the internet.

- **Integration with Azure services**   Azure vNET supports integration with Azure services such as Azure SQL Database and Azure Storage using Azure Private Link and service endpoints for secure communication over public and private networks.

Design concepts and deployment considerations

vNETs are a backbone of any Azure deployment. It is important to understand the design concepts behind vNETs to deploy them in an optimal manner to achieve scale, security, and redundancy.

Address space

An address space is a private IP address range or series of ranges allocated to a vNET and is used to provide IP addresses to resources hosted in the vNET. For example, if you create a private address space of 10.10.10.0/24, VMs hosted in that vNET would obtain IP addresses between 10.10.10.1 to 10.10.10.251.

Subnets

You can split or segment an address space into multiple network subnets and assign portions of the address space to each subnet. You can then host different Azure resources in different subnets, and apply different routing, traffic-management, and security policies to each subnet based on its resource requirements.

You can extend your current on-premises network address space to Azure to maintain the same IP series in both locations. You should do this only if there are IP dependencies for applications being migrated to Azure, as this type of setup requires careful planning and integration to avoid routing issues.

You can also set up subnet delegation to integrate Azure PaaS services directly into an Azure vNET. This gives full control to the Azure service to set up rules for access to the service via that vNET subnet. You can choose to set up specific subnets just for delegation to such services.

vNET peering

An Azure vNET is scoped to a single region. So, resources that must be hosted in different regions cannot be set up within the same vNET. You can only achieve this using multiple vNET setups in each Azure region where resources must be hosted. However, vNETs *can* be connected to other vNETs using peering. This enables VMs on vNETs in the same or different Azure region to communicate with each other securely. This allows organizations to set up resources as close as possible to the intended target audience, but consolidate key services such as monitoring, logging, data warehousing, and so on in a single region by enabling all resources across vNETs to be able to talk to each other.

> **NOTE** A vNET can be part of only a single Azure subscription. However, a single Azure subscription can host multiple vNETs.

Routing

Azure supports several different types of routing types:

- Default system routes
- Optional system routes
- User-defined routes

The following sections offer details about each of these routing types to give you a better understanding of each one and how best to use them.

Default system routes

Default system routes are automatically created and assigned to every subnet in a vNET. These routes are created and managed by the Azure service itself. Table 1-1 outlines the default system routes defined automatically by Azure whenever a vNET is created. Each default system route defines the source network, address prefix, and next-hop type.

TABLE 1-1 Default system routes

Source	Address prefix	Next-hop type
Default	Unique to the vNET	vNET
Default	0.0.0.0/0	Internet
Default	10.0.0.0/8	None
Default	192.168.0.0/16	None
Default	100.64.0.0/10	None

> **NOTE** You cannot manually modify, add, or delete any default system route.

Table 1-1 notes various next-hop types. These depend on the purpose of the address prefix, as detailed here:

- **vNET** If an address space contains multiple IP ranges or subnets, Azure creates an individual route for each subnet, and routes traffic between them without requiring the use of a gateway. When the next-hop type is vNET, the traffic for those IP address ranges will be contained within the vNET itself.

- **Internet**   This is the default route for all traffic to the internet, including any traffic that does not have a specific route defined in the route table. The only exception to this is traffic to Azure services, which is routed using the Microsoft Azure backbone network instead.
- **None**   Azure automatically creates default routes to the following three reserved address prefixes. If the next-hop type is None, it implies the traffic is dropped:
  - **10.0.0.0/8**   Reserved for private use in RFC 1918.
  - **192.168.0.0/16**   Reserved for private use in RFC 1918.
  - **100.64.0.0/10**   Reserved in RFC 6598.

> **NOTE**   If any of these IP address ranges are used in a vNET address space, Azure changes the default route configuration to vNET instead of None to ensure traffic routing for that network is working.

When traffic exits a subnet, Azure matches the destination address prefix to the default route defined for that address prefix and routes accordingly. If multiple routes are defined for the same IP address prefix or if overlapping IP prefixes exist, Azure has a pre-defined algorithm and logic to determine the best course of action. (For more on this, see the section "Route selection in Azure" later in this chapter.)

Optional system routes

Beyond the default routes that are added to every subnet, optional routes are added after you enable specific Azure capabilities. Azure adds these routes to specific subnets or to the entire vNET, depending on the capability enabled. Table 1-2 shows an example of how these optional default routes are added. Each route defines the source, address prefix, next-hop type, and subnet with which the route is associated.

TABLE 1-2   Optional system routes

Source	Address prefix	Next-hop type	Subnet within VNet to which route is added
Default	Unique to the vNET (for example, 10.10.10.0/24)	vNET peering	All
vNET gateway	Prefix advertised from on-premises via BGP or configured in the local network gateway	vNET gateway	All
Default	Multiple	VirtualNetworkServiceEndpoint	Only the subnet for which a service endpoint is enabled

The next-hop type depends on the purpose of the route, as explained here:

- **vNET gateway**   When a vNET gateway is added to a vNET, optional routes are added based on the subnet defined in the gateway configuration or on the routes propagated from the on-premises network gateway using the BGP.

- **vNET peering** As discussed, you can use peering to connect different Azure vNETs. When peering is established, a route for each address range is added to the route table.
- **VirtualNetworkServiceEndpoint** If you integrate an Azure PaaS service to a vNET using a service endpoint, Azure adds a route for the service endpoint to the route table. Azure adds routes only for the subnets for which the service endpoint is enabled. Azure maintains this information automatically when changes are made to subnet associations.

Custom routes

In addition to default and optional system-generated and system-managed routes, you can set up custom routes to direct traffic to on-premises networks or other services, per your requirements. There are two ways to do this, as follows:

- User-defined routes
- Border Gateway Protocol (BGP) routes

USER-DEFINED ROUTES

User-defined routes are custom routes that you define to override the default system routes created by Azure or as additional routes to address specific routing requirements for your environment for compliance or monitoring purposes. To create a user-defined route, you create a route table that contains a series of routing rules; you then associate this route table with one or more subnets.

As mentioned, user-defined routes either override system-defined routes or work alongside them. This implies that user-defined routes take precedence over system-defined routes in the event of a conflict.

User-defined routes support some of the same next-hop types as default and optional system routes, such as vNET, Internet, None, and vNET gateway. In addition, they support a next-hop type called virtual appliance, which routes traffic to vNET appliances such as firewalls. However, user-defined routes do not support vNET peering VirtualNetworkServiceEndpoint next-hop types.

BORDER GATEWAY PROTOCOL (BGP) ROUTES

BGP routes are another type of user-defined route. These are supported only in scenarios where an Azure virtual gateway S2S VPN or Azure ExpressRoute connection is used to establish connectivity with on-premises networks.

With BGP routes, the initial route exchange occurs when a connection between an on-premises gateway and an Azure VPN gateway is established. This allows either end to automatically propagate the required routes and maintain them as changes occur, without manual intervention.

Route selection in Azure

Now that you have a better understanding of the different routing types available in Azure, it is important to understand how the routing algorithm selects the most appropriate route for outbound traffic from a subnet.

If there is only a single route defined for a destination IP address, the logic for the algorithm is extremely simple: It must use that single available route. However, if multiple routes exist for the same destination IP address, Azure must identify which route's IP address prefix most closely matches the destination IP address. If multiple routes contain the same address prefix, and that IP address prefix is the one that most closely matches the destination IP address, Azure selects the route based on the following priorities, in order:

1. User-defined route.
2. BGP route.
3. Default or optional system route.

Network security groups (NSGs)

You can use NSGs to set up inbound and outbound traffic-filtering rules to and from Azure resources in an Azure vNET. You can set up each rule to allow or deny traffic, inbound or outbound, and identify other parameters such as source and destination, port, and protocol.

An NSG can be applied on a subnet level and another applied on a resource level, such as an Azure VM. In such scenarios, traffic is evaluated against the rules configured in both NSGs, and the more restrictive action of the two is applied.

> **NOTE**   A network security group can contain zero or as many rules as desired.

Availability zones support

vNETs span across all availability zones in a defined Azure region. There is no requirement or even possibility to spread them across different availability zones. This is by design. Any resources set up to use availability zones can use the same vNET without additional configuration.

vNET network address translation (NAT)

Network address translation (NAT) helps route inbound or outbound traffic using a set of static public IP addresses to or from specific internal hosts. In the case of an Azure vNET NAT, outbound internet-based traffic is routed via a single or range of static public IP addresses. This eliminates the need to associate a public IP address with each VM requiring a static outbound IP or using a load balancer for outbound traffic routing.

NAT can be set up for a single or multiple subnets in a vNET. All subnets can use the same NAT, or separate NATs can be set up for every subnet in the vNET. Once defined, NAT is set as the default internet destination of a subnet.

Integrations for enhanced security

Azure vNETs support integration with Azure PaaS services to restrict access to the service from specific networks and endpoints. You can achieve this by using one of the following methods, depending on your environment's access requirements:

- **Network isolation using dedicated vNETs or subnet segmentation**   You can create a dedicated vNET on which to deploy Azure services and use NSGs or Azure firewall services to control traffic, depending on your organization's security requirements. You can also segment subnets to create services in their own subnet and set up NSGs to restrict access as needed.

- **Private endpoints and Private Link**   You can use private endpoints and Private Link services to enable private access to Azure services over an internal network instead of the public internet. You can securely connect to Azure PaaS services over peered Azure networks and interconnected on-premises networks. This is a one-way communication from internal networks to Azure services and does not support outbound connections from PaaS services to on-premises resources.

- **Service endpoints**   Service endpoints allow access to Azure PaaS services over the Azure backbone without completely exposing the service to all internet-based endpoints. You can integrate Azure vNETs with the service endpoint connected to the service, thereby providing secure access to the service even from customer environments.

Service tags

Service tags are pre-defined groups of IP addresses created and managed by Microsoft for different Azure services. For example, the AzureActiveDirectory service tag contains all IP address prefixes used by the Azure Active Directory service. If the IP address prefixes for a service change over time, the service tag automatically notes the change when used to define network access controls.

The VirtualNetwork service tag defines all IP address prefixes associated with the vNET, any peered vNETs, any on-premises address spaces connected over VPN or ExpressRoute, and any default and user-defined routes.

Disaster recovery planning

If a disaster brings an Azure region offline, the vNETs in that region will not automatically be available in another. If facing such a scenario, you have a few options to consider:

- You can preconfigure the same vNET address space and subnets in another Azure region. However, the two regions cannot be connected to or communicate with each other, as the network addresses overlap.

- You can set up a different vNET address space and subnet configuration in another Azure region and replicate, pre-create, or automatically provision all the related Azure resources when necessary. In such a scenario, both regions can be connected and communicate with each other. You'll need to take resource-level conflicts into consideration separately during the redundancy planning for each workload.

vNET walkthrough

The following sections walk you through the process of creating a vNET using the Azure Portal, Azure PowerShell, and the Azure CLI. If you are following along, be sure to select resources and resource names based on your environment, including a unique vNET name for each of your deployments. Also be sure to delete any unwanted resources after you have completed testing to reduce charges levied by Microsoft for these resources.

USING THE AZURE PORTAL

To create a vNET using the Azure Portal, follow these steps:

1. Log into the Azure Portal, type **virtual networks** in the search box to locate the service, and select it from the list that appears. (See Figure 1-1.)

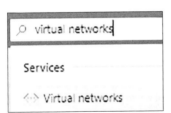

FIGURE 1-1 Create a virtual network.

2. Click **Create** or **Create Virtual Network** to start the Create Virtual Network wizard. (See Figure 1-2.)

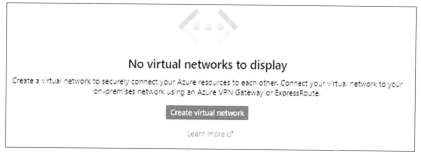

No virtual networks to display

Create a virtual network to securely connect your Azure resources to each other. Connect your virtual network to your on-premises network using an Azure VPN Gateway or ExpressRoute.

Create virtual network

Learn more ⬚

FIGURE 1-2   Click Create Virtual Network.

3. In the **Basics** tab of the Create Virtual Network wizard (see Figure 1-3), enter the following information and click **Next**:

 ■ **Subscription**   Select the subscription to host the vNET.

 ■ **Resource Group**   Select the resource group you want to host the vNET. Alternatively, click the **Create New** link and follow the prompts to create a new resource group.

 ■ **Name**   Type a name for the vNET. If the name you type is already in use, the wizard will prompt you to enter another name.

 ■ **Region**   Select the Azure region in which you want to create the vNET.

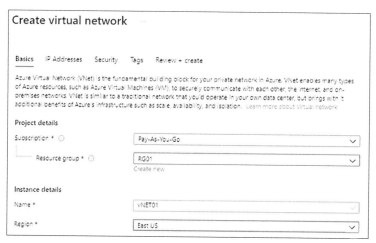

FIGURE 1-3   The Basics tab of the Create Virtual Network wizard.

4. In the **IP Addresses** tab of the Create Virtual Network wizard, review the default IPv4 address space defined by the Azure service. To associate a different address space with the vNET, replace the current address space with the one you want. (See Figure 1-4.)

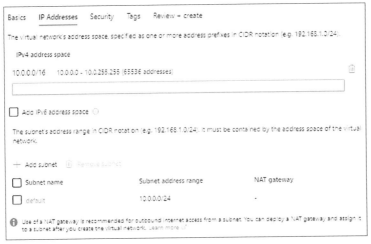

FIGURE 1-4   The IP Addresses tab of the Create Virtual Network wizard.

5. Review the default subnet defined by the Azure service and change it if needed. Then click **Next**.

6. In the **Security** tab, leave the default settings as is (set to **Disable** for all services) and click **Next**. (See Figure 1-5.)

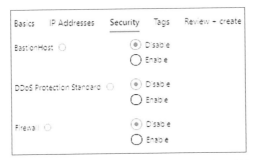

FIGURE 1-5   The Security tab of the Create Virtual Network wizard.

7. In the **Tags** tab, enter any tags required for the vNET or leave the fields blank (see Figure 1-6) and click **Next**.

FIGURE 1-6   The Tags tab of the Create Virtual Network wizard.

8. In the **Review + Create** tab (see Figure 1-7), review your settings and click **Create**.

FIGURE 1-7 The Review + Create tab of the Create Virtual Network wizard.

9. When the deployment is complete, click **Go to Resource** to access the vNET setup. (See Figure 1-8.)

FIGURE 1-8 Click Go to Resource.

USING AZURE POWERSHELL

You can create a vNET using Azure PowerShell with the `New-AzVirtualNetwork` command and various switches to set the vNET's parameters. The following code shows you how. Use this snippet to create the same vNET as you did in the Azure Portal; when you do, be sure to either delete the previous network or give this new network a different name:

```
#Define variables
$vnetName = 'vNET01"
$rg = "RG01"
$location = "East US"
$Subnet = New-AzVirtualNetworkSubnetConfig -Name default -AddressPrefix "10.0.0.0/24"
#Create virtual network with the default subnet configuration
New-AzVirtualNetwork -Name $vnetName -ResourceGroupName $rg -Location $location
-AddressPrefix "10.0.0.0/16" -Subnet $default
```

USING THE AZURE CLI

You can create a vNET using the Azure CLI with the `az network vnet` command and various switches to set the vNET's parameters. The following Bash script shows you how. Use this snippet to create the same vNET as you did in the Azure Portal; when you do, be sure to either delete the previous network or give this new network a different name:

```
#Define variables
vnetname = "vNET01"
rg = "RG01"
location = "East US"
subnet = "default"
#Create virtual network with the default subnet configuration
az network vnet create -g $rg -n $vnetname -location $location --address-prefix
10.0.0.0/16 --subnet-name $subnet --subnet-prefix 10.0.0.0/24
```

Best practices

Following are some general best practices for designing and securing vNETs in Azure:

- **Identify unique address spaces across the organization** Be sure to use Azure address spaces that do not overlap with others already in use in the on-premises or other connected cloud environments. Although you can use the same address spaces if necessary, this requires careful planning, execution, and maintenance to avoid routing issues.

- **Size address spaces for long-term use** When sizing address spaces in Azure, take into account long-term goals and requirements. Don't use all address ranges for subnets right away, with no room for expansion later. Although you can add more address spaces to the vNET at a later stage, considering this during initial planning can reduce issues in the future.

- **Consolidate into fewer larger vNETs** Although it is possible to connect multiple vNETs, it is a better practice to consolidate, such that you have fewer larger vNETs that cover the necessary requirements. This reduces the environment's complexity and management overhead.

- **Secure internal traffic** Use NSGs to secure internal traffic between Azure and on-premises networks to ensure that the only networks that can communicate with each other are the ones you require to do so. Isolate critical networks in their own subnets or vNETs and ensure that access to those subnets or vNETs is restricted to only the required source and destination endpoints, protocols, and ports. Finally, use Azure ExpressRoute instead of an S2S VPN if you require all internal communications to route over a completely private network.

- **Protect against DDoS attacks** Use Azure Firewall and Azure Security Center to detect and prevent distributed denial of service (DDoS) attacks from known malicious IP ranges. You can set up the environment to automatically respond to such threats once detected or simply alert you so you can take action manually. (See Figure 1-9.)

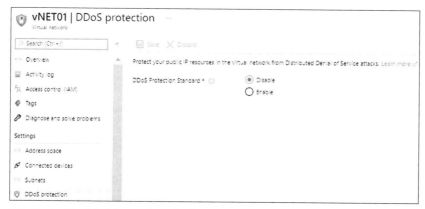

FIGURE 1-9 The DDoS Protection tab of the Azure vNET.

- **Use Log Analytics to analyze vNET flow logs** This will provide you with a better understanding of traffic on the vNET. Set up Log Analytics integration to gain deeper visibility into the traffic on a vNET to make better decisions about vNET security and the routing setup.

- **Use Azure Firewall's Threat Intelligence capabilities** Azure Firewall is connected to the Microsoft Threat Intelligence feed, which is constantly updated from different sources regarding ongoing and new threat vectors around the globe. By enabling this for a firewall instance connected to an Azure vNET, you can better protect your environment from known bad actors on the internet.

- **Use service tags to reduce complexity in network security rules** Service tags are a great way to manage traffic rules associated with Azure services. Use service tags whenever possible to reduce the management overhead of tracking and maintaining service changes that could potentially affect communications within your vNET.

- **Use tags to document vNET configuration**   Label different components and vNET security rules to easily identify or filter them as required.

- **Use Azure Policy to standardize the vNET configuration**   Azure Policy can help you enforce vNET security standards, including policy requirements, policy documentation, and so on, to ensure that all vNETs across an organization are created with the same set of guidelines.

- **Use automated logging and monitoring**   You can use Azure Activity Logs and Azure Monitor to track and alert on events on an Azure vNET, such as configuration changes. It is a good practice to set up alerts for critical events that could have a detrimental impact on your environment. You can also integrate Azure Log Analytics to store logs for longer periods of time for historical reporting and comparisons.

## Chapter 2

Azure Application Gateway

Overview

Azure Application Gateway is an ideal load balancer for web servers and applications that require HTTP/HTTPS traffic load-balancing and routing. It operates at the application layer (OSI layer 7 of the TCP and UDP stack) and can therefore analyze incoming traffic for custom routing based on URL paths and host headers in the incoming request. (See Figure 2-1.)

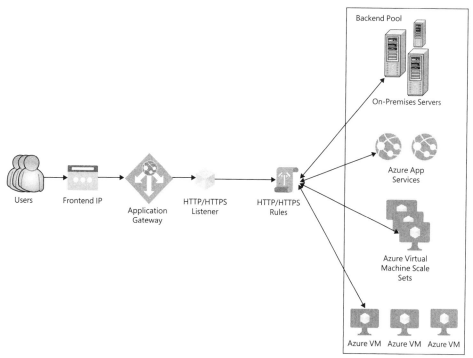

FIGURE 2-1 The Azure Application Gateway handles incoming traffic using routing rules to back-end services.

Traditional load balancers operate at OSI layer 4, meaning they can only route traffic with limited parameters, such as the source IP or port and the destination IP and port. Due to these limitations, complex application traffic routing is difficult on traditional load balancers. In contrast, Azure Application Gateway can route traffic based on the URL in the header information of the incoming traffic request. This makes it possible to route traffic for the same host header, directed to the same Azure Application Gateway IP, to a different server or server pool. For example, a request with the URL *www.contoso.com/videos* can be routed to one server or server pool hosting video-based content, a request for *www.contoso.com/images* can be routed to another server or server pool hosting image-based content, and so on. (See Figure 2-2.) This can help you design and optimize a web application server pool based on the content hosted by the pool.

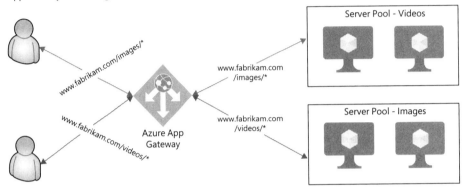

FIGURE 2-2 Azure Application Gateway URL-based routing.

You can deploy an Azure Application Gateway in one of two ways:

- **As an internal-only Azure Application Gateway**   This is ideal for environments in which the application must be accessible only over internal virtual networks (vNETs). The gateway has an internal IP address, and the DNS records for it are set up in an internal or custom DNS server or service that is accessible only via vNETs for client connectivity.

- **As an internet-facing Azure Application Gateway**   This has a public IP, which publicly exposes the gateway. So, back-end applications can be publicly accessed by clients by way of the internet. The DNS name for a public-facing load balancer is added to the public DNS by the Azure service.

Azure Application Gateway features

The following list outlines the main features of the Azure Application Gateway. These features help explain how this service can be a key component of any web application design:

- **Web application firewall (WAF)**   The Azure Application Gateway can act as a WAF, monitoring incoming traffic from clients and intercepting any malicious activities to provide centralized protection from well-known vulnerabilities for multiple web applications in your environment. You can host an application behind the WAF even if you have not yet been able to patch the vulnerabilities on the web servers themselves. You can centrally protect an application or even a large server farm that needs patching from a known vulnerability by patching the WAF. This serves as an interim solution until the application or server farm itself can be updated.

NOTE WAF rules are based on Open Web Application Security Project (OWASP) core rule sets 3.1 (WAF v2), 3.0 (WAF v1 and v2), and 2.2.9 (WAF v1 and v2).

- **Multiple-site hosting** Azure Application Gateway supports the use of multiple host, domain, or subdomain names on the same application gateway. So, you can use a single application gateway to handle web traffic for multiple web applications. This enables you to maximize your investment in the service by using each instance to its fullest capacity. You can map more than 100 web applications to a single application gateway. And, by using multi-site listeners, you can route traffic sent to a single public IP to different back-end server pools based on the URL request or host header.

- **Web-traffic redirection** By redirecting web traffic meant for one port to another, you can mask the application ports used internally on the web application servers, which can improve the security of your web applications. Traffic redirection also enables you to centrally route HTTP traffic to HTTPS, ensuring that no unencrypted communication occurs between your clients and web services. Web-traffic redirection supports the following scenarios:

    - **Global traffic redirection** This type of redirection enables you to redirect all traffic from HTTP to HTTPS on a site or to any other non-standard port required by the web application.

    - **Path-based redirection** With this type of redirection, you can redirect HTTP to HTTPS or any other non-standard port only on specific site areas, such as traffic to /videos/* or /checkout/*.

    - **Redirection to an external site** This type of redirection allows you to redirect traffic to an external site.

- **Secure Sockets Layer/Transport Layer Security (SSL/TLS) termination** You can use Azure Application Gateway to offload SSL/TLS processing for your web applications. This helps reduce the overhead of SSL/TLS encryption/decryption as well as server resource consumption. Traffic between the application gateway to the web application hosted internally behind it can be unencrypted. In some scenarios, however, you might need the back-end traffic to be encrypted for compliance or application-design reasons. Azure Application Gateway supports these types of end-to-end encryption scenarios, too.

- **Session affinity handling** You can set up Azure Application Gateway to support cookie-based session affinity, thereby ensuring that any sessions that are interrupted or dropped will reconnect to the same server as before. This can be a critical requirement for some applications where a user's session state is stored locally on the server.

- **Static virtual IP (VIP) assignment** The Standard_v2 version of Azure Application Gateway supports the use of static VIP addresses, ensuring the VIP is maintained as-is for the lifetime of the application gateway.

- **Zone redundancy** You can set up Azure Application Gateway to span multiple availability zones, thereby improving the gateway's SLA and resiliency.

NOTE Currently, only the Standard_v2 version of Azure Application Gateway supports zone redundancy.

■ **Path-based routing** This enables you to analyze and route traffic based on the path indicated in the incoming web request. You can set up the application gateway to route traffic to different back-end servers or server pools based on the paths found in the request. So, content for different paths of a URL can be hosted on different servers or server pools, and the content itself can be optimized to deliver the best end-user experience possible.

■ **Automatic scaling** You can set up Azure Application Gateway to automatically scale up or down based on traffic load at any given time. You need not select the "perfect" size for the application gateway when you provision it, because the gateway can scale as needed as traffic grows over time.

■ **Support for WebSocket and HTTP/2 traffic** Azure Application Gateway natively supports WebSocket and HTTP/2 protocols. WebSocket is enabled by default and cannot be turned off. It allows full duplex communication between the web application server and client over long-running TCP connections, which can be optimized and used for multiple requests and responses. HTTP/2 protocols can be used only for client-to-application gateway communications. HTTP/2 is designed to function more efficiently than HTTP-based communications by eliminating the need for the constant polling required by HTTP to keep long-running sessions alive, which reduces the application gateway's overhead with client communications. Both protocols are designed to work over ports 80 and 443, so you can easily incorporate them into an environment without making firewall changes.

Design concepts and deployment considerations

Azure Application Gateway consists of a number of components that come together to filter traffic and provide secure routing services for your web applications. The main components of the Azure Application Gateway service are as follows (see Figure 2-3):

■ Front-end IP addresses

■ Back-end pools

■ Listeners

■ Request routing rules

■ HTTP settings

■ Health probes

It is important to have a solid understanding of each of these components to be able to design and deploy them appropriately based on your environment's requirements. In addition, you should have a strong grasp of sizing and scaling as well as TLS policy. This section covers all of these topics.

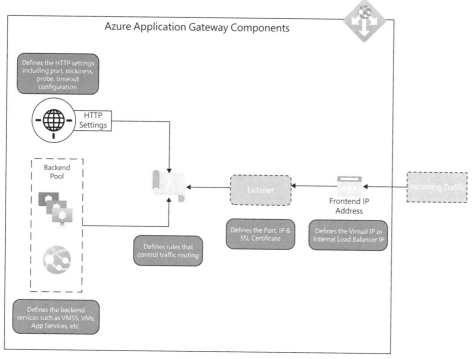

FIGURE 2-3 Azure Application Gateway components.

Front-end IP addresses

A front-end IP address is the ingress point for the application gateway to receive web application traffic. It is referenced in the internal and/or public DNS and used to route application traffic. The front-end IP address can be an internal private IP address, a public IP address, or both.

If a private IP address is to be used, the gateway should be deployed in the same region as the vNET with which it is associated. Similarly, you should create any public IP that must be associated as the front-end IP address in the same region as the application gateway.

The application gateway supports both static and dynamic IP addresses for the private and public IP addresses. However, based on the SKU of the gateway, the support varies for each. SKU v1 supports dynamic public IP addresses and static or dynamic private IP addresses; there is no support for static public IP addresses. SKU v2 supports static and dynamic private and public IP addresses. You cannot set up a static private IP address along with a dynamic public IP address, but you can set up a static public IP address with a dynamic private IP address if required.

Back-end pools

Back-end pools are back-end servers or services to which web traffic requests from clients are routed. They serve the client request with the required application response via the application gateway.

Back-end pools support the following types of services:

- Virtual network interfaces
- Virtual machine scale sets (VMSS)
- Public IP addresses associated with Azure virtual machines (VMs) or services
- Internal IP addresses associated with Azure or on-premises servers or services
- Fully qualified domain names (FQDNs)
- Azure services, such as App Service

Back-end pools can be located across Azure regions, across different clusters, or outside Azure in a client's or third-party datacenter. As long as the application gateway can reach the back-end endpoint over TCP/IP, it can serve as a front-end to that web application.

For communications with on-premises servers, a VPN gateway or Azure ExpressRoute connection is necessary. For communication with Azure VMs and services over their private internal IPs, vNET peering or VPN gateway integration is needed.

Listeners

Every application gateway requires a minimum of one listener and can contain multiple listeners. A listener helps you define the protocol, port, hostname, and source IP address that is allowed to communicate with the back-end pool. Based on the configuration of the listeners defined on the application gateway, traffic is passed through or dropped. If the listener allows traffic through, the gateway evaluates it against routing rules configured to route traffic to the correct back-end pool.

There are two types of listeners:

- **Basic**   A basic listener can listen for requests only for a single domain.
- **Multi-site**   A multi-site listener can listen to requests for multiple host names or domain names. This type of listener can support more than 100 websites, which you can route to their own back-end pool.

Both types of listeners support the following ports:

- **SKU V1**   Ports 1 – 65502
- **SKU V2**   Ports 1 – 65199

In addition, they support the following protocols:

- HTTP
- HTTPS
- HTTP/2
- WebSocket

There are a few caveats to be aware of, as follows:

- WebSocket protocol support is enabled by default and cannot be turned off.
- HTTP/2 protocol support is disabled by default and must be turned on manually.
- HTTP/2 protocol support is limited to the client and application gateway communications. Any back-end communications occur over HTTP/1.1.

Request routing rules

A request routing rule defines how traffic received by the application gateway should be routed. It binds the listener to a back-end server pool based on the HTTP settings defined to monitor in the request. One listener can be attached to only one rule.

Routing to the back-end pool depends on the rule configuration that defines which back-end pool binds to which URL or URL path. The routing rule also specifies whether any request must be rewritten before being routed to the back-end pool.

There are two types of request routing rules:

- **Basic**   A basic request routing rule forwards all traffic to the associated back-end pool based on the HTTP settings associated with the rule.
- **Path-based**   A path-based request routing rule analyzes the URL path in the request to identify the back-end pool to which to route the request. The rule contains different URL paths, set up to route to different back-end pools. If the incoming request does not match any of the rules, the traffic is routed to the default back-end pool based on associated HTTP settings.

A request routing rule is evaluated based on the priority assigned to that rule. By default, the priority is automatically assigned based on the order of rule creation (unless a specific priority is provided at the time of rule creation or set later on).

It is important to take priority into consideration in case there are rules that contain domains that overlap—for example, *.fabrikam.com and blogs.fabrikam.com. In such cases, wildcard rules should be lower in priority to ensure the individual domain rules are evaluated before the wildcard rules. Otherwise, requests will be routed to the back-end pools associated with the wildcard domains only.

Redirection support

In addition to routing traffic to back-end pools, request routing rules can be set up to redirect traffic to and from any port to a redirection target. The redirection could be to another listener or an external site. Redirection routing helps redirect HTTP traffic to HTTPS, or traffic from a standard web port (such as 80) to a non-standard port.

Azure Application Gateway supports different types of redirection:

- 310 Permanent Redirect
- 302 Found
- 303 See Other
- 307 Temporary Redirect

Rewriting of HTTP headers and URLs

Azure Application Gateway allows HTTP request and response headers to be modified before the packet is sent to the back-end pool. So, the URL can be rewritten with custom security header fields, removing sensitive header information such as port information on X-Forwarded-For (XFF) headers. This feature can apply these changes only when certain conditions are met, so you can target rewrites to address any complex scenario as required.

HTTP settings

HTTP settings define the back-end servers' port number, protocol, encryption settings, and other details. The application gateway uses these settings to route traffic to back-end servers when it receives a matching request.

HTTP settings are also used to define other settings, such as the following:

- **Cookie-Based Session Affinity**   This setting instructs the gateway to use affinity to always route requests from the same client to the same hosts (assuming the host is online).
- **Connection Draining**   This setting instructs the application gateway to gracefully drain connections on back-end servers, as they may be taken down for maintenance.
- **Custom Health Probe**   This setting helps the gateway understand how it should validate the health of the back-end pool.

Health probes

Monitoring the health of back-end pool instances is a critical function. It helps the service decide which back-end pool instances are healthy and usable for request routing and which ones need to be taken out of service to avoid application outages. Health probes provide the application gateway with the hostname, URL path, probe interval, and failed response limits to help it identify unhealthy back-end pool instances. The application gateway performs health monitoring by default. However, custom health probes help the gateway target the right parameters to evaluate instance health. Therefore, it is highly recommended to define custom health probes for each individual back-end pool.

Sizing and scaling

The v1 SKU offers different gateway sizes:

- **Small**   Appropriate for test and dev scenarios.
- **Medium**   Appropriate for small environments with a few hundred users accessing a web application.
- **Large**   Recommended for most enterprise or multi-site scenarios, to handle higher loads.

With the v2 SKU, autoscaling is available, eliminating the need for different gateway sizes. In this case, you use manual scaling or auto-scaling configurations to handle load instead of attempting to determine the right instance size at the outset.

TLS policy

With Azure Application Gateway, you can offload SSL/TLS. This way, SSL connections from clients are terminated on the application gateway, and internal communications with the application back-end can be encrypted or unencrypted (thereby reducing overhead on instances of the application). If the back-end instances are set up to communicate with the application gateway in an unencrypted manner, application certificates can be deployed and managed only on the application gateway. This makes it easier to track, maintain, and update them.

A TLS policy defines the different TLS protocol versions and cipher suites to be used during a TLS handshake. The order of the ciphers specifies the order in which they are evaluated at the time of the handshake. There are two mechanisms to control this, as follows:

- **Using a predefined TLS policy**   Every application gateway interface includes three predefined TLS policies—each one defined to support different TLS protocol versions and cipher suites. The names of the policies indicate the dates on which they were introduced; it's recommended that you use the newer ones.
- **Using a custom TLS policy**   If a predefined policy does not meet your requirements, you can customize a policy to include the TLS protocols and cipher suites (and their priority) based on your needs.

With both predefined and custom TLS policies, SSL 2.0 and 3.0 are set to disabled, and you cannot override this. However, with a custom policy, you can set up any of the three TLS protocol versions (v1_0, v1_1, or v1_2) as the minimum required version. You can also set up all three of these with no minimum requirement if needed.

Application gateway walkthrough

The following sections walk you through the process of creating an application gateway using the Azure Portal, Azure PowerShell, and the Azure CLI. If you are following along, be sure to select resources and resource names based on your environment, including a unique application gateway name for each of your deployments. Also be sure to delete any unwanted resources after you have completed testing to reduce charges levied by Microsoft for these resources. Finally, to complete this walkthrough, you need to have created at least two back-end VMs with IIS web services to integrate with the Application Gateway. Microsoft provides Windows Server templates in the Azure Marketplace that install and set up IIS with the default configuration; alternatively, you can create a custom configuration based on your requirements.

USING THE AZURE PORTAL

To create an application gateway using the Azure Portal, follow these steps:

1. Log into the Azure Portal, type **application gateway** in the search box to locate the service, and select it from the list that appears.

2. Click **Create** or **Create Application Gateway** to start the Create Application Gateway wizard. (See Figure 2-4.)

No application gateways to display

Azure Application Gateway gives you application-level routing and load balancing services that let you build a scalable and highly-available web front end in Azure. You control the size of the gateway and scale your deployment based on your needs. Learn more about Application gateway ⌐

Create application gateway

FIGURE 2-4   Click Create Application Gateway.

3. In the **Basics** tab of the Create Application Gateway wizard (see Figure 2-5), enter the following information and click **Next: Frontends**:

   ■ **Subscription**   Select the subscription to host the application gateway.

   ■ **Resource Group**   Select the resource group you want to host the application gateway. Alternatively, click the **Create New** link and follow the prompts to create a new resource group.

- **Name**   Type a name for the application gateway. If the name you type is already in use, the wizard will prompt you to enter another name.
- **Region**   Select the Azure region in which you want to create the application gateway.
- **Tier**   Choose **Standard V2**.
- **Enable Autoscaling**   Select the **Yes** option button.
- **Minimum Instance Count**   Enter the minimum number of hosts to set up.
- **Maximum Instance Count**   Enter the maximum number of hosts to which the gateway should scale.
- **Availability Zone**   Leave this set to **None**.
- **HTTP2**   Leave this set to **Disabled**.
- **Virtual Network**   Select an existing vNET for which you have created back-end VMs.
- **Subnet**   Select a subnet for the application gateway.

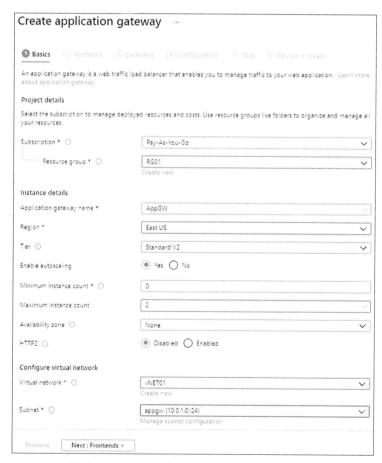

FIGURE 2-5   The Basics tab of the Create Application Gateway wizard.

4. In the **Frontends** tab of the Create Application Gateway wizard (see Figure 2-6), for **Frontend IP Address Type**, select the **Public** option button.

FIGURE 2-6 The Frontends tab of the Create Application Gateway wizard.

5. Under the **Public IP Address** box, click the **Add New** link.

6. On the **Add a Public IP** page, in the **Name** box, type a name for the public IP address. (See Figure 2-7.) Then click **OK**.

FIGURE 2-7 The Add a Public IP dialog box.

7. In the **Frontends** tab of the Create Application Gateway wizard, click **Next: Backends**.

8. In the **Backends** tab of the Create Application Gateway wizard (see Figure 2-8), click the **Add a Backend Pool** link.

FIGURE 2-8 The Backends tab of the Create Application Gateway wizard.

9. In the **Add a Backend Pool** dialog box (see Figure 2-9), enter the following information and click **Add**:

- **Name** Type a name for the back-end pool.
- **Add Backend Pool Without Targets** Click **No**.

- **Target Type** Select **Virtual Machine**.
- **Target** Select one of the VMs you created for this walkthrough.

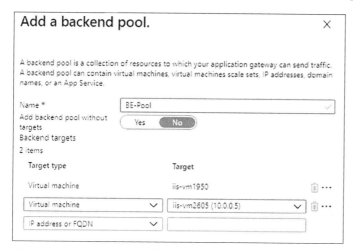

FIGURE 2-9 The Add a Backend Pool dialog box.

10. In the **Backends** tab of the Create Application Gateway wizard (see Figure 2-10), verify that the back-end pool configuration is correct and click **Next: Configuration**.

FIGURE 2-10 The updated Backends tab of the Create Application Gateway wizard.

11. In the **Configuration** tab of the Create Application Gateway wizard (see Figure 2-11), click **Add a Routing Rule** to create a routing rule for incoming traffic.

FIGURE 2-11 The Configuration tab of the Create Application Gateway wizard.

12. In the **Listener** tab of the **Add a Routing Rule** settings (see Figure 2-12), enter the following information:

■ **Rule Name**   Type a name for the rule.

■ **Listener Name**   Type a name for the listener.

■ **Frontend IP**   Select **Public**.

■ **Protocol**   Select the protocol used by your application.

■ **Port**   Type the port used by your application.

■ **Listener Type**   Select the **Basic** option button.

■ **Error Page URL**   Select the **No** option button.

FIGURE 2-12   The Listener tab in the Add a Routing Rule settings.

13. Click the **Backend Targets** tab (look ahead to Figure 2-13).

14. For **Target Type**, select the **Backend Pool** option button.

15. Open the **Backend Target** drop-down list and select the back-end pool target.

16. Under **HTTP Settings**, click the **Add New link**.

17. In the **Add a HTTP Setting** settings (see Figure 2-14), enter the following information and click **Add**. (Leave the other settings as is.)

■ **HTTP Settings Name**   Enter a name for the HTTP settings.

■ **Backend Protocol**   Select the back-end protocol used by the application.

■ **Backend Port**   Type the back-end port used by your application.

■ **Cookie-Based Affinity**   Select the **Disable** option button.

■ **Connection Draining**   Select the **Disable** option button.

■ **Request Time-Out (Seconds)**   Enter a request time-out value (in seconds) that reflects the responsiveness of your application.

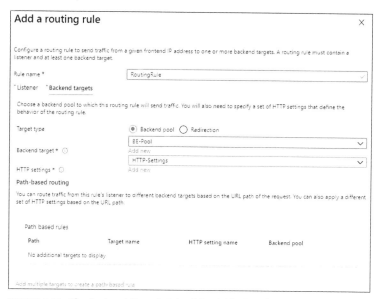

FIGURE 2-13 The Backend Targets tab of the Add a Routing Rule settings.

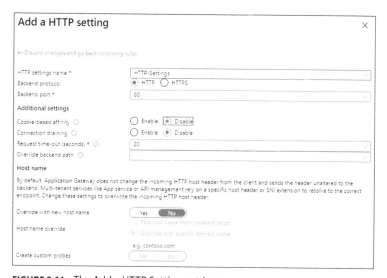

FIGURE 2-14 The Add a HTTP Setting settings.

18. In the **Configurations** tab (see Figure 2-15), confirm that the configuration is correct and click **Next: Tags**.

FIGURE 2-15 The updated Configuration tab of the Create Application Gateway wizard.

19. In the **Tags** tab, enter any tags required for the application gateway or leave the fields blank (see Figure 2-16) and click **Next: Review + Create**.

✓ Basics ✓ Frontends ✓ Backends ✓ Configuration ⑤ Tags ⑥ Review + create

Tags are name/value pairs that enable you to categorize resources and view consolidated billing by applying the same tag to multiple resources and resource groups. Learn more

Note that if you create tags and then change resource settings on other tabs, your tags will be automatically updated.

Name ⓘ   Value ⓘ

[   ] : [   ]

FIGURE 2-16 The Tags tab of the Create Application Gateway wizard.

20. On the **Review + Create** tab (see Figure 2-17), review your settings, and click **Create**. You can now test whether your application is accessible by accessing the application gateway URL. (The URL will be visible in the application gateway's Overview tab.)

FIGURE 2-17 The Review + Create tab of the Create Application Gateway wizard in the Azure Portal.

USING AZURE POWERSHELL

You can create an application gateway using Azure PowerShell with the `New-AzVirtualNetworkGateway` and `New-AzVirtualNetworkGatewayConnection` commands and various switches to set the application gateway's parameters. The following code shows you how. Use this snippet to create the same application gateway as you did in the Azure Portal. (Replace all the variables and on-premises firewall configuration as per your environment.) When you do, be sure to either delete the previous application gateway or give this new application gateway a different name:

```
#Define variables
$agSubnetConfig = New-AzVirtualNetworkSubnetConfig `
  -Name myAGSubnet `
  -AddressPrefix 10.21.0.0/24
$backendSubnetConfig = New-AzVirtualNetworkSubnetConfig `
  -Name myBackendSubnet `
  -AddressPrefix 10.21.1.0/24
New-AzVirtualNetwork `
  -ResourceGroupName myResourceGroupAG `
  -Location eastus `
  -Name myVNet `
  -AddressPrefix 10.21.0.0/16 `
  -Subnet $agSubnetConfig, $backendSubnetConfig
New-AzPublicIpAddress `
  -ResourceGroupName myResourceGroupAG `
  -Location eastus `
  -Name myAGPublicIPAddress `
  -AllocationMethod Static `
  -Sku Standard
#Create IP Config and front-end port
$vnet    = Get-AzVirtualNetwork -ResourceGroupName myResourceGroupAG -Name myVNet
$subnet = Get-AzVirtualNetworkSubnetConfig -VirtualNetwork $vnet -Name myAGSubnet
$pip     = Get-AzPublicIPAddress -ResourceGroupName myResourceGroupAG -Name
myAGPublicIPAddress
$gipconfig = New-AzApplicationGatewayIPConfiguration `
  -Name myAGIPConfig `
  -Subnet $subnet
$fipconfig = New-AzApplicationGatewayFrontendIPConfig `
  -Name myAGFrontendIPConfig `
  -PublicIPAddress $pip
$frontendport = New-AzApplicationGatewayFrontendPort `
  -Name myFrontendPort `
  -Port 80
#Create backend pool
$backendPool = New-AzApplicationGatewayBackendAddressPool `
  -Name myAGBackendPool
$poolSettings = New-AzApplicationGatewayBackendHttpSetting `
```

```
  -Name myPoolSettings `
  -Port 80 `
  -Protocol Http `
  -CookieBasedAffinity Enabled `
  -RequestTimeout 30
#Create listener and add rule
$defaultlistener = New-AzApplicationGatewayHttpListener `
  -Name myAGListener `
  -Protocol Http `
  -FrontendIPConfiguration $fipconfig `
  -FrontendPort $frontendport
$frontendRule = New-AzApplicationGatewayRequestRoutingRule `
  -Name rule1 `
  -RuleType Basic `
  -HttpListener $defaultlistener `
  -BackendAddressPool $backendPool `
  -BackendHttpSettings $poolSettings
#Create application gateway
$sku = New-AzApplicationGatewaySku `
  -Name Standard_v2 `
  -Tier Standard_v2 `
  -Capacity 2
New-AzApplicationGateway `
  -Name myAppGateway `
  -ResourceGroupName myResourceGroupAG `
  -Location eastus `
  -BackendAddressPools $backendPool `
  -BackendHttpSettingsCollection $poolSettings `
  -FrontendIpConfigurations $fipconfig `
  -GatewayIpConfigurations $gipconfig `
  -FrontendPorts $frontendport `
  -HttpListeners $defaultlistener `
  -RequestRoutingRules $frontendRule `
  -Sku $sku
```

USING THE AZURE CLI

You can create an application gateway using the Azure CLI with the `az network vnet-gateway create` command and various switches to set the application gateway's parameters. The following Bash script shows you how. Use this snippet to create the same application gateway as you did in the Azure Portal. (Replace all the variables and on-premises firewall configuration as per your environment.) When you do, be sure to either delete the previous application gateway or give this new application gateway a different name:

```
#Define variables
#Create network
az network vnet create \
```

```
    --name myVNet \
    --resource-group myResourceGroupAG \
    --location eastus \
    --address-prefix 10.21.0.0/16 \
    --subnet-name myAGSubnet \
    --subnet-prefix 10.21.0.0/24
 az network vnet subnet create \
    --name myBackendSubnet \
    --resource-group myResourceGroupAG \
    --vnet-name myVNet    \
    --address-prefix 10.21.1.0/24
 az network public-ip create \
    --resource-group myResourceGroupAG \
    --name myAGPublicIPAddress \
    --allocation-method Static \
    --sku Standard
#Create application gateway
address1=$(az network nic show --name myNic1 --resource-group myResourceGroupAG | grep
"\"privateIpAddress\":" | grep -oE '[^ ]+$' | tr -d '",')
address2=$(az network nic show --name myNic2 --resource-group myResourceGroupAG | grep
"\"privateIpAddress\":" | grep -oE '[^ ]+$' | tr -d '",')
 az network application-gateway create \
    --name myAppGateway \
    --location eastus \
    --resource-group myResourceGroupAG \
    --capacity 2 \
    --sku Standard_v2 \
    --public-ip-address myAGPublicIPAddress \
    --vnet-name myVNet \
    --subnet myAGSubnet \
    --servers "$address1" "$address2"
```

Best practices

Following are some recommended practices for deploying and managing your application gateway environment. These practices can help you make the most of your investment in this service:

- **Monitor and plan instance count to avoid resource crunch**   Azure Application Gateway v2 supports auto-scaling, but if you are using Azure Application Gateway v1, you will have to scale manually. The v1 SKU supports scaling up to 32 instances. To identify the right instance count, monitor CPU utilization for the application gateway for at least a month and identify the peak CPU usage. Then add a buffer of 15% to 20% to handle unexpected spikes and growth. Finally, select your instance count based on this sizing.

- **Upgrade to the v2 SKU as soon as possible**   As mentioned, Azure Application gateway v1 supports manual scaling only—which is not the most efficient or cost-effective way to manage your gateway instances. In addition to auto-scaling, the v2 SKU offers other performance benefits, including SSL/TLS offloading, improved deployment performance, zone redundancy, and many others. You should upgrade to the v2 SKU as soon as you can so you can benefit from all these (and other) features.

- **Set the maximum instance count in the v2 SKU**   Because the v2 SKU supports auto-scaling, and because charges are levied based on how many units are used, it is important to consider budgetary requirements when setting the maximum instance count. The v2 SKU supports a maximum of 125 instances—which means unplanned spikes can result in more instances being activated than are budgeted for.

- **Size the gateway subnet for future growth**   Size the subnet in which you plan to host application gateway instances to take into account future scalability requirements. Changes to the subnet configuration are not currently supported and require a redeployment of the service, resulting in possible disruption.

- **Set the minimum instance count for v2 SKU**   Bringing additional instances online to accept traffic when auto-scaling does take some time—usually between six and seven minutes. Any unexpected spikes during this period can result in traffic drops or higher response latency. You should monitor CPU usage for at least a month to identify the minimum instances required, and maintain a buffer of 15% to 20% to allow for unexpected spikes.

- **Monitoring and alerting**   Set up alerts for different gateway metrics to monitor CPU usage, instance scaling, and network utilization so you can be notified of any anomalies that might cause potential outages. Examples of alerts could include average CPU usage spiking by 75% to 80% for a sustained period of time, too many failed requests, gateway not responding, logs containing numerous 4xx or 5xx errors (indicating response issues), and too many unhealthy back-end hosts.

- **Set up geo-filtering to block unwanted countries/regions**   The v2 SKU supports geo-filtering, which enables you to allow or block traffic from specific countries or regions. It is a good practice to use this feature to prevent (or allow) traffic from certain locales to connect to your web applications to reduce your attack surface.

- **Set up bot protection to prevent attacks**   The v2 SKU has a feature to prevent traffic from known bot networks. Enable this feature to intercept known malicious traffic before it reaches your web applications.

- **Set up diagnostics logging and long-term retention**   Collect firewall, performance, and access logs for your application gateway instances and save them in Azure storage, Log Analytics, or an event stream. These logs can help you identify potential issues and take proactive action. Set up retention policies based on historical data storage comparison and compliance requirements for your organization.

- **Set up the latest TLS policy version for extra security**   Use the latest TLS policy version (currently AppGwSslPolicy20170401S) to enforce TLS 1.2 and stronger ciphers.

## Chapter 3

Azure VPN gateway

Overview

A virtual private network (VPN) gateway is a device that you can use to connect different networks over the internet for secure communications. These can include on-premises networks connected to Azure virtual networks (vNETs) or one Azure vNET connected to another Azure vNET. IPSec/IKEv2 is used to encrypt traffic between networks. In Azure, the service to create VPN gateways is known as the virtual network gateway service.

Azure VPN gateway features

Following are some key concepts and benefits of using a VPN gateway in your Azure design:

- **Managed gateway**   When a VPN gateway is deployed in an Azure vNET, the Azure service provisions two or more VMs in an associated subnet called the gateway subnet. These VMs are set up with gateway routing services, route tables based on the configuration of the VPN tunnel, and the Azure vNET in which the gateway is provisioned. The Azure service itself sets up and manages these VMs; you cannot modify or otherwise manage them yourself.

- **High availability**   Each Azure vNET supports the use of only one VPN gateway. For high-availability, you can set up the gateway in an active-active architecture and connect it to multiple remote gateways at the same time. The total bandwidth available for use on the VPN gateway depends on its SKU and is shared across all active connections.

- **Coexistence with ExpressRoute gateway**   Azure supports two types of gateways: VPN gateways and ExpressRoute gateways. An ExpressRoute gateway enables secure connectivity to on-premises networks over a private connection; in contrast, the VPN gateway uses the public internet to connect networks. After you use the VPN gateway to establish an IPsec/IKE VPN tunnel between two sites, Azure creates routes in the route table based on the subnets defined in the VPN configuration or propagated automatically when the connection is established.

NOTE A vNET can have one VPN gateway and one ExpressRoute gateway at the same time.

- **Support for remote work scenarios using a point-to-site VPN connection**   In addition to a site-to-site (S2S) VPN connection, a VPN gateway also allows you to create a point-to-site (P2S) VPN connection, using OpenVPN, IKEv2, or SSTP. This allows you to connect to the vNET directly over your home or remote network to access resources using their private internal IPs.
- **Support for availability zones**   Azure VPN gateway supports deployment in availability zones, bringing the scalability, resiliency, and redundancy features associated with availability zones to the VPN gateway. When a VPN gateway is deployed in an availability zone, it is physically and logically separated within a region, thereby protecting the service against zonal failures.
- **Support for Azure PowerShell, Azure CLI, and ARM templates**   In addition to using the Azure Portal to manage the VPN gateway, you can use Azure PowerShell, Azure CLI, and ARM templates.

NOTE The Azure VPN gateway service uses Azure Blob storage to automatically replicate the system metadata and store it securely using encryption-at-rest features.

Design concepts and deployment considerations

Before setting up a VPN gateway, it is important to identify all your requirements for connectivity. This includes the end clients in scope, throughput required, protocols supported, on-premises firewall or VPN devices available, and support, resiliency, redundancy, and authentication mechanisms required.

After you've identified these requirements, you can use the following table to identify what will be the best solution, including the type of VPN connection (P2S or S2S), the gateway SKU, deployment models, protocols, and so on.

	Point-to-Site	Site-to-Site
Azure-Supported Services	Cloud services and virtual machines (VMs)	Cloud services and VMs
Typical Bandwidths	Based on the gateway SKU	Typically < 1 Gbps aggregate
Protocols Supported	Secure Sockets Tunneling Protocol (SSTP), OpenVPN, and Internet Protocol Security (IPsec)	IPsec
Routing	Route-based (dynamic routing)	Policy-based (static routing) and route-based (dynamic routing)
Connection Resiliency	Active-passive	Active-passive and active-active
Typical Use Case	Secure access to Azure vNETs for remote users	Dev, test, and lab scenarios and small- to medium-scale production workloads for cloud services and VMs

The following sections discuss in more detail the various components and design elements to consider in order to design and deploy the most appropriate VPN solution for your environment.

VPN types

Azure supports two types of VPNs: route-based and policy-based. The type of VPN you select will depend on your VPN connection requirements. P2S connections support only route-based VPNs, whereas S2S connections support both route-based and policy-based VPNs.

Policy-based VPNs support only one VPN tunnel and require the use of the Basic SKU, so it has fewer use cases. In contrast, route-based VPNs support both P2S and S2S connections simultaneously, although other available features and tunnels depend on the gateway SKU.

There's one more important difference between these VPN types: In a policy-based VPN, static routing is defined using an access list, whereas in a route-based VPN, routes are dynamically added (or removed) from the route table when a connection is established (or shut down).

Gateway SKUs

There are different SKUs available for VPN gateways. The one you choose will be based on your organization's throughput, features, and SLA requirements.

The Basic SKU is recommended for test and dev workloads. Other SKUs, starting with VPNGw1, are recommended for production environments. Which of these SKUs you choose will depend on the feature set you require. For example, the VpnGw1AZ SKU supports availability zones, whereas the VpnGw2 SKU does not. However, the VpnGw2 SKU allows for greater throughput (1 Gbps compared to 650 Mbps).

You can switch between SKUs in the same generation. For example, you can switch from a VpnGw1 gateway to a VpnGw2 gateway. However, you cannot switch from a VpnGw1 gateway to a VpnGw2AZ gateway.

> **NOTE** You can upgrade a legacy Basic gateway to a VPNGw1 gateway, but you will have to delete the Basic gateway and then create a new VPNGw SKU gateway.

Connection types

VPN gateway devices support four connection types, as follows:

- **IPsec**   Use this to establish an S2S connection with an on-premises gateway device.
- **Vnet2Vnet**   Use this to interconnect two Azure vNETs using a VPN gateway.
- **ExpressRoute**   Use this when the gateway type is set to ExpressRoute to establish connections between secure private networks and Azure.
- **VPNClient**   Use this to establish a P2S connection between a client device and the VPN gateway device.

Gateway subnet

Before you provision a VPN gateway, you need to create a special subnet, called a gateway subnet, to host it. The gateway subnet is set up as part of the Azure vNET address space. It can be a subnet as small as /29, but it is generally recommended to size it to /26 or /27 to handle active-active configuration scenarios that require the deployment of additional VMs to handle redundancy.

Border Gateway Protocol (BGP)

Border Gateway Protocol (BGP) is a standard routing protocol that supports route exchange between connected networks called BGP peers or neighbors. This requires both ends of the connection to support BGP; its use with Azure VPN gateways is optional.

The primary advantages of using BGP are as follows:

- **Dynamic routing**   BGP enables the Azure VPN gateway to support dynamic routing. Route exchange can then occur to update either end of the connection, in the event modifications to the routing paths occur due to network changes or outages.

- **Better control over network access**   BGP allows you to declare only the IP address prefixes to which you want to give access instead of opening access to the entire IP address prefix in the on-premises or Azure network. This allows you to better control traffic between both sites.

- **Support for multiple active tunnels**   After you set up BGP on the on-premises network, you can set up multiple active-active or active-standby connections to the on-premises network or Azure network to increase redundancy and resiliency in both environments. Traffic is automatically routed via the active tunnels on either end.

- **Support for transit routing**   Regardless of whether networks are connected to each other directly or indirectly, BGP enables gateways to automatically learn and propagate IP address prefixes across all networks. This enables you to set up transit routing between the Azure VPN and on-premises networks and other interconnected networks.

Local network gateways

Local network gateways are gateways set up in Azure that represent your on-premises gateway device and corresponding networks. It is referenced in the gateway configuration when you set up the VPN tunnel. Generally, you need only define the public IP address of the on-premises VPN gateway, the shared secret to use for the connection, and the IP address prefixes to allow from the on-premises network.

However, if you use BGP, additional configuration is required. Specifically, you must define a BGP peer IP address and an autonomous system number (ASN). You need not, however, define the IP address prefixes located in the on-premises network; BGP allows these IP ranges to be added to the route table in Azure automatically.

VPN gateway redundancy

Even when you deploy Azure VPN gateway without the active-active configuration, the service deploys two VPN instances in an active-standby configuration to facilitate any planned or unplanned events that might hamper the functioning of the active instance.

While the switchover to the standby instance is automatic, it does cause a brief interruption in service as all the S2S VPN tunnels are re-established. In a planned maintenance scenario, this can take up to 15 seconds, but might be longer if the outage is unplanned. In that scenario, it can take up to 3 minutes to bring the VPN services back online.

Be aware that any active P2S connections are dropped during such an event, and they are not reestablished automatically. Rather, the end client must initiate the reestablishment of the connection.

Deployment models

VPN gateway connections support different deployment models. You select a deployment model based on your organization's security, redundancy, and connectivity requirements. To help you make a more-informed decision, the following sections review these deployment models.

> **NOTE** The following sections cover basic topologies for each scenario, but more complex configurations are possible. Use each of the topology diagrams in these sections as an initial reference point rather than as a set limitation for various use cases.

Site-to-site VPN gateway connections

You set up a site-to-site (S2S) VPN gateway connection over IPsec/IKE to connect on-premises gateway devices to Azure VPN gateway devices. Both the on-premises gateway device and the Azure gateway device must be associated with a public IP address. You can configure an Azure VPN gateway in active-standby mode or active-active mode, depending on your redundancy requirements and cost limitations.

SINGLE-SITE ACTIVE-STANDBY MODE

In an active-standby configuration, both tunnels are configured as online, but only one tunnel is active; the other is in standby mode. (See Figure 3-1.) If the active tunnel goes down, the standby tunnel becomes active and is then used to route traffic.

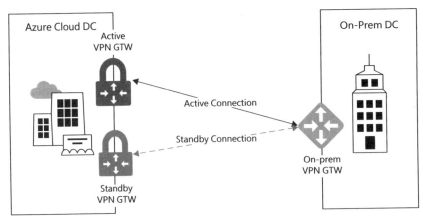

Single-site active-standby VPN mode

FIGURE 3-1 Single-site active-standby mode.

MULTI-SITE ACTIVE-ACTIVE MODE

A variation on the S2S VPN gateway connection is a multi-site VPN connection in which a single active VPN gateway in Azure is connected to multiple on-premises devices in different sites. (See Figure 3-2.) This requires the use of a route-based VPN type, so it does not work with the Basic VPN gateway SKU. The overall throughput available to the gateway device (which is based on its SKU) is shared across all the established connections.

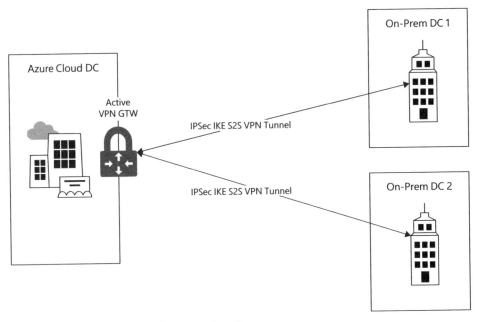

S2S VPN with multiple on-premises sites

FIGURE 3-2 S2S VPN with multiple on-premises sites.

HIGH AVAILABILITY (HA) IN ACTIVE-STANDBY MODE

In this scenario, the Azure VPN gateway is simultaneously connected to two VPN devices in the same on-premises location. (See Figure 3-3.) The same routes are propagated over both connections, and traffic is routed to the on-premises network using both connections to increase the throughput to the on-premises network. (Note that both on-premises devices must support the use of BGP.) Throughput on the Azure end is restricted based on the gateway SKU selected.

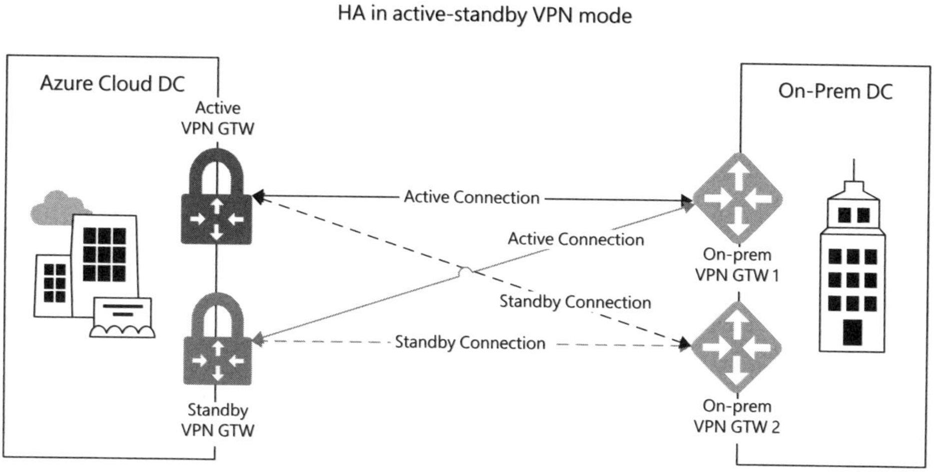

HA in active-standby VPN mode

FIGURE 3-3   HA in active-standby mode.

ACTIVE-ACTIVE MODE

To set up active-active mode, you set the Azure VPN gateway to active-active mode. This results in multiple active connections to the Azure VPN gateway from each on-premises location, and traffic is routed through all of them. (See Figure 3-4.) If any tunnel goes offline, traffic is automatically switched to a tunnel that is still active. This must be set up on both the Azure end and on the on-premises end to ensure that routes involving the inactive tunnel are diverted and removed automatically. (Note that BGP is required for both the Azure gateways and the on-premises ones for route propagation.) This mode increases redundancy and resiliency on the Azure end and ensures there is no disruption in services during planned or unplanned maintenance activities in Azure.

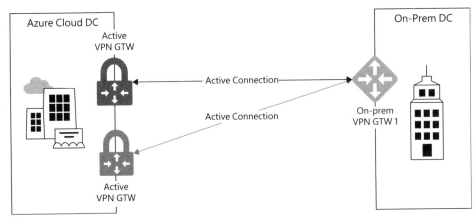

Azure VPN Gateway in active-active mode

FIGURE 3-4 Azure VPN Gateway in active-active mode.

HA IN ACTIVE-ACTIVE MODE

With this "full mesh" mode, two Azure gateways are connected to two on-premises gateways. Any failure in any device on either end will automatically result in the routing of traffic via devices that are still active. (Note that BGP is required for route propagation.) In the scenario shown in Figure 3-5, four S2S tunnels are used. It is important to take this into consideration when choosing gateway SKUs and the limits associated with each.

> **NOTE** This is the recommended design to adopt if it meets your requirements. This design ensures maximum redundancy on both the Azure and on-premises network.

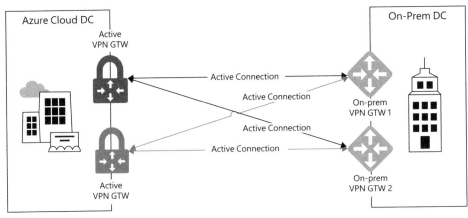

On-premises to Azure VPN gateway connectivity in HA

FIGURE 3-5 On-premises to Azure VPN gateway connectivity in HA.

Point-to-site VPN gateway connections

P2S VPN gateway connections help organizations address work-from-home or remote-work scenarios in which employees must be able to securely connect and access internal resources hosted in Azure or on interconnected on-premises networks. With P2S connections, devices need not be directly connected over a public IP. Client devices simply require an active internet connection and the ability to connect to the Azure endpoint over SSL.

SUPPORTED PROTOCOLS

The following protocols are supported for P2S connections:

- **OpenVPN Protocol**   The OpenVPN protocol is an SSL/TLS-based VPN protocol that works over most firewalls because it requires only port 443 (which most firewalls leave open). You can use the OpenVPN protocol to connect from Android, iOS (versions 11.0 and above), Windows, Linux, and Mac devices (macOS versions 10.13 and above).
- **Secure Socket Tunneling Protocol (SSTP)**   SSTP is a proprietary TLS-based VPN protocol. Like the OpenVPN protocol, SSTP works over most firewalls because it requires only port 443. The difference: Only Windows devices use SSTP. Azure supports all versions of Windows that have SSTP and support TLS 1.2 (Windows 8.1 and later).
- **IKEv2 VPN**   IKEv2 VPN is a standards-based IPsec VPN protocol that can be used to connect from Windows, Android, iOS, and Mac devices (macOS versions 10.11 and above).

AUTHENTICATION

P2S VPN gateway connections (see Figure 3-6) support three types of authentication mechanisms:

- **Remote Authentication Dial-In User Service (RADIUS) authentication**   This requires integration with a RADIUS server for successful authentication.
- **Native Azure certificate authentication**   This involves the generation of an enterprise certificate or a self-signed certificate, deployed to the Azure device and to the various end clients to use as part of their connection request.
- **Native Azure AD authentication**   This requires the use of the OpenVPN protocol, Windows 10– and Windows 11–based clients, and the Azure VPN client.

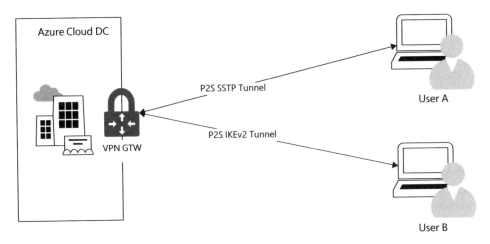

FIGURE 3-6 P2S VPN Gateway tunnels.

VNET-TO-VNET CONNECTIONS (IPSEC/IKE VPN TUNNEL)

Connecting two Azure vNETs using a VPN gateway on either end establishes a vNET-to-vNET connection. This is similar to connecting an Azure VPN gateway to an on-premises network gateway device but enables you to connect Azure vNETs in the same or different regions, in the same or different subscriptions, and in the same or different deployment models (classic and ARM). (See Figure 3-7.)

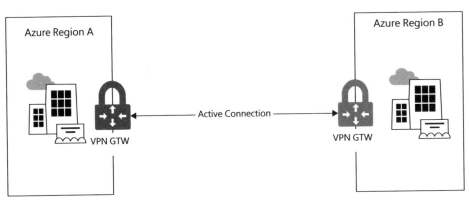

FIGURE 3-7 Azure vNET-to-vNET connections using VPN gateway.

HIGHLY AVAILABLE VNET-TO-VNET

Similar to the full-mesh S2S HA in active-active mode, the vNET-to-vNET design supports an active-active gateway between two vNETs. (See Figure 3-8.) This allows for the establishment of four tunnels between the two VPN gateways connected to two vNETs to provide higher availability and resiliency. (Note that BGP is optional in this setup unless transit routing is required.)

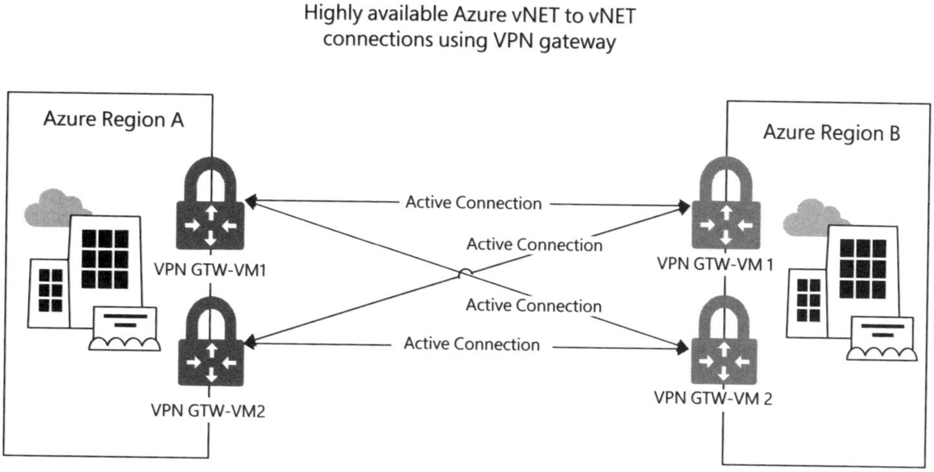

Highly available Azure vNET to vNET
connections using VPN gateway

FIGURE 3-8   Highly available Azure vNET-to-vNET connections using VPN gateways.

ExpressRoute

This book does not discuss ExpressRoute in detail. Still, it is important to know that ExpressRoute is a connectivity option available for your environment, based on your use case. ExpressRoute allows you to extend your on-premises networks with the help of a connectivity provider directly into the Microsoft cloud over a private connection.

> **NOTE**   Connections to Microsoft cloud services are not limited to Microsoft Azure. Connectivity to other Microsoft services such as Microsoft 365 and Dynamics 365 is also allowed.

With ExpressRoute, all connectivity occurs over a private network with the most stringent possible SLAs. This makes ExpressRoute connections more secure and reliable than S2S VPN connections. ExpressRoute also provides higher throughputs and lower latency, making it ideal for large organizations and for organizations whose security and compliance requirements call for its use.

ExpressRoute and site-to-site VPN gateways can co-exist on the same Azure vNET and can be implemented with an active-failover design, such that issues with ExpressRoute will result in an automated failback to the S2S VPN. The other option is to leverage S2S VPNs for sites that are not covered by ExpressRoute connections. It is important to be aware of this compatibility so that you can take it into account when designing for larger environments in which reliability and redundancy are critical for business.

Zonal and zone-redundant VPN gateways

Azure VPN gateway devices support deployment in Azure availability zones. This extends all the redundancy, scalability, and availability features of availability zones to the vNET gateway devices. When gateway devices are deployed in Azure availability zones, they are separated physically and logically within an Azure region to protect against zone-level failures.

There are two options for availability zones:

- **Zonal gateways**   When a VPN gateway is deployed in an availability zone and the availability zone configuration is specified, all instances of the gateway are deployed in that same availability zone. These are called zonal gateways.
- **Zone-redundant gateways**   If the availability zone configuration is set to automatic, the VPN gateway is deployed across availability zones, making them zone-redundant to provide higher resiliency.

> **NOTE**   The two VPN gateway instances will be deployed in any two out of the three availability zones in a region.

Azure VPN gateway walkthrough

The following sections walk you through the process of creating an Azure VPN gateway using the Azure Portal, Azure PowerShell, and the Azure CLI. If you are following along, be sure to select resources and resource names based on your environment, including a unique Azure VPN gateway name for each of your deployments. Also be sure to delete any unwanted resources after you have completed testing to reduce charges levied by Microsoft for these resources.

USING THE AZURE PORTAL

To create an Azure VPN gateway using the Azure Portal, follow these steps:

1. Log into the Azure Portal, type **virtual network gateway** in the search box to locate the service, and select it from the list that appears. (See Figure 3-9.)

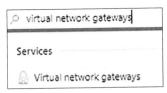

FIGURE 3-9   Selecting the virtual network gateway in the Azure Portal.

2. Click **Create** or **Create Virtual Network Gateway** to start the Create Virtual Network Gateway wizard. (See Figure 3-10.)

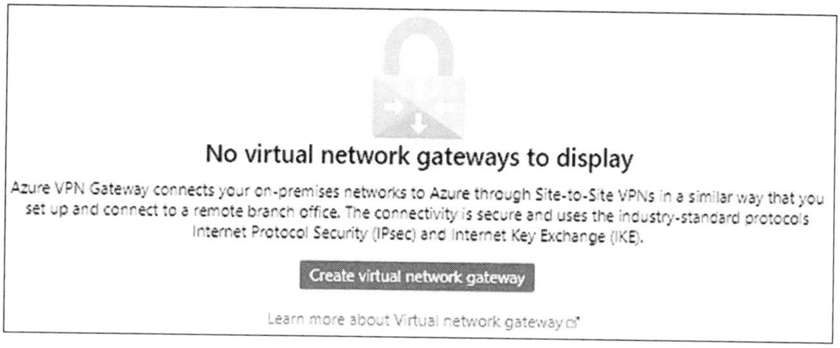

No virtual network gateways to display

Azure VPN Gateway connects your on-premises networks to Azure through Site-to-Site VPNs in a similar way that you set up and connect to a remote branch office. The connectivity is secure and uses the industry-standard protocols Internet Protocol Security (IPsec) and Internet Key Exchange (IKE).

Create virtual network gateway

Learn more about Virtual network gateway ⧉

FIGURE 3-10   Creating the virtual network gateway.

3. In the **Basics** tab of the Create Virtual Network Gateway wizard (see Figure 3-11), enter the following information and click **Next**:

■ **Subscription**   Select the subscription to host the vNET gateway.

■ **Name**   Type a name for the vNET gateway. If the name you type is already in use, the wizard will prompt you to enter a different name.

■ **Region**   Select the Azure region in which you want to create the VPN gateway.

NOTE   Selecting an Azure region automatically populates the Resource Group setting.

■ **Gateway Type**   Select the **VPN** option button.

■ **VPN Type**   Select the **Route-Based** option button.

■ **SKU**   Choose the **VpnGw1** SKU. Alternatively, for higher throughput, choose a higher SKU.

■ **Generation**   Select the SKU's generation. (The options available will depend on the SKU you choose.)

■ **Virtual Network**   Select the virtual network you want to use to host the VPN gateway. Alternatively, click the Create New link and follow the prompts to create a new vNET.

■ **Gateway Subnet Address Range**   Enter an address range for the gateway subnet. This will be used to assign a private IP address to your VPN gateway.

■ **Public IP Address**   Select whether to create a new public IP address or use an existing one. If you want to select an existing IP, you will have to ensure that it is a static public IP on the Standard SKU.

NOTE   If you select the Create New option button, you'll need to add a unique name for the new public IP address in the Public IP Address Name box. If the name you type is already in use, the wizard will prompt you to enter a different one.

- **Enable Active-Active Mode** Select the **Disabled** option button.
- **Configure BGP** Select the **Disabled** option button (unless BGP is required for the on-premises firewall that you will integrate).

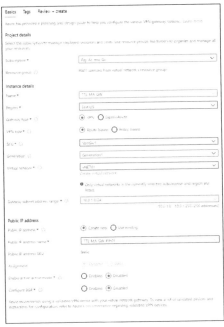

FIGURE 3-11 The Basics tab of the Create Virtual Network Gateway wizard.

4. In the **Tags** tab (see Figure 3-12), enter any tags required for the vNET gateway or leave the fields blank. Then click **Next: Review + Create**.

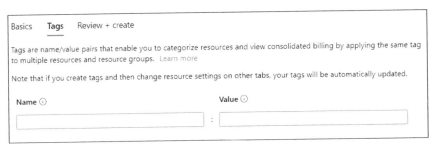

FIGURE 3-12 The Tags tab of the Create Virtual Network Gateway wizard.

5. On the **Review + Create** tab (see Figure 3-13), review your settings and click **Create**.

FIGURE 3-13 The Review + Create tab of the Create Virtual Network Gateway wizard in the Azure Portal.

Azure builds the new vNET gateway. Be aware that this can take 30 to 45 minutes.

6. After Azure builds the new vNET gateway, click **Go to Resource**.

7. In the left pane of the vNET gateway's configuration blade, click **Connections**. (See Figure 3-14.)

FIGURE 3-14 Creating connections in the vNET gateway.

8. Click **Add** to create a new site-to-site VPN tunnel.

The Add Connection options open. (See Figure 3-15.)

FIGURE 3-15 The Add Connection options.

9. In the **Name** box, enter a unique name for the connection. If the name you type is already in use, the dialog box will prompt you to enter a different name.

10. Open the **Connection Type** drop-down list and select **Site-to-Site (IPsec)**.

The Azure service automatically adds the vNET gateway. Now you need to create a new local network gateway to contain the details of your on-premises firewall.

11. In the Add Connection options, click **Local Network Gateway**.

12. Under **Choose Local Network Gateway**, click **Create New**. (See Figure 3-16.)

FIGURE 3-16 Creating a new local network gateway.

13. In the **Create Local Network Gateway** options (see Figure 3-17), enter the following information. Then click **OK**:

- **Name** Enter a unique name for the local network gateway. If the name you type is already in use, you will be prompted to enter a different name.

- **Endpoint** Choose **IP Address** or **FQDN**, depending on your on-premises firewall requirements.

- **IP Address** Enter the IP address for the on-premises firewall that you will integrate with.

NOTE The IP address shown in Figure 3-18 is for illustrative purposes only. It is not available for integration.

- **Address Space** Enter the address space for the on-premises networks that should be allowed to connect to Azure resources via this VPN connection.

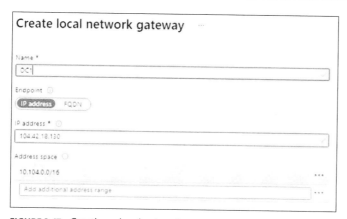

FIGURE 3-17 Creating a local network gateway.

14. Back in the **Add Connection** options, enter the following information and click **OK**:

- **Shared Key (PSK)** Enter the shared key that will be used to connect with the on-premises firewall.

- **Use Azure Private IP Address** Leave this unchecked.

- **Enable BGP** Leave this unchecked unless your on-premises firewall supports BGP.

- **IKE Protocol** Select the IKE protocol that is suitable for your on-premises firewall.

- **Ingress NAT Rules** Leave this at the default setting.

- **Egress NAT Rules** Leave this at the default setting.

15. After Azure creates the connection, click the **Download Configuration** button in the connection's blade. (See Figure 3-18.) This downloads the instructions for setting up your on-premises firewall with the VPN gateway in Azure.

FIGURE 3-18   Downloading the instructions to set up the on-premises firewall with the VPN gateway in Azure.

16. Follow the instructions you just downloaded to configure the on-premises firewall.

   After you configure the on-premises firewall, Azure changes the status of the connection to **Connected**. (See Figure 3-19.)

FIGURE 3-19   The status of the connection is Connected.

USING AZURE POWERSHELL

You can create a vNET gateway and connection using Azure PowerShell with the New-AzVirtualNetworkGateway and New-AzVirtualNetworkGatewayConnection commands and various switches. The following code shows you how. Use this snippet to create the same VPN gateway and connection as you did in the Azure Portal. (Replace all the variables and on-premises firewall configuration as per your environment.) When you do, be sure to either delete the previous vNET gateway or give this new vNET gateway a different name:

```
#Define variables
$rg = "RG01"
$location = "East US"
$vpngwname = "TTL_MA-GW"
$vnet = "vNET01"
#Create GatewaySubnet
Add-AzVirtualNetworkSubnetConfig -Name 'GatewaySubnet' -AddressPrefix 10.0.1.0/24
-VirtualNetwork $vnet
#Create public IP for VPNGW
$gwpip= New-AzPublicIpAddress -Name TTL-MA-GW-PIP -ResourceGroupName $rg -Location
$location -AllocationMethod Dynamic
#Create VPNGW configuration
$subnet = Get-AzVirtualNetworkSubnetConfig -Name 'GatewaySubnet' -VirtualNetwork $vnet
$vpngwipconfig = New-AzVirtualNetworkGatewayIpConfig -Name vpngwipconfig1 -SubnetId
$subnet.Id -PublicIpAddressId $gwpip.Id
#Create the VPN GW
```

```
New-AzVirtualNetworkGateway -Name $vpngwname -ResourceGroupName $rg -Location $location
-IpConfigurations $gwipconfig -GatewayType Vpn -VpnType RouteBased -GatewaySku VpnGw1
#Create Local Network Gateway
$local = New-AzLocalNetworkGateway -Name DC1 -ResourceGroupName $rg -Location $location
-GatewayIpAddress 104.42.18.130 -AddressPrefix "10.104.0.0/24"
#Create site-to-site connection
New-AzVirtualNetworkGatewayConnection -Name MA-DC1 -ResourceGroupName $rg -Location
$location -VirtualNetworkGateway1 $vpngwname -LocalNetworkGateway2 $local -ConnectionType
Ipsec -RoutingWeight 10 -SharedKey 'abcde12345'
```

USING THE AZURE CLI

You can create a vNET gateway using the Azure CLI with the `az network vnet-gateway create` command and various switches to set the VPN gateway's parameters. The following Bash script shows you how. Use this snippet to create the same VPN gateway as you did in the previous sections. (Replace all the variables and on-premises firewall configuration as per your environment.) When you do, be sure to either delete the previous vNET gateway or give this new vNET gateway a different name:

```
#Define variables
$rg = "RG01"
$location = "East US"
$vpngwname = "TTL_MA-GW"
$vnet = "vNET01"
#Create GatewaySubnet
az network vnet subnet create --vnet-name $vnet  -n GatewaySubnet -g $rg
--address-prefix 10.0.1.0/24
#Create public IP for VPNGW
az network public-ip create -n TTL-MA-GW-PIP -g $rg --allocation-method Dynamic
#Create VPNGW gateway
az network vnet-gateway create -n $vpngwname -l $location --public-ip-address
TTL-MA-GW-PIP -g $rg --vnet $vnet --gateway-type Vpn --sku VpnGw1 --vpn-type RouteBased
--no-wait
#Create Local Network Gateway
az network local-gateway create -g $rg -n DC1 --gateway-ip-address 104.42.18.130 --local-
address-prefixes 10.104.0.0/24
#Create site-to-site connection
az network vpn-connection create --name MA-DC1 --resource-group $rg --vnet-gateway1
$vpngwname -l $location --shared-key abcde12345 --local-gateway2 DC1
```

Best practices

Following are some best practices for maintaining and managing Azure VPN gateways:

- **Enable logging for VPN gateway routing activities**   VPN gateway logs all network traffic that it processes for customers. However, you should also activate NSG flow logging to capture and monitor this traffic for better visibility and management.

- **Set up resource logging**   Use Azure Security Center and Azure Monitor to capture all activity logs for the VPN gateway to assist in investigations when required.

- **Standardize with Azure Policy**   Azure Policy helps in standardizing the Azure environment to match company policies and standards for workload deployment and maintenance. Use Azure Policy to ensure that VPN gateways are deployed in line with those standards.

- **Perform penetration testing**   Conduct regular penetration-testing attacks against the VPN gateway to identify weaknesses or possible loopholes. These controlled simulations can help you proactively identify and address weaknesses and defend the company from breaches and attacks.

- **Integrate with Log Analytics for long-term log retention**   Integrate Azure VPN gateway devices with Azure Log Analytics workspaces to store VPN gateway logs for an extended duration to facilitate historical analysis of network patterns, trends, and planning.

- **Integrate with SIEM for security monitoring**   Azure VPN gateway has no built-in features to monitor or manage security. To monitor VPN gateway traffic logs for security breaches and threats, you need to forward those logs to a security information and event management (SIEM) solution, such as Azure Sentinel or a third-party provider.

## Chapter 4

Azure Load Balancer

Overview

Azure provides a load balancer service that enables you to build scalable application architectures with multiple application or web servers where client traffic is distributed based on different algorithms suitable for your environment. The Azure Load Balancer service works on layer 4 of the OSI model to provide secure load balancing for internal applications from the public internet and internal networks.

You can deploy two types of load balancers in Azure (see Figure 4-1):

- **Public load balancer** A public load balancer helps you securely publish internal applications or web servers or services to internet-based clients without exposing the back-end service or virtual machine (VM) directly. Clients connect to the public load balancer and, based on the load-balancing algorithm defined on the load balancer, traffic is routed to the appropriate back-end service.

- **Internal load balancer** An internal load balancer helps you provide secure access to internal applications, web servers, or services to internal-only clients. The clients can be connected directly to the virtual network (vNET) in Azure or via hybrid-connectivity solutions such as a site-to-site (S2S) VPN, point-to-site (P2S) VPN, or ExpressRoute. Direct public access to the load balancer is not possible.

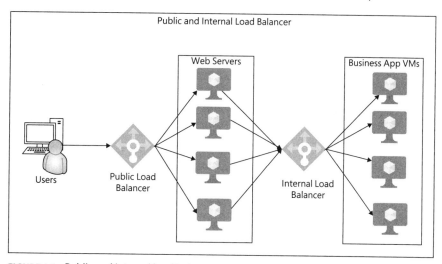

FIGURE 4-1 Public and internal load balancers.

Azure Load Balancer features

Following are some key concepts and benefits of using the Azure Load Balancer service:

- **Support for both public and internal load-balancing options** Azure Load Balancer supports both public and internal-only load-balancing options, which enables it to address various application scenarios that may or may not require public exposure.

- **Highly scalable** Azure Load Balancer is highly scalable. The service scales up automatically as connection requests to back-end services increase.

- **Support for availability zones** The standard Azure Load Balancer supports the use of availability zones to enhance the service's resiliency and availability.

- **Secure access by default** The standard Azure Load Balancer is designed to block all incoming traffic by default unless traffic is explicitly allowed through the use of network security groups (NSGs). The basic Azure Load Balancer, on the other hand, is open to public networks by default and requires configuration to block incoming traffic.

- **Outbound traffic management** You can use Azure Load Balancer to manage egress of all outbound traffic from VMs and to better control that traffic.

- **Support for multiple load-balancing algorithms** There are multiple load-balancing algorithms available to define the most appropriate routing method for your application. You can switch from one load-balancing algorithm to another as the needs of your application evolve.

- **Support for IPv6** Azure Load Balancer supports IPv6 connectivity availability. So, you can set up Azure Load Balancer to accommodate applications that require IPv6 for client connectivity.

- **Support for multiple ports and IP addresses** Azure Load Balancer supports the use of multiple IP addresses and ports to load-balance traffic for multiple application back ends.

- **Support for TCP and UDP flows** Azure Load Balancer supports both TCP and UDP traffic load balancing.

Design concepts and deployment considerations

It is important to understand the different components that comprise Azure Load Balancer to appropriately design and deploy it for your various application requirements. The following sections review each of these components in more detail.

> **NOTE** Azure Load Balancer supports the use of the Azure Portal, Azure PowerShell, the Azure CLI, and ARM Templates for deployment and management.

Front-end IP address

As mentioned, Azure Load Balancer works with both public and internal-only access. To support these scenarios, you can set up the load balancer with either a public IP address or a private IP address. The IP address you assign dictates whether the load balancer is a public or an internal load balancer, as this is the ingress point for your clients to connect to the application or service.

> **NOTE** Both basic and standard load balancers support the use of public or private IP addresses. You determine which will work based on your application's requirements.

Multiple front ends

A load balancer can support multiple front ends, but they have to all be of the same type. For example, if a load balancer has been set up as an internal load balancer, additional IP addresses assigned to it must be internal, too. The same applies to a public load balancer. Incoming traffic is routed based on defined load-balancing rules. In other words, the load balancer identifies the source, protocol, ports, and destination requirements of incoming traffic to select the appropriate back end.

Back-end pool

The back-end pool refers to the VM scale set (VMSS) or VMs that are hosting the web service or application that you want to route traffic. As you add more instances of VMs to the back-end pool, the load balancer automatically incorporates those into its algorithm and routes traffic to the new instances based on routing logic defined in the rules.

In the case of a VMSS, this routing recalculation is automatic, as the VMSS adds or removes instances dynamically. With VMs, the recalculation occurs when you add or remove a VM from the back-end pool.

Health probes

Health probes define parameters that Azure Load Balancer must use to determine the health status of instances in the back-end pool. Depending on the type of load balancer provisioned, the types of health probes supported are as follows:

- **Standard load balancer**   TCP, HTTP, and HTTPS
- **Basic load balancer**   TCP and HTTP

Health probe parameters include the frequency, expected responses, and thresholds to help the load balancer determine when a back-end instance is unhealthy. In such cases, the load balancer stops routing new traffic to the unhealthy instance until subsequent health probes confirm that the instance is once again in a healthy state.

Be aware that with a standard load balancer, any connections that already exist will continue to be routed to the unhealthy instance until the flow is disconnected, terminated, or times out. With a basic load balancer, however, when the instance is deemed unhealthy, TCP flows are disconnected regardless of the connection state.

Load-balancing rules

Load-balancing rules dictate how ingress traffic is managed based on the source IP, source port, destination IP, destination port, and IP protocol details in the connection flow. The rule connects a front-end IP address, public or private, and a port to multiple back-end IP addresses and ports. (See Figure 4-2.) The load-balancing algorithm selected is used thereafter to route the traffic to the back-end pool. Be aware that all load-balancer front-end and back-end endpoints must reside in the same Azure vNET. vNET spanning is not supported.

NOTE ICMP is not a supported protocol.

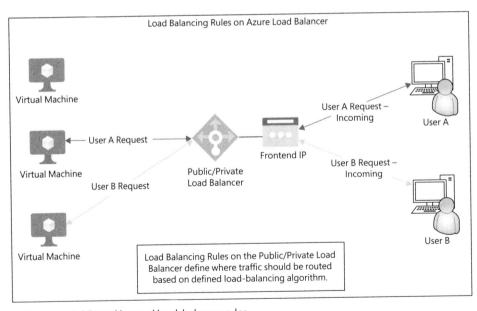

FIGURE 4-2 Public and internal load-balancer rules.

High-availability (HA) ports load-balancing rule

The high-availability (HA) ports load-balancing rule instructs the Azure service that all traffic for all protocols on all ports must be routed in a load-balanced manner, regardless of the port number. This rule is configured when the protocol is set to all, and front-end and back-end ports are set to 0. With this rule, load-balancing decisions are still made per flow based on the five-tuple connection logic that includes the source IP address, source port, destination IP address, destination port, and protocol. (See Figure 4-3.)

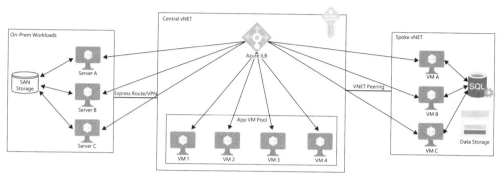

FIGURE 4-3   Azure internal load balancer with HA rules.

Inbound network address translation (NAT) rules

You can set up inbound network address translation (NAT) rules to forward incoming traffic to a specific back-end VM based on the combination of the front-end IP address and the port. (See Figure 4-4.) Traffic can be routed to one or more VMs in a VMSS as part of a NAT pool setup.

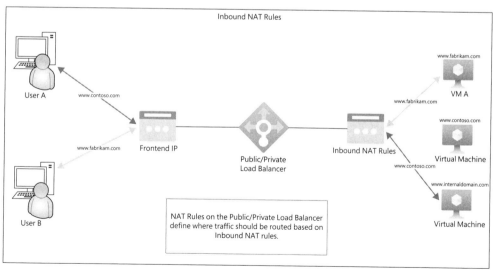

FIGURE 4-4   Inbound NAT rules.

Outbound source network address translation (SNAT) rules

You can set up a standard public load balancer with outbound source network address transla-tion (SNAT) rules for all back-end VM or VMSS resources for any internet-bound egress traffic as well as traffic to other endpoints. (See Figure 4-5.) This helps present the public IP of the load balancer to any external endpoint without exposing IP address information associated with the back-end instance itself.

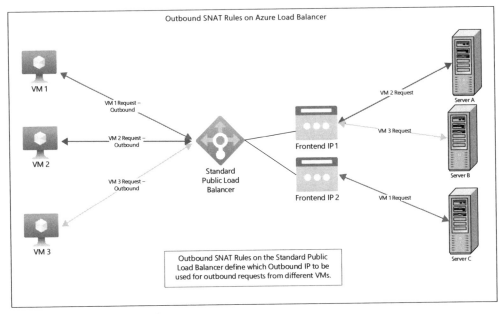

FIGURE 4-5 Outbound SNAT rules.

You can set up a public IP prefix to provide the load balancer with a public IP pool. This can then be used to scale the number of outbound connections across all IPs and ports. You can also map back-end resources to individual public IP addresses or set them up to use any IP address in the pool to prevent port exhaustion. This improves redundancy and scalability.

> **NOTE** Basic load balancers do not support outbound SNAT rules. Standard internal load balancers do not support outbound SNAT rules for internet routing.

Load-balancing algorithms

There are two load-balancing algorithms to route incoming traffic to back-end resources. Each algorithm provides a different level of redundancy and session persistence. The algorithm you select will depend on your use case. The two load-balancing algorithms are as follows:

- **Hash-based** This algorithm generates a unique hash based on a combination of the source IP, source port, destination IP, destination port, and protocol type. Any connection from the same source IP using a different source port to the same application back end will result in a new hash, which might route traffic to a different back-end endpoint each time. This type of routing is useful in scenarios where the application does not require stickiness for all sessions originating from a particular client. It can also help improve responsiveness, as a larger number of sessions from a smaller number of source clients will be evenly distributed across a back-end pool.

- **Source IP affinity**   With this algorithm, traffic from the same source IP to the same destination IP, using the same protocol type, is routed to the same endpoint each time. This helps ensure that a back-end endpoint that is already managing active client sessions responds to any additional incoming client sessions with the same source IP, destination IP, and protocol. You can set up the source IP affinity algorithm to check the source IP and destination IP of incoming requests, or to check the source IP, destination IP, and protocol type, before determining which back-end instance the connection should be routed to.

> **NOTE**   There are different use cases for the source IP affinity algorithm. One is when Azure Load Balancer is used to handle incoming client connections to Remote Desktop Gateway servers. Another is when the client application requires all client traffic to be directed to a single back-end endpoint for the duration of the session.

Availability zones

The standard Azure Load Balancer supports the use of availability zones to increase redundancy and availability in the event of a zone failure. You can set up availability zones to route traffic across zones, and to failover to a different active zone if a zone you are using goes offline.

You can set up Azure Load Balancer to use availability zones for redundancy in three ways:

- **Zone redundant**   If the Azure region on which Azure Load Balancer is deployed supports availability zones, you can set the front-end IP address as zone redundant. That way, if there is a failure within a zone, the IP address will survive it, and will route new incoming requests to the back-end pool. (Of course, this assumes there are resources in the back-end pool that are set up in a similar zone-redundant manner and are online in case of a zone failure.) It is recommended that you use a zone-redundant Azure Load Balancer for your production workloads.

- **Zonal**   With zonal redundancy, the load balancer is redundant within a single zone. If that zone experiences a failure, the load balancer does not failover to another zone. It remains offline for the duration of the zone's outage. You might use zonal redundancy in scenarios in which different IP addresses are set up in different zones within a region to expose an application and use a traffic-management service like Azure Traffic Manager. In this case, traffic is routed across all zones, depending on their availability. This enables you to monitor the health and availability of each zone independently, as each front end in a zone has its own unique public IP.

- **Non-zonal**   Here, the load balancer is set up in a "no-zone" front-end configuration with zero redundancy. This is not a recommended configuration for production workloads.

> **CAUTION**   Public IP addresses upgraded from basic to standard are non-zonal by default. You must take this into consideration if you perform such an upgrade.

Azure Load Balancer walkthrough

The following sections walk you through the process of creating an Azure Load Balancer using the Azure Portal, Azure PowerShell, and the Azure CLI. If you are following along, be sure to select resources and resource names based on your environment, including unique Azure Load Balancer and VM names. Also be sure to delete any unwanted resources after you have completed testing to reduce charges levied by Microsoft for these resources.

USING AZURE PORTAL

To create a public Azure Load Balancer using the Azure Portal, follow these steps:

1. Log into the Azure Portal, type **load balancer** in the search box to locate the service, and select it from the list that appears. (See Figure 4-6.)

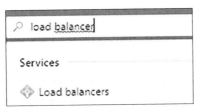

FIGURE 4-6   Creating an Azure Load Balancer in the Azure Portal.

2. Click **Create** or **Create Load Balancer** to start the Create Load Balancer wizard. (See Figure 4-7.)

No load balancers to display

With built-in load balancing for cloud services and virtual machines, you can create highly-available and scalable applications in minutes. Azure Load Balancer supports TCP/UDP-based protocols such as HTTP, HTTPS, and SMTP, and protocols used for real-time voice and video messaging applications.

Create load balancer

Learn more about Load balancers

FIGURE 4-7   Creating the load balancer.

3. In the **Basics** tab of the Create Load Balancer wizard (see Figure 4-8), enter the following information and click **Next**:

- **Subscription**   Select the subscription to host the Azure Load Balancer.

- **Resource Group**   Select the resource group you want to host the Azure Load Balancer. Alternatively, click the **Create New** link and follow the prompts to create a new resource group.

- **Name**   Type a name for the Azure Load Balancer. If the name you type is already in use, the wizard will prompt you to enter a different name.

- **Region**   Select the Azure region in which you want to host the Azure Load Balancer.

- **SKU**   Select the **Standard** option button.

- **Type**   Select the **Public** option button.

- **Tier**   Select the **Regional** option button.

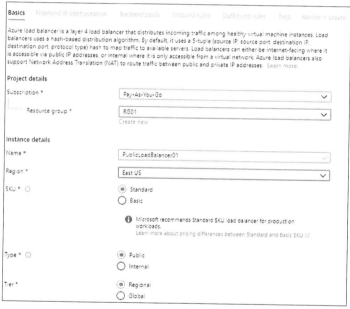

FIGURE 4-8   The Basics tab of the Create Load Balancer wizard.

4. In the **Frontend IP Configuration** tab of the Create Load Balancer wizard (see Figure 4-9), click **Add a Frontend IP Configuration** to create a front-end IP address.

FIGURE 4-9   The Frontend IP Configuration Tab in the Create Load Balancer wizard.

5. In the **Add Frontend IP Address** options (see Figure 4-10), enter the following information:

- **Name**   Enter a name **for the front-end IP address.** If the name you type is already in use, you'll be prompted to enter a different name.
- **IP Version**   Select the **IPv4** option button.
- **IP Type**   Select the **IP Address** option button.
- **Public IP Address**   Select an existing public IP address from the drop-down list. Alternatively, click the **Create New** link.

FIGURE 4-10   Add front-end IP address.

Clicking the **Create New** link opens the **Add a Public IP Address** options.

6. In the **Add a Public IP Address** options (see Figure 4-11), enter the following information and click **OK**:

- **Name**   Enter a name for your public IP address. If the name you type is already in use, you'll be prompted to enter a different name.
- **Availability Zone**   Specify whether you want to set up an availability zone and, if so, which kind—in this case, **Zone-Redundant**.
- **Routing Preference**   Select the option button for your routing preference—in this case, **Microsoft Network**.

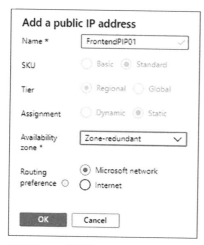

FIGURE 4-11 Adding a public IP address.

7. In the **Add Frontend IP Address** options, click **OK**. Then click **Next** in the **Frontend IP Configuration** tab in the Create Load Balancer wizard.

8. In the **Backend Pools** tab of the Create Load Balancer wizard (see Figure 4-12), click **Add a Backend Pool**.

FIGURE 4-12 The Backend Pools tab of the Create Load Balancer wizard.

9. In the **Add Backend Pool** options (see Figure 4-13), enter the following information:

- **Name** Enter a name for the back-end pool. If the name you type is already in use, you'll be prompted to enter a different name.
- **Virtual Network** Select the vNET on which you want to create the back-end pool.
- **Backend Pool Configuration** Select the **NIC** option button.
- **IP Version** Select the **IPv4** option button.

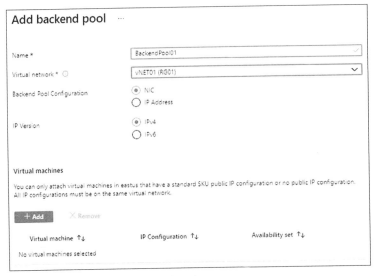

FIGURE 4-13   The Add Backend Pool settings.

10. Under **Virtual Machines**, click the **Add** button.

11. In the **Add Virtual Machines to Backend Pool** settings (see Figure 4-14), select the VMs you want to set up in the back-end pool.

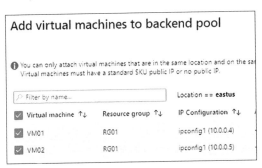

FIGURE 4-14   Add virtual machines to the back-end pool.

12. Confirm that the VMs you selected are listed in the **Virtual Machines** section of the **Add Backend Pool** settings. (See Figure 4-15.) Then click **Next**.

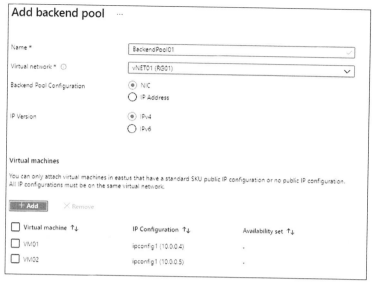

FIGURE 4-15 The Add Backend Pool settings with the selected VMs listed.

13. In the **Inbound Rules** tab of the Create Load Balancer wizard (see Figure 4-16), click **Add a Load Balancing Rule**.

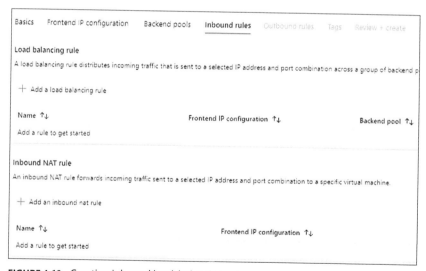

FIGURE 4-16 Creating inbound load-balancing rules.

14. In the **Add Load Balancing Rule** settings (see Figure 4-17), enter the following information:

- **Name**   Enter a name for the load-balancing rule. If the name you type is already in use, you'll be prompted to enter a different name.
- **IP Version**   Select the **IPv4** option button.

- **Frontend IP Address**   Select the front-end IP you created earlier.
- **Backend Pool**   Select the back-end pool configuration you created earlier.
- **Protocol**   Select the appropriate protocol—in this example, **TCP**.
- **Port**   Enter the port to use for load-balancing—in this case, **80**.
- **Backend Port**   Enter the back-end port to use for load-balancing—again, **80**.
- **Health Probe**   Click the **Create New** link.

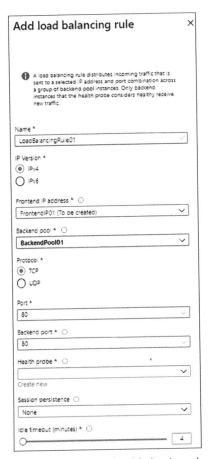

FIGURE 4-17   Add the load-balancing rule.

15. In the **Add Health Probe** settings (see Figure 4-18), enter the following information and click **OK**:

- **Name**   Enter a name for the health probe. If the name you type is already in use, you'll be prompted to enter a different name.
- **Protocol**   Select the appropriate protocol—in this example, **HTTP**.
- **Port**   Enter the port to use for testing—here, **80**.
- **Path**   Enter the path to use for testing—in this case, **/**.

- **Interval** Enter the interval to use for testing—in this example, **5**.
- **Unhealthy Threshold** Enter the threshold to determine whether an instance is unhealthy—here, **2**.

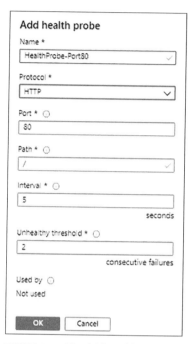

FIGURE 4-18 The Add Health Probe settings.

16. Back in the **Add Load Balancing** settings, open the **Session Persistence** drop-down list and select the persistence you want to use. (See Figure 4-19.)

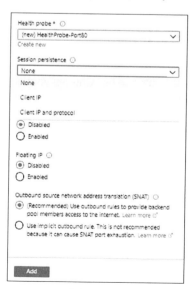

FIGURE 4-19 Selecting a Session Persistence option in the Add Load Balancing Rule settings.

17. Leave the rest of the settings in the **Add Load Balancing Rule** options as is and click **Add**.

18. In the **Outbound Rules** tab of the Create Load Balancer wizard (see Figure 4-20), leave the default settings as is, and click **Next**.

FIGURE 4-20 The Outbound Rules tab in the Create Load Balancer wizard.

19. In the **Tags** tab of the Create Load Balancer wizard (see Figure 4-21), enter any tags required for the load balancer or leave the fields blank. Then click **Next**.

FIGURE 4-21 The Tags tab in the Create Load Balancer wizard.

20. On the **Review + Create** tab, review your settings, and click **Create**.

    Azure creates the load balancer.

21. After Azure builds the new load balancer, click **Go to Resource**.

22. In the left pane of the load balancer's blade, click **Frontend IP Configuration**.

23. Click the link for the front-end IP address you just created to test whether your application's load-balancing is working as expected. (See Figure 4-22.)

FIGURE 4-22 Front-end IP configuration.

USING AZURE POWERSHELL

You can create a load balancer using Azure PowerShell with the `New-AzLoadBalancer` command and various switches. The following code shows you how. Use this snippet to create the same load balancer configuration as you did in the Azure Portal. (Replace all variables and configuration as per your environment.) When you do, be sure to delete the previous load balancer or give this new load balancer a different name:

```
#Define variables
$Region = 'eastus'
$RG = 'RG01'
$LBName = 'PublicLoadBalancer01'
$LBPIP = 'FrontendPIP01'
$BEPool = 'BackendPool01'
#Create zone redundant Public IP
$LBpublicip = @{
    Name = '$LBPIP'
    ResourceGroupName = 'RG01'
    Location = $location
    Sku = 'Standard'
    AllocationMethod = 'static'
    Zone = 1,2,3
}
New-AzPublicIpAddress @LBpublicip
#Create public load balancer
# Place public IP into a variable
$azlbpublicIp = Get-AzPublicIpAddress -Name $LBPIP -ResourceGroupName $RG
# Create load balancer front-end configuration
$azLBfrontend = New-AzLoadBalancerFrontendIpConfig -Name $LBPIP -PublicIpAddress
$azlbpublicIp
# Create back-end address pool configuration
$azlbbepool = New-AzLoadBalancerBackendAddressPoolConfig -Name $BEPool
# Create the health probe
$healthprobe = @{
    Name = 'HealthProbe-Port80'
    Protocol = 'http'
    Port = '80'
    IntervalInSeconds = '360'
    ProbeCount = '5'
    RequestPath = '/'
}
$httphealthprobe = New-AzLoadBalancerProbeConfig @healthprobe
# Create the load-balancer rule
$azloadbalancingrule = @{
    Name = 'LBRule-HTTP-01'
    Protocol = 'tcp'
    FrontendPort = '80'
    BackendPort = '80'
```

```
        IdleTimeoutInMinutes = '15'
        FrontendIpConfiguration = $azlbfrontend
        BackendAddressPool = $azlbbepool
}
$lbhttprule = New-AzLoadBalancerRuleConfig @azloadbalancingrule -EnableTcpReset
-DisableOutboundSNAT
## Create the load balancer
$loadbalancer = @{
        ResourceGroupName = $RG
        Name = $LBName
        Location = $Region
        Sku = 'Standard'
        FrontendIpConfiguration = $frontend
        BackendAddressPool = $azlbbepool
        LoadBalancingRule = $lbhttprule
        Probe = $httphealthprobe
}
New-AzLoadBalancer @loadbalancer
## Add VM01 to the back-end pool
$lb = Get-AzLoadBalancer `
        -ResourceGroupName $RG `
        -Name $LBName
$nic1 = Get-AzNetworkInterface `
        -ResourceGroupName $RG `
        -Name "VM01*"
$nic1.IpConfigurations[0].LoadBalancerBackendAddressPools=$lb.BackendAddressPools[0]
Set-AzNetworkInterface -NetworkInterface $nic1
## Add VM02 to the back-end pool
$nic2 = Get-AzNetworkInterface `
        -ResourceGroupName $RG `
        -Name "VM02*"
$nic2.IpConfigurations[0].LoadBalancerBackendAddressPools=$lb.BackendAddressPools[1]
Set-AzNetworkInterface -NetworkInterface $nic2
```

USING THE AZURE CLI

You can create a load balancer using the Azure CLI with the `az network lb create` command and various switches to set its parameters. The following Bash script shows you how. Use this snippet to create the same load balancer as you did in the previous sections. (Replace all variables and configuration as per your environment.) Be sure to either delete the previous load balancer or give this new one a different name:

```
#Define variables
region='eastus'
rg='RG01'
publicip='FrontendPIP01'
lbname='PublicLoadBalancer01'
```

```
#Create public IP address
az network public-ip create \
    --resource-group $rg \
    --name $publicip \
    --sku Standard \
    --zone {1,2,3} \
    --tier Regional \
    --location $region
#Create load balancer
az network lb create \
    --resource-group $rg \
    --name $lbname \
    --sku Standard \
    --public-ip-address FrontendPIP01 \
    --frontend-ip-name Frontend \
    --backend-pool-name BackEndPool01 \
    --location $region
#Create health probe
az network lb probe create \
    --resource-group $rg \
    --lb-name $lbname \
    --name HealthProbe-Port80 \
    --protocol tcp \
    --port 80
#Create load balancing rule
az network lb rule create \
    --resource-group $rg \
    --lb-name $lbname \
    --name LBRule-HTTP \
    --protocol tcp \
    --frontend-port 80 \
    --backend-port 80 \
    --frontend-ip-name Frontend \
    --backend-pool-name BackEndPool01 \
    --probe-name HealthProbe-Port80 \
    --disable-outbound-snat true \
    --idle-timeout 15
## Add VM01 and VM02 network cards to the back-end pool
array=(VMNIC01 VMNIC02)
  for vmnic in "${array[@]}"
  do
    az network nic ip-config address-pool add \
      --address-pool BackEndPool01 \
      --ip-config-name ipconfig1 \
      --nic-name $vmnic \
      --resource-group $rg \
      --lb-name $lbname
  done
```

Best practices

Following are some best practices recommended for Azure Load Balancer that can help you better deploy and manage the service in your environment:

- **Upgrade to standard**   It is highly recommended that you upgrade from the basic Azure Load Balancer to the standard Azure Load Balancer as soon as possible. The standard option provides a number of benefits compared to the basic option. These include the following:
    - 99.99% SLA
    - Support for multiple inbound and outbound front ends
    - Support for availability zones
    - Support for health probes for the HTTPS protocol
    - Large number of front-end configurations
    - Larger back-end pool sizes
- **Use multiple front ends**   Using multiple front ends can help you scale the number of connections supported for load balancing on specific ports or IP addresses. In addition, this feature offers more benefits, such as zone redundancy, by setting up your front ends in separate zones for higher resiliency.
- **Integrate with Azure Firewall**   You can integrate Azure Load Balancer with Azure Firewall. This enables you to use Azure Firewall's threat intelligence feature to protect web applications in the back-end pool. If your web application is used to manage critical business data, it is highly recommended that you use this feature to protect against known and evolving threats.
- **Setup Network Watcher**   Network Watcher is an Azure service that enables you to identify, analyze, and monitor any issues on the network level to or from an Azure service. It is a good practice to set up Network Watcher in the regions where load balancers are created and to set up alerts to flag anomalous activities on the network.
- **Use service tags in NSG rules**   You can use NSG rules to block inbound traffic to back-end pool resources—*except* inbound traffic that originates from a load balancer. Load balancers can still connect with back-end pool resources to monitor health and route traffic. However, any changes to the load balancer's IP address can break this connectivity if the corresponding rules are not updated in the NSG. To resolve this, you can use service tags. These Microsoft-managed tags contain all the address prefixes associated with an Azure service. In this case, Microsoft manages the AzureLoadBalancer service tag and keeps it up to date. It is a good practice to use service tags in place of IP addresses in NSG rules to ease management overhead.
- **Use Azure Activity log to identify and track service changes**   Azure Activity log keeps track of changes to the Azure Load Balancer configuration. Logs are stored for 90 days. It is a good practice to set up Azure Activity log to monitor for critical changes

and alert you when they occur. This enables you to proactively address unplanned or unauthorized changes.

■ **Configure central security log management** To keep Azure Activity logs for longer than 90 days (for example, for compliance, analytics, or reference purposes), integrate these logs with Azure Monitor and export them to a Log Analytics workspace to perform analytics. You can also integrate with a security information and event management (SIEM) solution such as Microsoft Sentinel for automated analytics and alerting on security incidents.

■ **Set up monitoring and alerts for load balancer metrics** The standard load balancer provides numerous key metrics that you can use to monitor the health of the load balancer and to set up alerts when the situation calls for a proactive response. Some key metrics include the following:

- ■ Data path availability
- ■ Health probe status
- ■ SNAT connection count
- ■ Allocated SNAT ports
- ■ Used SNAT ports
- ■ Packet count
- ■ Byte count

It is a good idea to integrate the load balancer with Azure Monitor and Log Analytics to track these metrics over time. This enables you to identify issues with the service response or setup.

Along with the load balancer, it is a good practice to set up monitoring and alerting for back-end resources used by the load balancer so you can address any service issues on the back-end pool.

Azure provides a dashboard for Azure Load Balancer called Load Balancer Insights. This dashboard provides detailed insights into the load balancer's health and performance. The dashboard consists of the following:

- ■ Functional dependency view
- ■ Metrics dashboard
- ■ Overview tab
- ■ Frontend and Backend Availability tab
- ■ Data Throughput tab
- ■ Flow distribution
- ■ Connection monitors
- ■ Metric definitions

## Chapter 5

Azure Firewall

Overview

Azure Firewall is a fully managed, highly available, highly scalable, stateful firewall provided as an Azure service. It enables you to centrally define network and application logging and to enforce policies to protect Azure virtual network (vNET) resources across multiple subscriptions. (See Figure 5-1.) The service complies with most international standards, including service organization controls (SOCs), International Organization for Standardization (ISO) standards, Payment Card Industry Data Security Standard (PCI DSS), the Health Information Trust Alliance Common Security Framework (HITRUST CSF), and others.

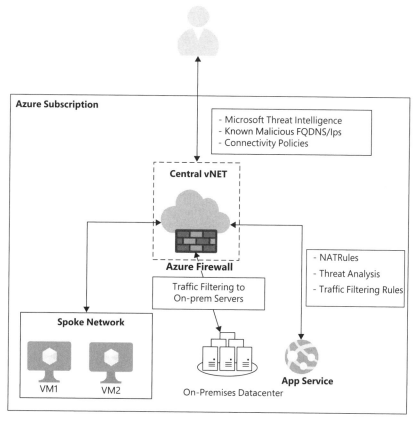

FIGURE 5-1   Azure Firewall features.

Azure Firewall features

Some key features and concepts of Azure Firewall include the following:

- **High availability by design**   Azure Firewall is highly available by design. The service uptime standard is 99.95%. Organizations need not perform additional setup or configuration to achieve high availability.

- **Unlimited scaling capabilities**   Azure Firewall has unlimited scaling capabilities to handle higher volumes of traffic as needed. So, organizations need not plan for or manually scale the firewall to handle peak loads.

- **Support for availability zones**   Azure Firewall supports deployment across multiple availability zones, allowing for 99.99% uptime. Azure Firewall costs remain the same regardless of the availability zone configuration. If a firewall spans multiple availability zones, there are additional charges associated with inbound and outbound data transfers between availability zones.

- **Fully stateful service**   Azure Firewall is a fully stateful service that provides layer 3 and 4 monitoring and filtering capabilities. Defining rules for what traffic should be allowed or denied based on source, destination IPs, protocols, or ports protects resources spread across multiple Azure subscriptions and vNETs.

- **Centralized management**   Azure Firewall allows for centralized management using Azure Firewall Manager. This makes it easy to configure and manage multiple Azure Firewalls from a single location.

- **Threat Intelligence**   Azure Firewall supports the automatic blocking of traffic from known malicious IPs and sources based on Microsoft Threat Intelligence feeds. You can easily enable this functionality if your organization requires it.

- **NAT support**   Azure Firewall service provides both inbound and outbound network address translation (NAT) capabilities, allowing traffic to be securely routed to and from internal resources without requiring public exposure for critical services.

- **Support for multiple IP addresses**   As many as 250 IP addresses can be assigned to Azure Firewall. So, you can configure inbound and outbound NAT for multiple virtual resources on the same ports using different IP addresses.

- **Centralized logging**   Azure Firewall supports centralized logging to Azure Monitor, enabling long-term retention of firewall and traffic logs for analysis and alerting.

- **Multiple deployment methods**   You can deploy and manage Azure Firewall using the Azure Portal and Azure PowerShell. You can also deploy Azure Firewall using ARM templates.

Design concepts and deployment considerations

It's important to gain a better understanding of the various features of Azure Firewall to design and deploy the service most effectively for your environment. The following sections discuss several firewall features in detail.

Support for availability zones

An availability zone is a unique physical location encompassing one or more datacenters. Multiple availability zones comprise each Azure region.

You can deploy Azure Firewall across multiple availability zones in a region when you create the firewall, but not after it has been created. Any firewall you've already created that needs to be part of an availability zone must be deleted and re-created in the availability zone.

The cost of the firewall is the same, whether it's within an availability zone or not. However, if a firewall spans multiple availability zones, additional charges apply for inbound and outbound data transfers across the availability zones.

> **NOTE** If you create an Azure Firewall that spans two or more availability zones, the service SLA jumps from 99.95% uptime to 99.99% uptime.

Inbound DNAT

Azure Firewall supports destination network address translation (DNAT). This allows the firewall to route incoming traffic for a specific public IP associated with the firewall, to an internal service. This allows secure publishing of internal services over the public internet.

DNAT allows traffic to be routed from standard public ports to non-standard internal ports, thereby obscuring the internal application ports. Internal applications can be securely exposed without fear of exposing the application front end to malicious attacks.

You can set up as many as 250 public IP addresses on Azure Firewall, making it possible to associate different public IPs with different internal services. This makes it easier to use the same ports for multiple internal applications if required.

Outbound SNAT

Azure Firewall also supports source network address translation (SNAT) for outbound traffic that originates from resources inside the network. With SNAT, traffic going to the public internet can be masked with a specific public IP or a set of public IPs. This makes it possible for people (such as remote employees) to access resources over the public internet. It also makes it possible to set up routing rules to enable specific SNAT configurations access to known-partner or third-party networks that require static IP associations.

SNAT can take advantage of Azure Firewall's multi-IP support, using multiple public IPs to limit the impact of port exhaustion for a single public IP. All public IPs associated with the firewall are randomly chosen at the time of the SNAT. Hence, any filtering performed downstream will require that all associated public IPs or the public IP prefix be allowed for any services that rely on this filtering.

Traffic filtering

With Azure Firewall, you can create different types of traffic-filtering rules to protect your environment and back-end services. You can perform traffic filtering in different ways:

- Network traffic-filtering rules using incoming network packet details
- Web-traffic filtering rules using web categories
- Application FQDN traffic-filtering rules to protect outbound traffic to pre-defined Microsoft-managed application FQDNs

Network traffic filtering

Azure Firewall can filter network traffic through the creation of rules that allow or deny traffic based on source IPs, destination IPs, port, or protocol. Because Azure Firewall is a fully stateful service, capable of monitoring and filtering layer 3 and layer 4 traffic, it can constantly analyze the context of traffic and data packets traversing the firewall. This enables it to filter based on not just source and destination IPs but also by port and protocol, providing more control over the network traffic allowed in and out of the network.

Web-traffic filtering

Azure Firewall also supports web-traffic filtering, allowing or restricting traffic based on pre-defined categories such as social media, search engine, religion, sports, and so on.

The standard Azure Firewall supports categorization and filtering up to the primary domain level of a web request only. For example, web requests for www.bing.com and www.bing.com/news would be categorized under search engine because the primary domain in both cases (bing.com) is a search engine.

NOTE If required, you can set up exceptions to allow or deny specific sites or sets of sites within a category.

Application FQDN traffic filtering

Azure Firewall enables you to limit outbound HTTP, HTTPS, and Azure SQL traffic to a pre-defined set of fully qualified domain names (FQDNs). This includes the ability to allow traffic based on wildcards to these FQDNs that are managed by Microsoft.

Groupings

Azure provides various methods to simplify grouping well-known services. These are frequently used for IP ranges, infrastructure services, and website categories, to enable them to be used effectively in filtering rules.

Tags

Tags make it easier to group resources, services, or objects to apply specific actions on them. There are two different types of tags available for use with Azure Firewall service: fully qualified domain name (FQDN) tags and service tags.

FQDN TAGS

An FQDN tag is applied to a pre-defined set of well-known Azure services to easily allow traffic to them. For example, the Windows Diagnostics FQDN tag is applied to all Windows Diagnostics endpoints. You can enable this tag to allow traffic to the Windows Diagnostics service instead of setting up all the IPs associated with this service to allow traffic.

> **NOTE** FQDN tags are managed and maintained by Microsoft. You cannot make changes to FQDN tags, nor can you create new ones.

The FQDN tags currently available in Azure include the following (Microsoft will add more FQDN tags in the future as the need arises):

- **Windows Update** This FQDN tag allows access to all Microsoft Update endpoints.
- **Windows Diagnostics** This FQDN tag allows access to all Windows Diagnostics endpoints.
- **Microsoft Active Protection Service (MAPS)** This FQDN tag allows access to all MAPS endpoints.
- **App Service Environment (ASE)** This FQDN tag allows access to ASE platform traffic. This tag, however, does not cover customer-specific storage and SQL endpoints created by ASE. Those need to be enabled via service endpoints or added manually.

> **NOTE** Applying these tags allows the corresponding access associated with each endpoint or service.

SERVICE TAGS

Service tags are created by Microsoft to manage groups of IP address prefixes associated with specific Azure services. For example, the AppService service tag applies to the Azure App Service, and any rules set up to use this tag would apply to all instances of that Service.

Other service tags include the following:

- **Storage**   This applies to the Azure Storage service.
- **SQL**   This applies to the Azure SQL service.
- **AzureActiveDirectory**   This applies to the Azure Active Directory service.

> **NOTE** Only Microsoft can create and manage service tags. New services tags are typically created when new services are brought online.

Infrastructure FQDNs

Every Azure Firewall instance contains a built-in collection of rules for infrastructure FQDNs that are set up to allow traffic for different Azure services and enabled by default. The following services are included in these FQDNs, are specifically for the Azure platform, and cannot be used for any other reason:

- Compute access to the storage Platform Image Repository (PIR)
- Managed disks status storage access
- Azure Diagnostics and Logging (MDS)

> **NOTE** You can override this collection of built-in rules by adding a Deny All Application Rules collection at the end of the list of firewall rules.

IP groups

You can use IP groups to assemble different IP addresses or IP ranges for use in Azure Firewall rules. An IP group could be used as a source address or destination address in network traffic rules, or as a source address in DNAT or application rules.

The same IP group can be used in multiple rules. This makes it easier to maintain and manage them and reduces management overhead. Each IP group can contain a single IP address, multiple IP addresses, or a range of IP addresses.

Web categories

Web categories are pre-defined sets of categories that contain a list of websites that are related based on their content or purpose. These categories make it easy for administrators to allow or deny traffic based on organizational policies. You can set up exceptions or exclusions for specific websites in a category to override your organization's policy for that category.

Forced tunneling

Forced tunneling involves routing all outbound internet traffic through a designated edge device or network virtual appliance instead of through the default internet gateway. This helps organizations process outbound traffic for compliance, audit, or security reasons before sending it to the internet.

You can set up forced tunneling only when you create an Azure Firewall instance. If you want to configure an existing Azure Firewall instance to use forced tunneling, you must delete that instance and re-create it with forced tunneling enabled. Similarly, if you want to disable forced tunneling for an Azure Firewall instance, you must delete the instance and re-create it with that setting disabled.

Traffic to manage the firewall service must be separated from client traffic to allow operational activities for the service to continue uninterrupted. You must use a dedicated subnet, AzureFirewallManagementSubnet, with a minimum subnet size of /26. This subnet requires a dedicated public IP address. Once this configuration is in place, you can set the AzureFirewallSubnet to route all traffic to any on-premises or dedicated appliance for processing as required.

Threat intelligence

Threat intelligence–based filtering is an advanced security feature available with Azure Firewall that sources information about malicious IPs and domains from the Microsoft Threat Intelligence feed. This feature is enabled by default in alert-only mode, although you can set it to alert-and-deny mode to alert you to a potential threat and block that threat when necessary.

When alert-and-deny mode is enabled, other network or application-filtering rules are ignored. This is because if this setting is enabled, Azure Firewall always analyzes Threat Intelligence rules for incoming or outgoing traffic first. Note that this order of operations cannot be changed.

In contrast, in alert mode, Azure Firewall also analyzes the traffic first, but because the service need only raise an alert, the rest of the network and application traffic-filtering rules continue to be applied for that traffic.

Azure Firewall Manager

Azure Firewall Manager is a management layer service that can be used to centrally configure policies and to route and manage instances of Azure Firewall deployed in multiple subscriptions and vNETs. For enterprises accustomed to employing a central console for firewall management, Azure Firewall Manager is the ideal solution for managing Azure Firewall instances. It can be used to centrally create, deploy, and manage network and application filtering rules across multiple Azure Firewall instances using firewall policies (discussed next).

Classic rules versus firewall policies

There are two ways to set up Azure Firewall rules:

- **Classic rules** Classic rules are standard application or network rules that are set up for individual Azure Firewall instances. These are available only on the standard SKU. Newer Azure Firewall features do not support classic rules.

- **Firewall policies** Firewall policies are collections of NAT rules, network traffic rules, application filtering rules, and Threat Intelligence settings that are stored on a global level and can be deployed across multiple Azure Firewall instances. This makes it easier to apply standards across an organization using policy inheritance and enforcement. New firewall policies can be created based on existing policies. In addition, you can create local policies for specific scenarios and apply them to individual Azure Firewall instances. To create and manage firewall policies, you use Azure Firewall Manager, Azure PowerShell, the Azure CLI, REST API, or ARM templates.

> **NOTE** Microsoft does not charge for firewall policies associated with zero or one firewall. Fixed-rate charges are levied only if there are multiple firewall associations.

It is highly recommended to migrate away from classic rules to firewall policies. One easy way to do this is to select the Migrate to Firewall Policy option in the Azure Portal.

Firewall rule processing

Now that you know all the different ways Azure Firewall can manage traffic—Threat Intelligence, inbound and outbound NAT rules, network and application rules—it is important to grasp the order in which they are processed.

> **NOTE** Azure Firewall will deny all traffic until some rules are defined to specify what traffic should be allowed in and out.

Incoming traffic

For incoming traffic, the order in which rules are processed depends on the type of firewall management in place.

For a firewall set up with classic rules, the order is as follows:

1. Threat Intelligence rules.
2. NAT rules.
3. Network rules, in order of priority (from the lowest number to the highest number).

For a firewall set up with firewall policies, the order is as follows:

1. Threat Intelligence rules.
2. NAT rules.

3. Rule collections or rule-collection groups, in order of priority (from the lowest number to the highest number). Inside each rule collection or rule collection group, network rules are processed using the same logic (from the lowest number to the highest number).

> **NOTE** There is one exception to this logic: Rule-collection groups inherited from a parent policy are always applied first, regardless of the priority set on the child rule collection or child rule-collection groups.

> **NOTE** Application rules do not apply to incoming traffic because Azure Firewall does not support this functionality. For application rule filtering, you should use Azure Web Application Firewall or Azure Front Door.

Outbound traffic

Like inbound traffic, the order in which rules for outbound traffic are applied depends on the type of firewall management in place. On each level, if there is a match to deny traffic, no further rules are applied. In addition:

- Application rules are analyzed only if there is no match for network rules.
- Infrastructure rules are analyzed only if there is no match for application rules.
- If there is no match for infrastructure rules, traffic is denied.

For a firewall set up with classic rules, the order is as follows:

1. Threat Intelligence rules.
2. NAT rules.
3. Network rules, in order of priority (from the lowest number to the highest number).
4. Application rules in order of priority (from the lowest number to the highest number).
5. Infrastructure rule collections.

For a firewall set up with Firewall Policy, the order is as follows:

1. Threat Intelligence rules.
2. NAT rules.
3. Rule collections or rule-collection groups in order of priority (from the lowest number to the highest number). Inside each rule collection or rule-collection group, network and application rules are processed using the same logic (from the lowest number to the highest number).
4. Infrastructure rule collections.

> **NOTE** There is one exception to this logic: Rule-collection groups inherited from a parent policy are always applied first, regardless of the priority set on the child rule collection or child rule-collection groups. In addition, application rules are processed only if the traffic uses the HTTP, HTTPS, or MSSQL protocol.

DNS proxy

You can configure Azure Firewall as a DNS proxy to resolve client DNS requests as an intermediary, with the help of an authorized DNS server.

Active FTP support

Azure Firewall supports active FTP. Support for active FTP is disabled by default to protect against FTP bounce attacks, but you can enable it if the firewall is deployed using Azure PowerShell, the Azure CLI, or an ARM template.

Azure Monitor logging

You can integrate Azure Firewall with Azure Monitor. This integration also provides support for logging events, archiving logs to a storage account for long-term retention, sending logs to Log Analytics, and event streaming to Event Hub.

Microsoft provides a pre-built template for Azure Monitor called Azure Firewall Workbook that you can use to analyze firewall data and create visualizations for reporting purposes. There are also numerous firewall metrics, activity logs, and diagnostic logs that you can incorporate into your monitoring solution for deeper analysis of firewall performance and ongoing issues.

Firewall metrics

Azure Monitor provides numerous metrics for various Azure services that you can use to monitor specific aspects of the service. These metrics enable you to detect related performance issues and other problems related to the service better than generic metrics alone.

Azure Monitor includes Azure Firewall–specific metrics to collect service-related information and raise alerts if issues are detected. Key metrics include the following:

- **Firewall Health State** Gauges the health of the firewall based on SNAT port availability.
- **Data Processed** Tracks the total amount of data traversing the firewall at various periods of time.
- **Throughput** Indicates the rate per second at which data is traversing the firewall.
- **Application Rules Hit Count** Gauges the number of times an application rule has been triggered by a request.
- **Network Rules Hit Count** Tracks the number of times a network rule has been triggered by a request.
- **SNAT Port Utilization** Indicates the percentage of SNAT ports currently in use by the firewall.

Azure Activity logs

Azure automatically collects Activity logs for all deployed services. These logs contain operational and audit data that records all changes and actions performed on a service for a given period of time. You can collect and analyze these logs to track change-management activities or administrative actions over time.

Diagnostic logs

There are various types of diagnostic logs available for Azure Firewall to monitor various features of the service to identify ongoing issues. These include the following:

- **Application Rule log** This records all connection requests that match an application rule.
- **Network Rule log** This records all connection requests that match a network rule.
- **DNS Proxy log** This records all DNS messages sent to a DNS server using the DNS proxy service configured on the firewall.

Each of these log types can be configured to store logs in one of three ways:

- Store them in an Azure Storage account
- Send them to Azure Monitor
- Stream them to Event Hubs

Azure Firewall deployment walkthrough

The following sections walk you through the process of creating an Azure Firewall using the Azure Portal and Azure PowerShell. (The functionality needed to use the Azure CLI to complete this task is under development, so it is not covered here.) If you are following along, be sure to select resources and resource names based on your environment, including a unique Azure Firewall name for each deployment. Also be sure to delete any unwanted resources after you have completed testing to reduce charges levied by Microsoft for these resources.

USING AZURE PORTAL

To create an Azure Firewall using the Azure Portal, follow these steps:

1. Log into the Azure Portal, type **firewall** in the search box to locate the service, and select it from the list that appears.

2. Click **Create** or **Create Firewall** to start the Create a Firewall wizard. (See Figure 5-2.)

No firewalls to display

Cloud-native network security, to protect your Azure Virtual Network resources. Learn more about Azure Firewall

Create firewall

FIGURE 5-2   Create a firewall.

3. In the **Basics** tab of the Create a Firewall wizard (see Figure 5-3), enter the following information and click **Next**:

   ■ **Subscription**   Select the subscription to host the Azure Firewall instance.

   ■ **Resource Group**   Select the resource group you want to host the firewall. Alternatively, click the **Create New** link and follow the prompts to create a new resource group.

   ■ **Name**   Type a name for the firewall. If the name you type is already in use, the wizard will prompt you to enter a different name.

   ■ **Region**   Select the Azure region in which you want to host the Azure Firewall instance.

   ■ **Availability Zone**   Select an availability zone for the firewall.

   ■ **Firewall Tier**   Select the **Standard** option button.

   ■ **Firewall Management**   Select the **Use a Firewall Policy to Manage This Firewall** option button.

   ■ **Firewall Policy**   Select the policy you want to associate with the firewall. Alternatively, click the **Create New** link and follow the prompts to create a new firewall policy.

   ■ **Choose a Virtual Network**   Select an existing vNET on which to deploy the firewall. Alternatively, click the **Create New** link and follow the prompts to create a new vNET.

   ■ **Public IP Address**   Select the public IP address you want to use. Alternatively, click the **Add New** link and follow the prompts (see Figure 5-4) to create a new IP address.

   ■ **Forced Tunneling**   Leave this set to **Disabled**.

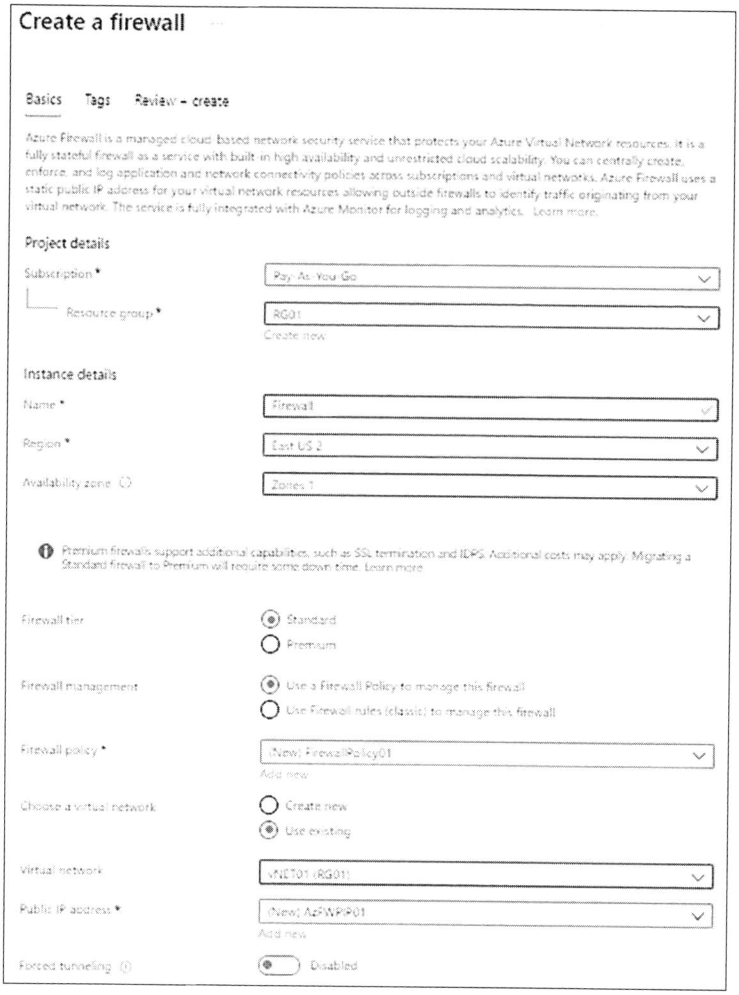

FIGURE 5-3 The Basics tab of the Create a Firewall wizard.

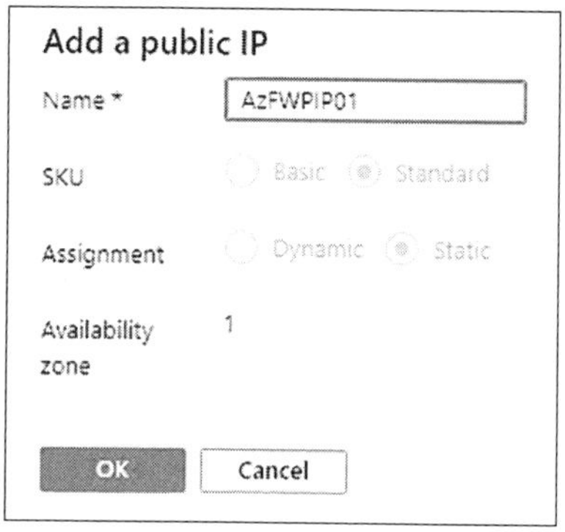

FIGURE 5-4 Adding a new public IP.

4. In the **Tags** tab of the Create a Firewall wizard (see Figure 5-5), enter any tags required for the firewall. Then click **Next**.

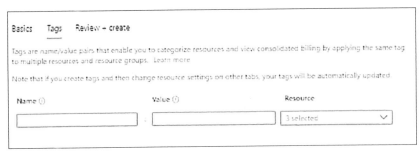

FIGURE 5-5   The Tags tab of the Create a Firewall wizard.

5. On the **Review + Create** tab, review your settings. Then click **Create**.

Now you need to create a default route and attach it to the required subnets to route traffic from resources in those subnets through the firewall.

6. In the Azure Portal, type **route tables** in the search box to locate the service and select it from the list that appears.

7. Click **Create** or **Create Route Table** to start the Create Route Table wizard. (See Figure 5-6.)

FIGURE 5-6   Create route table.

8. In the **Basics** tab of the Create Route Table wizard (see Figure 5-7), enter the following information and click **Next**:

- **Subscription**   Select the subscription to host the route table.
- **Resource Group**   Select the resource group in which you want to create the route table. Alternatively, click the **Create New** link and follow the prompts to create a new resource group.
- **Region**   Select the Azure region in which you want to create the route table.

- **Name**   Type a name for the route table. If the name you type is already in use, the wizard will prompt you to enter a different name.
- **Propagate Gateway Routes**   Select the **Yes** option button.

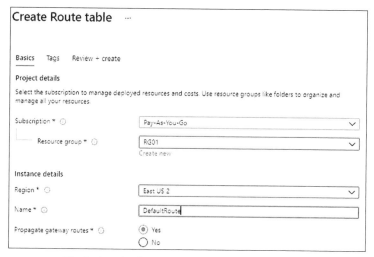

FIGURE 5-7   The Basics tab of the Create Route Table wizard.

9. In the **Tags** tab of the Create Route Table wizard (see Figure 5-8), enter any tags required for the route table. Then click **Next**.

FIGURE 5-8   Enter the tags.

10. On the **Review + Create** tab, review your settings. Then click **Create**.

11. When the route table has been created, click **Go to Resource**.

12. In the left pane of the new route table's configuration blade, click **Subnets**. Then click the **Associate** button in the right pane. (See Figure 5-9.)

FIGURE 5-9 Associating the subnet in the route table.

13. In the **Associate Subnet** settings (see Figure 5-10), enter the following information. Then click **OK**:

- **Virtual Network**   Select the appropriate vNET.
- **Subnet**   Select the subnet you want to associate with the route table.

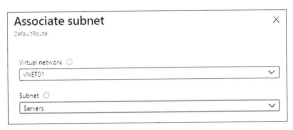

FIGURE 5-10 The Associate Subnet options.

14. After the subnet has been associated with the route table, click **Routes** on the left side of the route table's configuration blade. Then click **Add** on the right side of the blade. (See Figure 5-11.)

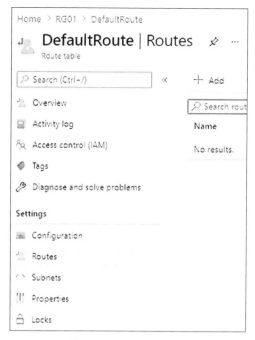

FIGURE 5-11 The Routes options.

15. In the **Add Route** settings, enter the following information and click **Add**:

   ■ **Route Name**   Enter a unique name for the route. If the name you type is already in use, you'll be prompted to enter a different name.

   ■ **Address Prefix**   Type **0.0.0.0/0** to set it as the default gateway.

   ■ **Next Hop Type**   Select **Virtual Appliance**.

   ■ **Next Hop Address**   Enter the firewall's private IP.

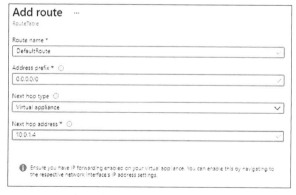

FIGURE 5-12 The Add Route options.

16. Type **firewall policies** in the Azure Portal search box. Then select **FirewallPolicy01** (created earlier in this walkthrough) from the list that appears.

17. On the left side of the configuration blade for FirewallPolicy01, click **Application Rules**. Then click **Add a Rule Collection** on the right side of the blade. (See Figure 5-13.)

FIGURE 5-13   The Application Rules options for the firewall policy.

18. In the **Add a Rule Collection** dialog box (look ahead to Figure 5-14), enter the following information:

   - **Name**   Enter a unique name for the rule collection—here, AppRule01. If the name you type is already in use, you'll be prompted to enter a different name.
   - **Rule Collection Type**   Select **Application**.
   - **Priority**   Enter a priority for the rule collection type—in this example, **100**.
   - **Rule Collection Action**   Select **Allow**.
   - **Rule Collection Group**   Leave this set to the default rule-collection group or select a different rule-collection group.

19. In the **Rules** section of the **Add a Rule Collection** dialog box (see Figure 5-14), enter the following information. When you're finished, click **Add**:

   - **Name**   Type a name for the first rule in the rule collection—here, **AllowWebBrowsing**.
   - **Source Type**   Choose **IP Address**.
   - **Source**   Enter the source's IP address.
   - **Protocol**   Enter the supported protocols in the **Protocol** box.
   - **Destination Type**   Select the destination type—in this case, **Web Categories**.
   - **Destination**   Select the destination. (You will see a list of destinations based on the destination type selected earlier.)

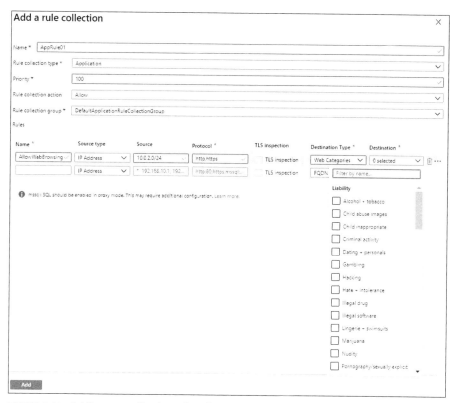

FIGURE 5-14   Adding an application rule collection.

20. On the left side of the FirewallPolicy01 blade, click **Network Rules**. Then click **Add a Rule Collection** on the right. (See Figure 5-15.)

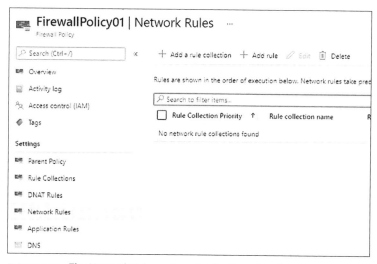

FIGURE 5-15   The Network Rules options for the firewall policy.

21. In the **Add a Rule Collection** dialog box (look ahead to Figure 5-16), enter the following information:

- **Name** Enter a unique name for the rule collection. If the name you type is already in use, you'll be prompted to enter a different name.
- **Rule Collection Type** Select **Network**.
- **Priority** Enter a priority for the rule collection type—in this example, **100**.
- **Rule Collection Action** Select **Allow**.
- **Rule Collection Group** Leave this set to the default rule-collection group or select a different rule-collection group.

22. In the **Rules** section of the **Add a Rule Collection** dialog box (see Figure 5-16), enter the following information. When you're finished, click **Add**:

- **Name** Type a name for the first rule in the rule collection—here, **AllowDomainNameResolution**.
- **Source Type** Choose **IP Address**.
- **Source** Enter the source's IP address.
- **Protocol** Enter the supported protocols in the **Protocol** box.
- **Destination Type** Select the destination type—in this case, **IP Address**.
- **Destination** Select the destination.

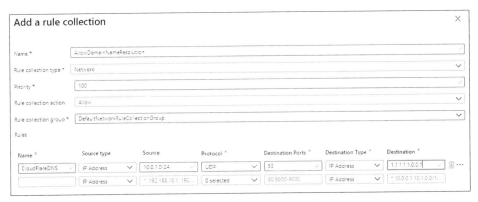

FIGURE 5-16 Adding a network rule collection.

23. On the left side of the FirewallPolicy01 blade, click **DNAT Rules**. Then click **Add a Rule Collection** on the right. (See Figure 5-17.)

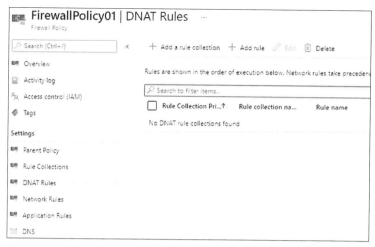

FIGURE 5-17 The DNAT Rules for the firewall policy.

24. In the **Add a Rule Collection** dialog box (look ahead to Figure 5-18), enter the following information:

■ **Name** Enter a unique name for the rule collection—here, **DNAT-AllowRDP-VM**. If the name you type is already in use, you'll be prompted to enter a different name.

■ **Rule Collection Type** Select **DNAT**.

■ **Priority** Enter a priority for the rule collection type—in this example, **100**.

■ **Rule Collection Type** This is automatically set to **Destination Network Address Translation (DNAT)** and cannot be changed.

■ **Rule Collection Group** Leave this set to the default rule-collection group or select a different rule-collection group.

25. In the **Rules** section of the **Add a Rule Collection** dialog box (see Figure 5-18), enter the following information. When you're finished, click **Add**:

■ **Name** Type a name for the first rule in the rule collection—here, **AllowRDP-VM**.

■ **Source Type** Choose **IP Address**.

■ **Source** Enter the source IP. (I typed * to choose all IPs.)

■ **Protocol** Enter the supported protocols in the **Protocol** box.

■ **Destination Ports** Enter the destination port.

■ **Destination Type** Select the destination type—in this case, **IP Address**.

■ **Destination** Select the destination.

■ **Translated Address** Enter the translated address of the destination address. I entered 10.0.0.4 (partially visible in Figure 5-18).

■ **Translated Port** Enter the translated address of the destination port. In my case, it was 3389 (not visible in Figure 5-18).

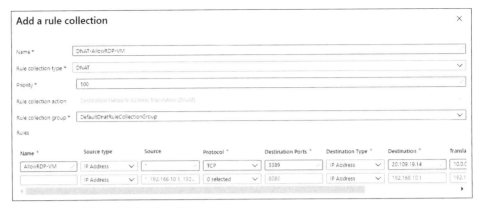

FIGURE 5-18 Adding a DNAT rule collection.

26. On the left side of the FirewallPolicy01 blade, click **Rule Collections**. Then, on the right, verify that the rule collections you created are listed and reflect your requirements. (See Figure 5-19.)

> **NOTE** You can edit any of the rule collections. Simply click the link for the collection and change its settings as needed.

FIGURE 5-19 Rule collections listed in the FirewallPolicy01 blade.

27. On the left side of the FirewallPolicy01 blade, click **Threat Intelligence**.

28. Enter the following information on the right side of the blade (see Figure 5-20) and click **Save**:

- **Threat Intelligence Mode** Choose between **Off**, **Alert Only**, and **Alert and Deny**, depending on your requirements.
- **Allow List Addresses** In the **IP Address, Range, or Subnet** box under **Allow List Addresses**, enter any IP address, range, or subnet whose traffic you want to allow-list or allow to pass through your firewall.
- **FQDNs** In the **FQDNs** box under **FQDNs**, enter any FQDNs you want to allow-list.

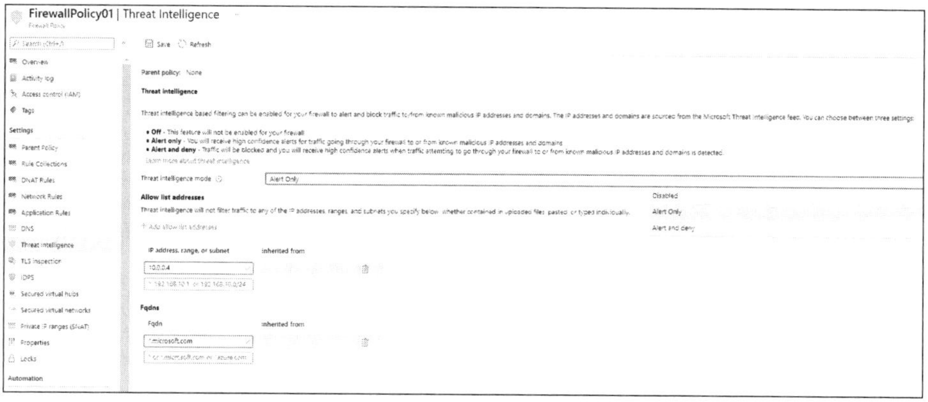

FIGURE 5-20 Applying Threat Intelligence settings.

USING AZURE POWERSHELL

You can create an Azure Firewall instance using Azure PowerShell with the `New-AzFirewall` command and various switches. The following code shows you how. Use this snippet to create the same Azure Firewall instance as you did in the Azure Portal. (Replace all variables and configuration as per your environment.) When you do, be sure to either delete the previous firewall or give this firewall a different name:

```
#Define variables
$RG="RG01"
$Region="EastUS2"
#Create new Firewall Policy
$AzFirewallpolicy = New-AzFirewallPolicy -Name FirewallPolicy -ResourceGroupName $RG
-Location $Region
#Create and Configure a firewall policy application rule
$FWAppRuleGroup = New-AzFirewallPolicyRuleCollectionGroup -Name DefaultApplicationRuleCol-
lectionGroup -Priority 100 -FirewallPolicyObject $AzFirewallPolicy
$FWApprule01 = New-AzFirewallPolicyApplicationRule -Name AllowWebBrowsing -SourceAddress
10.0.1.0/24 -Protocol http, https -WebCategory "Business"
$FWAppCollection01 = New-AzFirewallPolicyFilterRuleCollection -Name AppRuleCollection01
-Priority 100 -Rule $FWAppRule01 -ActionType "Allow"
Set-AzFirewallPolicyRuleCollectionGroup -Name $FWAppRuleGroup.Name -Priority 100
-RuleCollection $FWAppcollection01 -FirewallPolicyObject $AzFirewallpolicy
#Create and configure a firewall policy network rule
$FWNWRuleGroup = New-AzFirewallPolicyRuleCollectionGroup -Name DefaultNetworkRuleCollec-
tionGroup -Priority 200 -FirewallPolicyObject $AzFirewallPolicy
$FWNetRule01 = New-AzFirewallPolicyNetworkRule -name CloudFlareDNS -protocol UDP
-sourceaddress 10.0.1.0/24 -destinationaddress 1.1.1.1,1.0.0.1 -destinationport 53
$FWNetCollection = New-AzFirewallPolicyFilterRuleCollection -Name AllowDomainNameResolu-
tion -Priority 100 -Rule $FWNetRule01 -ActionType "Allow"
Set-AzFirewallPolicyRuleCollectionGroup -Name $FWNWRuleGroup.Name -Priority 200
-RuleCollection $FWNetCollection -FirewallPolicyObject $AzFirewallPolicy
```

```
#Deploy the Azure Firewall
# Create a Public IP for the firewall
$AzFWPubIP = New-AzPublicIpAddress -Name "AzFWPIP01" -ResourceGroupName $RG -Location
$Region -AllocationMethod Static -Sku Standard
# Create the firewall
$vnet = Get-AzVirtualNetwork -ResourceGroupName $RG -Name "vNET01"
$Azfirewall = New-AzFirewall -Name Firewall -ResourceGroupName $RG -Location $Region
-VirtualNetwork $vnet -PublicIpAddress $AzFWPubIP -FirewallPolicyId $AzFirewallpolicy.Id
$AzFWPrivIP = $AzFirewall.IpConfigurations.privateipaddress
#Create and configure DNAT policy
$FWNATRuleGroup = New-AzFirewallPolicyRuleCollectionGroup -Name DefaultDNATRuleCollection-
Group -Priority 300 -FirewallPolicyObject $AzFirewallPolicy
$FWNATRule01 = New-AzFirewallPolicyNatRule -Name DNAT-AllowRDP-VM -SourceAddress * -Pro-
tocol TCP -DestinationAddress $AzFWPubIP -DestinationPort 3389 -TranslatedAddress 10.0.0.4
-TranslatedPort 3389
$FWDNATCollection = New-AzFirewallPolicyNatRuleCollection -Name DNAT-Rules -Priority 100
-Rule $FWNATRule01 -ActionType "Dnat"
Set-AzFirewallPolicyRuleCollectionGroup -Name $FWNATRuleGroup.Name -Priority 300
-RuleCollection $FWDNATCollection -FirewallPolicyObject $AzFirewallPolicy
#Create route table
$RouteTbl = New-AzRouteTable -Name RouteTable -ResourceGroupName $RG -location $Region `
#Create the default route
 Add-AzRouteConfig -Name "DefaultRoute" `
  -RouteTable $RouteTbl `
  -AddressPrefix 0.0.0.0/0 `
  -NextHopType "VirtualAppliance" `
  -NextHopIpAddress $AzFWPrivIP
#Set route table
Set-AzRouteTable -routetable $RouteTbl
#Associate the route table to the subnet
Set-AzVirtualNetworkSubnetConfig -VirtualNetwork $vnet `
  -Name 'Servers' `
  -AddressPrefix 10.0.1.0/24 `
  -RouteTable $RouteTbl
```

Best practices

Following are several recommended best practices for Azure Firewall to help you better deploy
and manage the service in your environment:

- **Integrate Azure Firewall with Azure Monitor**   As discussed, you can integrate
  Azure Firewall with Azure Monitor to store and analyze firewall logs. Doing so is highly
  recommended to monitor the firewall metrics to gauge its performance and identify
  issues. You can store your logs in a storage account, send them to Log Analytics, or
  stream them to Event Hub. Then, you can use tools like Log Analytics, Microsoft Excel,

and Microsoft Power BI to analyze them. You can also set up alerts for various metrics to automatically identify attacks or performance issues.

- **Set priority of rules in increments of 100**   When you create a new rule, it's a good practice to set its priority to 100. That way, as you add more rules over time, you can easily insert them between existing rules without having to modify the priority of those rules.

- **Avoid wildcards as sources for DNATs**   It is better to specify source IPs for incoming DNATs, if possible, instead of using wildcards. That way, only traffic from the sources you specify is allowed in and routed to the internal application.

- **Consider global peering**   Azure Firewall is typically deployed using a hub-and-spoke model, in which the firewall is deployed in a central vNET, with all other vNETs in the region peered with the central network. This allows for centralized control of traffic for all peered vNETs without requiring the deployment of a firewall in each one. This works well for vNETs that spread globally, but if traffic traverses different Azure regions before reaching its final destination, performance or latency issues might crop up. To rectify this, consider using global peering for firewalls only. Just be sure to test it first to ensure it meets the latency and performance requirements of the application and your organization.

- **Use Azure Firewall side-by-side with network security groups (NSGs)**   Azure Firewall and NSGs work together in a complementary way to provide in-depth network security. Even if you are deploying Azure Firewall to protect resources across all subscriptions and vNETs, be sure to take advantage of the distributed network layer traffic filtering provided by NSGs to limit traffic to resources within vNETs.

- **Use Azure Security Center**   Azure Security Center provides better management of your security posture management as well as protection from specific threats. Consider following the network-protection recommendations provided by Security Center to secure network resources related to Azure Firewall. When combined with a Log Analytics Workspace, you can set up monitoring and alerting for anomalous activity so you can respond to threats in a timely manner.

- **Enable Threat Intelligence**   As noted, Threat Intelligence–based filtering can alert you to and block traffic from and to well-known malicious IP addresses and domains. Consider using this functionality to enhance protection for your environment.

- **Reduce administrative overhead, where possible**   Where possible, use service tags, IP groups, and FQDN tags instead of IP addresses or IP ranges when setting up network security rules. This reduces management and maintenance of the network configuration as well as administrative overhead.

- **Standardize security configurations**   Standardize the configuration of your organization's security policies. Then, set up Azure services to ensure they are effectively maintained. Azure Firewall Manager and Azure Blueprints can help you achieve this objective. Azure Firewall Manager can help you standardize the security configuration, but Azure Blueprints goes much further by packaging all artifacts such as ARM templates, Azure RBAC controls, and policies in a single definition that, when deployed, can monitor and maintain your security policy standards.

- **Use automated tools to monitor network resource configurations and detect changes** Azure Activity log keeps track of all configuration changes to an Azure resource. You can (and should) set up alerts in Azure Monitor to trigger if there are changes to critical resources.

- **Consider Azure Sentinel for advanced monitoring needs** If your organization needs to monitor all security, diagnostic, and activity logs in a centralized repository—perhaps for monitoring and analyzing change-management efforts or to troubleshoot some future problem—consider using Azure Sentinel or a third-party SIEM solution. You can use these to capture all required logs for centralized storage, analysis, and review.

- **Configure security log storage retention as per organizational compliance requirements** It is important to identify your organization's compliance requirements regarding the retention of log data and ensure that the design of your environment takes them into consideration. With Log Analytics, you can store data for up to two years. However, you have two other options for storing logs for longer: storage accounts and SIEM solutions. You can use these to store logs for much longer durations if your organization requirements exceed the capabilities of Log Analytics. Furthermore, SIEM solutions can be customized to meet your organization's needs.

- **Ensure regular automated backups** Azure Firewall has no backup feature. However, you can ensure regular automated backups by using Azure Automation to export the firewall and related resources in a JSON template. You can also use the Export Template feature in the Azure Portal to manually export the Azure Firewall configuration in before change-management activities.

- **Enable locks** You can enable locks on Azure Firewall and policy resources to ensure that they aren't deleted accidentally or otherwise. Considering that a firewall is a critical resource in any environment—and that if it experiences an outage, it can bring the entire environment offline—it is advisable to protect it as best as you can.

## Chapter 6

Azure DNS

Overview

Azure DNS is a domain name hosting and resolution service provided in Microsoft Azure. Customers can add public domain names that they own to Azure DNS and use Azure DNS to manage their DNS records using their Azure AD credentials.

Azure DNS is a completely managed service hosted across the Azure global network of DNS servers, providing an SLA of 100%. It uses AnyCast networking. This enables clients to obtain name-resolution services from the closest available Azure DNS server, reducing latency on DNS queries.

You can manage the Azure DNS service using the Azure Portal, Azure PowerShell, the Azure the CLI, the REST API, and SDKs, allowing integration with applications that require automated DNS-management functionality.

Azure DNS features

Azure DNS provides a number of key features that make it a compelling service to use for most environments. These key features include the following:

- **Global scale and reduced latency**   Azure DNS stores customer DNS domains in its global DNS name server network. This ensures that an outage in a single region does not take public DNS services for customers offline. Azure DNS uses AnyCast networking, reducing latency for DNS queries and improving performance for client connections.

- **Unbeatable SLA**   Because of the global redundancy of the DNS domains, outage in one region does not bring the DNS domain offline on a global level. Azure DNS guarantees a valid DNS request response from at least one of its DNS servers 100% of the time.

- **Seamless access management and monitoring**   Azure's role-based access control (RBAC) provides access to Azure DNS for complete management or specific actions. Any changes in the DNS service configuration or DNS records are monitored and tracked to detect unwanted changes.

- **Easy billing management**   Azure DNS billing is integrated with the billing for all other Azure services, making it easier to keep track of expenses related to your public domain infrastructure. Service charges are based on the number of hosted domains and the number of DNS queries received, providing pay-as-you-go functionality. Using other third-party DNS-hosting services can add overhead with respect to monitoring and managing for service availability, contract renewals, and billing.

- **Support for private domains**   One of the key features provided by Azure DNS is the support for private DNS domain hosting. This makes it possible to integrate private virtual networks and use the DNS services to host private custom domains through the integration.

- **Alias records**   Alias record sets help to create references to Azure resources such as Traffic Manager profiles, Azure CDN endpoints, and Public IP addresses hosted in Azure. Alias record sets can be set up using Azure DNS, and the integration supports automatic updates to any IP address changes occurring for each of the services.

- **Management and integration**   You can manage Azure DNS using the Azure Portal, Azure PowerShell, and the Azure CLI. In addition, Azure DNS has integration capabilities using REST APIs and SDKs for automated DNS management.

- **Private DNS**   Azure DNS allows integration with Azure virtual networks to host private DNS zones, which you can use to provide name-resolution services in the virtual network. In addition, VMs can automatically register and update their DNS records, providing name-resolution services within the environment without requiring the use of other DNS services.

Azure DNS limitations

As of this writing, Azure DNS has a few limitations. Some key limitations are listed here:

- **DNSSEC**   Azure DNS does not currently support DNSSEC. The current guidance for organizations that require DNSSEC is to use a third-party DNS hosting service instead of Azure DNS.

- **Domain name procurement**   You cannot use Azure DNS to buy new domain names. Customers must procure domain names from a third-party domain name registrar, using Azure DNS only for the hosting services and record management.

- **Zone transfers**   Azure DNS does not support zone transfers, which enable the migration of DNS services from one DNS hosting provider to another using REST APIs. You can use the Azure CLI to import DNS records into Azure DNS or make entries using Azure Portal or Azure PowerShell, however.

- **URL redirection**   Some third-party DNS providers offer URL redirection as part of their DNS services. This enables companies to set up HTTP redirections for their web applications. Although many organizations find this to be a useful service, because the redirection is on the HTTP traffic layer instead of the DNS, it is not considered a real DNS feature. So, at this stage, URL redirection is not offered as part of the Azure DNS feature set.

Design and configuration considerations

You'll want to consider a few features provided by Azure DNS when setting up the service. The following sections discuss these in more detail.

Types of DNS zones

Azure DNS provides two types of DNS zone services: public and private. Both zone types address specific use cases, and both could be used in the same Azure environment to host the same DNS zone.

Public DNS zones allow for the hosting of publicly available domain names—for example, contoso.com. This type of zone generally contains DNS records for public-facing services, such as web servers, mail servers, and so on. Public DNS zones allow access over the public internet for name resolution of DNS records hosted by an organization for external consumption by customers or vendors and for internal consumption by employees. Examples of scenarios in which DNS records might be set up in public DNS zones might be as follows:

- An organization hosting a public-facing website could set up its WWW DNS address (A) record in a public DNS zone.

- To provide access to its email services, an organization could host its mail server A records in a public DNS zone.

- All organizations would set up their mail exchange (MX) records in a public DNS zone for other DNS servers to identify and route emails to their mail servers.

Private DNS zones allow for the hosting of internal DNS zones required for name resolution between Azure VM resources. A private zone can contain the following types of DNS records:

- WWW A DNS records with internal IPs of web servers and web applications

- A DNS records with internal IPs (if available) for mail servers

- A records for VMs hosted within the virtual network

- Pointer (PTR) records for VMs hosted within the virtual network

The zones are interlinked to virtual networks, and name resolution works only for those networks in which the link is in place. No internet-based name resolution of private DNS zones is possible. This provides a secure and reliable way to provide DNS services for VMs hosted in a virtual network without requiring the setup of other DNS solutions to host those custom private zones.

A few notes to keep in mind:

- The same domain can be hosted as a public DNS zone and a private DNS zone. This supports split-horizon DNS scenarios for name resolution of the same services with varying internal and external records to enable them to talk efficiently via internal and public networks.

- Azure DNS does not support single-labeled private DNS zones. All zones must have two labels separated by a dot (contoso.com), with a maximum of 34 labels.

- You must create child domains as separate private DNS zones, as zone delegation is currently not supported.

DNS zone walkthrough

The following sections walk you through the process of creating a DNS zone using the Azure Portal, Azure PowerShell, and the Azure CLI. If you are following along, be sure to select resources and unique resource names based on your environment for each of your deployments. Also, be sure to delete any unwanted resources after you have completed testing to reduce charges levied by Microsoft for these resources.

The steps for creating a public DNS zone in the Azure Portal are nearly identical to those for creating a private one. The difference is that you use the DNS Service to create a public DNS zone, and you use the Private DNS Zones service to create a private one. (See Figure 6-1.) Because the following sections cover more private DNS zone features than public DNS zone ones, the subsequent sections focus on creating private DNS zones.

FIGURE 6-1   DNS services in Azure.

USING THE AZURE PORTAL

To create a private DNS zone using Azure Private DNS service using the Azure Portal, follow these steps:

1. Log in to the Azure Portal, type **private DNS zone** in the search box to locate the service, and select it from the list that appears.

2. Click the **Create Private DNS Zone** button to start the Create Private DNS Zone wizard. (See Figure 6-2.)

FIGURE 6-2   Initiate the creation of a private DNS zone.

3. In the **Basics** tab of the Create Private DNS Zone wizard, enter the following information (see Figure 6-3), and click **Next**:

- **Subscription**   Select the subscription that will host the private DNS zone.

- **Resource Group**   Select the resource group you want to use to host the private DNS zone. Alternatively, to create a new resource group, click the **Create New** link and follow the prompts.

- **Name**   Type a name for the private DNS zone.

- **Resource Group Location**   This will be populated automatically based on the location of the resource group you just selected.

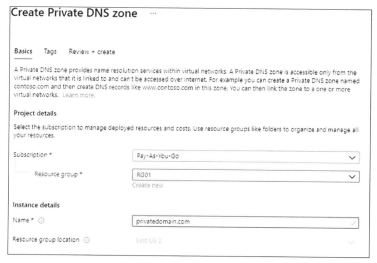

FIGURE 6-3   The Basics tab of the Create Private DNS Zone wizard.

4. In the **Tags** tab, enter any tags required for the private DNS zone or leave the fields blank (see Figure 6-4), and click **Next**.

FIGURE 6-4   Set up tags.

5. In the **Review + Create** tab (see Figure 6-5), review your settings and click **Create**.

FIGURE 6-5 Review and create a private DNS zone.

USING AZURE POWERSHELL

You can create a private DNS zone with Azure PowerShell using the `New-AzPrivateDNSZone` command with various switches to set the zone's parameters. For example, to create the same private DNS zone as you did in the preceding section, you use the first two lines of code below. If you want to create a public DNS zone instead, use the second two lines of code, and replace the domain name with one that you own:

```
#Create private DNS zone
New-AzPrivateDnsZone -Name privatedomain.com -ResourceGroupName RG01


#Create public DNS zone
New-AzDnsZone -Name publicdomain.com -ResourceGroupName RG01
```

USING THE AZURE CLI

You can create a private DNS zone with the Azure CLI using the `az network private-dns zone create` command with various switches to set the zone's parameters. The first two lines of code below show you how to set up the same zone you created in the preceding sections with the Azure CLI. If you want to create a public DNS zone instead, use the second two lines of code, and replace the domain name with one that you own:

```
#Create private DNS zone
az network private-dns zone create --resource-group RG01 --name privatedomain.com


#Create public DNS zone
Az network dns zone create --resource-group RG01 --name publicdomain.com
```

Linking with Azure virtual networks

You can link a private DNS zone to one or more Azure virtual networks. This enables VMs hosted in the virtual network(s) to use Azure DNS to resolve the names of any private DNS zones hosted in the service. (See Figure 6-6.)

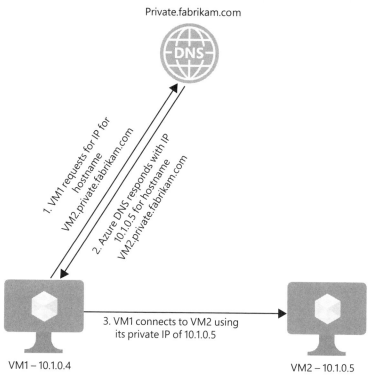

FIGURE 6-6   DNS name resolution after linking with a virtual network.

> **NOTE**   There is no explicit requirement to set up virtual network peering for multiple virtual networks linked to the same private DNS zone.

Virtual network link walkthrough

The following sections walk you through the process of linking the private DNS zone you created in the "DNS zone walkthrough" section to a virtual network using the Azure Portal, Azure PowerShell, and the Azure CLI.

USING THE AZURE PORTAL

To set up the virtual network link using the Azure Portal, follow these steps:

1. In the left pane of the private DNS zone's configuration page, under **Settings**, click **Virtual Network Links**. Then, in the right pane, click the **Add** button to start the Add Virtual Network Link wizard. (See Figure 6-7.)

2. In the Add Virtual Network Link wizard, enter the following information (see Figure 6-8) and click **OK**:

   - **Link Name**   Enter a unique name to identify the virtual network link.

   - **Subscription**   Select the subscription for which the link will be created.

   - **Virtual Network**   Select the virtual network you want to link to the private DNS zone.

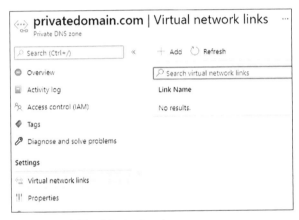

FIGURE 6-7   Add a virtual network.

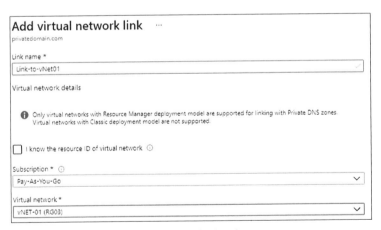

FIGURE 6-8   The Add Virtual Network Link wizard.

3. Repeat these steps for any other virtual networks you want to link to the DNS zone.

USING AZURE POWERSHELL

You can link a virtual network to a private DNS zone using Azure PowerShell with the `New-AzPrivateDNSVirtualNetworkLink` command and various switches to set the link's parameters. The following code shows you how:

```
#Define variables
$rg = "RG01"
$name = "Link-To-vNET01"
$vnet = "vNET-01"
#Create the virtual network link
New-AzPrivateDNSVirtualNetworkLink -ZoneName privatedomain.com -ResourceGroupName $rg
-Name $name -VirtualNetworkId $vnet.id
```

USING THE AZURE CLI

You can link a virtual network to a private DNS zone using the Azure CLI with the `az network private-dns link create` command and various switches to set the link's parameters. The following Bash script shows you how:

```
#Define variables
rg = "RG01"
name = "Link-To-vNET01"
vnet = "vNET-01"
#Create the virtual network link
az network private-dns link vnet create --resource-group $rg --name $rg --zone-name
privatedomain.com --virtual-network $vnet
```

Auto registration

Private DNS zones support the use of auto registration to automatically register and update VM DNS records for accurate name resolution between different VMs running on the same virtual network. This involves setting up an A and a PTR record for each VM that already exists or is newly created on the virtual network for which the feature is enabled. When a VM is deleted, the service also deletes the corresponding A and PTR records for the VM.

You can set up multiple virtual networks to use auto registration to the same private DNS zone. However, every virtual network can be connected to only a single private DNS zone if auto-registration is enabled. Here are a few other limitations to this feature to consider:

- Auto registration works only for the primary network card on a VM. The remaining network cards require manual DNS record creation and management.

- Auto registration will not work if a VM is set to a static IP. Only VMs using DHCP on their primary network card are supported.

- Auto registration supports only VMs. Any other Azure service, such as an internal load balancer, requires manual DNS record creation and management.

- IPv6 (AAAA) DNS records are not supported.

Auto-registration walkthrough

The following sections walk you through the process of using the Azure Portal, Azure Power-Shell, and the Azure CLI to enable auto-registration for the private DNS zone you created in the "DNS zone walkthrough" section when linking it to a virtual network.

> **NOTE** Recall that you can link a private DNS zone to multiple virtual networks. You've already linked the private DNS zone you created to one virtual network; here, you will link it to a different one.

USING THE AZURE PORTAL

To set up auto registration using the Azure Portal, follow these steps:

1. In the left pane of the private DNS zone's configuration page, under **Settings**, click **Virtual Network Links**. Then, in the right pane, click the **Add** button to start the Add Virtual Network Link wizard.

2. In the Add Virtual Network Link wizard, type a name for the link, select your subscription, and select the virtual network to which you want to link, as you did earlier in the "Virtual network link walkthrough" section.

3. Under **Configuration**, select the **Enable Auto Registration** check box (see Figure 6-9). Then click **OK**.

FIGURE 6-9 Enable auto registration.

USING AZURE POWERSHELL

You can enable auto registration during the virtual network link–creation process using Azure PowerShell with the `New-AzPrivateDNSVirtualNetworkLink` command and the `-EnableRegistration` switch. The following code shows you how:

```
#Define variables
$rg = "RG01"
$name = "Link-To-vNET01"
$vnet = "vNET-01"
#Create the virtual network link
New-AzPrivateDnsVirtualNetworkLink -ZoneName privatedomain.com -ResourceGroupName $rg
-Name $name -VirtualNetworkId $vnet.id -EnableRegistration
```

USING THE AZURE CLI

You can enable auto registration during the virtual network link–creation process using the Azure CLI with the `az network private-dns link create` command and the `--registration-enabled` parameter. The following code shows you how:

```
#Define variables
rg = "RG01"
name = "Link-To-vNET01"
vnet = "vNET-01"
#Create the virtual network link
az network private-dns link vnet create --resource-group $rg --name $rg --zone-name
privatedomain.com --virtual-network $vnet --registration-enabled true
```

Alias record sets

Alias record sets are references created in Azure Public DNS zones to public IPs associated with Azure services such as Azure Traffic Manager, Azure CDN, Azure Front Door, Azure App Service with Static IP, and Azure Public IP Address. You can associate an alias record set with any of these resources. Then, during the name-resolution process, the alias record will query and return the current IP address of the associated service.

The DNS record set changes automatically as the public IP of the service changes. This helps to ensure that DNS records are always up-to-date and that no stale or incorrect records can result in unplanned downtimes.

Azure DNS currently supports the following DNS record types:

- A
- AAAA
- CNAME

Alias record sets walkthrough

The following section walks you through the process of creating a public DNS zone and alias record set using the Azure Portal.

USING THE AZURE PORTAL

To create an alias record set, you first create a public DNS for the DNS domain you own. To do both these things using the Azure Portal, follow these steps:

1. Log in to the Azure Portal, type **DNS zone** in the search box to locate the service, and select it from the list that appears.

2. Click the **Create DNS Zone** button to start the Create DNS Zone wizard. (See Figure 6-10.)

FIGURE 6-10   Create a reverse DNS lookup zone.

3. In the **Basics** tab of the Create DNS Zone wizard, enter the following information (see Figure 6-11), and click **Next**:

- **Subscription**   Select the subscription to host the DNS zone.
- **Resource Group**   Select the resource group you want to use to host the reverse lookup DNS zone. Alternatively, to create a new resource group, click the **Create New** link and follow the prompts.
- **Name**   Enter a name for the DNS domain that you own.
- **Resource Group Location**   This will be populated automatically based on the location of the resource group you just selected.

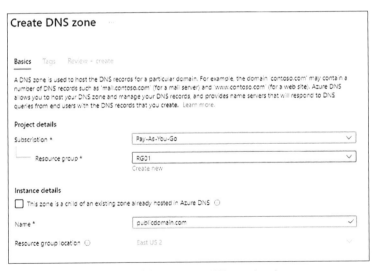

FIGURE 6-11   The Basics tab of the Create DNS Zone wizard.

4. In the **Tags** tab, enter any tags required for the DNS zone or leave the fields blank (see Figure 6-12). Then click **Next**.

FIGURE 6-12 Set up tags.

5. In the **Review + Create** tab, review your settings and click **Create**.

6. After the zone has been created, open its blade in the Azure Portal. Then, in the **Overview** tab, click the **Record Set** button. (See Figure 6-13.)

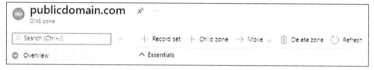

FIGURE 6-13 The Record Set button in the Overview tab.

7. In the **Add Alias Record Set** dialog box, enter the following information, and click **OK**. (See Figure 6-14.)

- **Name** Enter a name for the record set.
- **Type** Select the type of DNS record you want to create—in this case, **A – Alias Record to IPv4 Address**.
- **Alias Record Set** Select the **Yes** option button to create an alias record set.
- **Alias Type** Select Azure Resource option button.
- **Subscription** Select the subscription in which to create the alias record set.
- **Azure Resource** Select the Azure resource to associate with the alias record set.
- **TTL** Enter the time to live (TTL) for the record set. (I typed **1**.)
- **TTL Unit** Select the TTL unit from the drop-down list. (I selected **Hours**.)

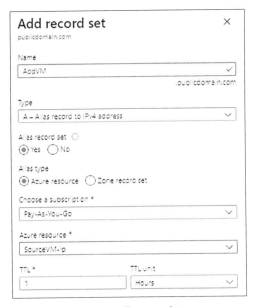

FIGURE 6-14 Create an alias record set.

Reverse DNS lookup

Azure private DNS zones support reverse DNS lookups using reverse DNS lookup zones for private IP addresses associated with VMs hosted in linked virtual networks. This can help in scenarios where applications require reverse lookups for verification purposes.

Reverse DNS lookups, which use Reverse DNS zones, return two FQDNs:

- The FQDN containing the name of the VM with a default suffix of *internal.cloudapp.net*.
- If auto-registration is enabled, an additional FQDN with the name of the VM and the suffix for the private DNS domain name.

Reverse DNS lookup zone walkthrough

The following section walks you through the process of creating a reverse DNS lookup zone using the Azure Portal, Azure PowerShell, and the Azure CLI.

USING THE AZURE PORTAL

To create a reserve DNS lookup zone using the Azure Portal, follow the steps as detailed here:

1. Log in to the Azure Portal, type **DNS zone** in the search box to locate the service, and select it from the list that appears.
2. Click the **Create DNS Zone** button to start the Create DNS Zone wizard. (See Figure 6-15.)

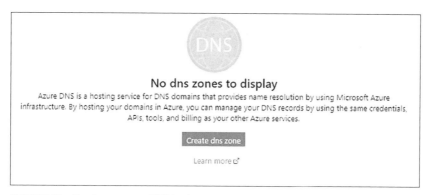

FIGURE 6-15   Create a reverse DNS lookup zone.

3. In the **Basics** tab of the Create DNS Zone wizard, enter the following information (see Figure 6-16), and click **Next**:

- **Subscription**   Select the subscription to host the DNS zone.
- **Resource Group**   Select the resource group you want to use to host the reverse lookup DNS zone. Alternatively, to create a new resource group, click the **Create New** link and follow the prompts.
- **Name**   Enter a name for the reverse DNS lookup zone in the format *<IPv4 network prefix in reverse order>*.**in-addr.arpa**.
- **Resource Group Location**   This will be populated automatically based on the location of the resource group you just selected.

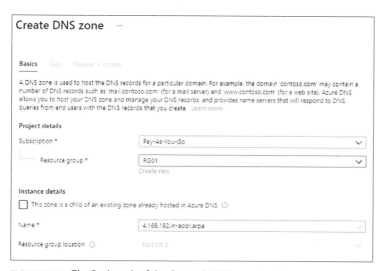

FIGURE 6-16   The Basics tab of the Create DNS Zone wizard.

4. In the **Tags** tab, enter any tags required for the reverse DNS lookup zone or leave the fields blank (see Figure 6-17), and click **Next**.

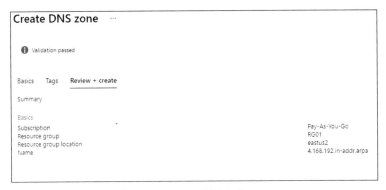

FIGURE 6-17   Set up tags.

5. In the **Review + Create** tab (see Figure 6-18), review your settings and click **Create**.

FIGURE 6-18   Review and create a reverse DNS lookup zone.

USING AZURE POWERSHELL

You can create a reverse DNS lookup zone with Azure PowerShell using the New-AzDNSZone command with various switches to set the zone's parameters. For example, to create the same reverse DNS lookup zone as you did in the preceding section, you use the following code:

```
#Create reverse DNS zone
New-AzDNSZone -Name 4.168.192.in-addr.arpa -ResourceGroupName RG01
```

USING THE AZURE CLI

You can create a reverse DNS lookup zone with the Azure CLI using the az network dns zone create command with various switches to set the zone's parameters. The following script shows you how to set up the same zone you created in the preceding sections with the Azure CLI:

```
#Create reverse DNS zone
az network dns zone create --resource-group RG01 --name 4.168.192.in-addr.arpa
```

Zone delegation

With Azure DNS, you can only host domains authoritatively. Azure DNS does not provide recursive DNS services. An authoritative DNS server is responsible for responding to all DNS queries related to the DNS records only in the zones hosted on it. A recursive DNS server does not host any DNS zones. It uses authoritative servers to respond to all DNS queries it receives.

To better understand this, consider a couple different scenarios. Imagine an environment in which the Azure DNS service hosts the domain contoso.com and receives different DNS queries:

- **DNS query for name resolution of www.contoso.com**   In this scenario, Azure DNS hosts the domain contoso.com, so it checks its record sets to identify whether there is a record for www. If so, it responds with the value for that record. If the record does not exist, it responds by stating no such record exists for that domain.

- **DNS query for name resolution of www.fabrikam.com**   In this scenario, Azure DNS does not host the DNS zone fabrikam.com. Hence, it is not able to respond to DNS queries, and the queries will fail.

Considering this, if name resolution for other non-authoritative domains is required for the VMs in an environment, you would have to set recursive DNS servers on the Azure VMs.

Best practices

Following are some best practices for the Azure DNS service that can help secure the service against attacks or unwarranted modifications:

- **Use Azure role-based access control (RBAC)**   Azure DNS supports Azure RBAC to control access to the DNS service. Use RBAC to limit access to the DNS service on the service, zone, or record level based on the access control requirements of the organization. Incorrect DNS records can result in application outages, so controlling access to avoid unwarranted changes to the DNS service is critical.

- **Use the DNS Zone Contributor role**   Azure provides a built-in role called DNS Zone Contributor. Users with this role can manage DNS resources—but that's all. Use this role if there are individuals in the organization who require access to the DNS service only for management purposes.

- **Use custom roles**   In addition to the DNS Zone Contributor role, you can create custom roles to limit access to specific DNS functions—for example, creating and modifying A records but not managing other record types. After you identify or create the required roles, you can ensure that access is assigned only on the required level. The available levels are as follows:

  - **Service-level Azure RBAC**   Permissions are assigned on the Azure DNS service level, enabling the user to manage all zones hosted in the service.

- **Zone-level Azure RBAC** Permissions are granted on the zone level, enabling the user to manage all records in that zone.
- **Record-set level Azure RBAC** Permissions are assigned on the record set level, enabling the user to manage specific record sets.

You manage all these permissions using the Azure Portal, Azure PowerShell, or the Azure CLI.

- **Use resource locks** Use the resource locks feature to prevent access for making changes to the DNS zones or protect them for deletion. Your options are as follows:
  - **Prevent all changes** Creating a read-only lock prevents any changes from being made to the DNS zone. This makes it possible to respond to DNS queries but prevents further changes to the records until the lock is modified or removed. (See Figure 6-19.)

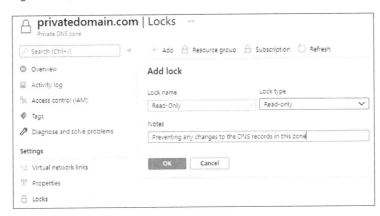

FIGURE 6-19 Create a read-only resource lock.

  - **Prevent individual records deletion** You can set resource locks on the record-set level to prevent changes to or deletions of individual DNS records. You can currently configure record set–level resource locks using Azure PowerShell only—not the Azure Portal or the Azure CLI. The following PowerShell snippet shows how to set up a lock on an individual DNS record:

```
#Define the required variables
$locklevel = "Read-only"
$lockname = "Read-only"
$dnsresource = "contoso.com/www"
$type = "Microsoft.Network/DNSZones/A"
$rg = "RG01"
# Lock a DNS record set
New-AzResourceLock -LockLevel $locklevel -LockName $lockname -ResourceName
$dnsresource -ResourceType $type -ResourceGroupName $rg
```

- **Prevent complete zone deletion** Creating a no-delete lock prevents the acciden-
tal or malicious deletion of a DNS zone. (See Figure 6-20.)

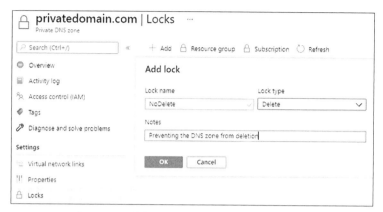

FIGURE 6-20 Create a no-delete resource lock.

- **Set up monitoring and alerting** Azure DNS provides metrics to monitor the performance of hosted DNS zones. In addition, you can integrate with Azure DNS with Azure
Monitor to monitor key metrics to gauge performance and identify bottlenecks. Some
key metrics include the following:

  - QueryVolume
  - RecordSetCount
  - RecordSetCapacityUtilization

  At a minimum, it is recommended that you set up alerting for performance parameters
  and critical administrative actions.

- **Integrate with other Azure services** If required, you can use Azure DNS to publish
custom domain records for other Azure services in use in the environment. This includes
Azure Application Gateway, Azure Load Balancer, Azure Traffic Manager, Azure App
Service, Azure Resource Manager VMs, and Azure Cloud Services. For each service,
based on its IP address configuration, you can create a corresponding DNS A or CNAME
record. You can create DNS CNAME records for services with dynamically allocated IP
addresses. For services using a static IP address, you can create DNS A records.

## Chapter 7

Azure Traffic Manager

Overview

Azure Traffic Manager is a service that performs DNS-based load balancing of incoming traffic to internet-facing endpoints. Traffic Manager service facilitates the distribution of traffic globally across applications hosted in various Azure regions or external endpoints hosted in client environments or other cloud services.

One of the most important aspects of Azure Traffic Manager is that it performs DNS-based redirects based on traffic-routing policies defined in the service. It does not act as a front-end gateway or proxy for application traffic. This implies that no application traffic passes through the service; it is simply redirected to designated endpoint(s), after which the client connects to the designated application endpoint directly. It also shows that Traffic Manager works on layer 7 (the application layer) of the OSI model.

You can define different types of endpoints for use with Traffic Manager. You can also deploy different routing algorithms to handle the incoming traffic based on your organization's unique availability requirements and application design. This is covered in more detail later in this chapter.

> **NOTE**   Microsoft designed Traffic Manager to be extremely resilient. Even an Azure region failure will not bring the service offline, because Microsoft built redundancy into the service to handle these types of scenarios.

Traffic Manager features

Traffic Manager has a number of key features to improve the availability, resiliency, and redundancy of client applications. These include the following:

- **Multiple routing algorithms to meet complex requirements**   Traffic Manager provides different traffic-routing algorithms that can be used in isolation or in combination based on the needs of the client environment. Each type of algorithm improves the redundancy and availability of the application in different ways. Combining routing methods can help address even the most complex scenarios.

- **Increased application resiliency and availability**   Traffic Manager continuously monitors application endpoints and automatically routes traffic based on endpoint availability. Traffic to offline endpoints is automatically paused until the endpoints come back online.

- **Enhanced application performance**   You can set up Traffic Manager to route traffic to endpoints that offer the lowest latency to the end client to improve the user experience.

- **Support for non–Azure-based endpoints**   Traffic Manager supports the use of public-facing endpoints hosted both inside and outside Azure (on-premises environments, other cloud services, etc.). A single Traffic Manager routing profile can contain endpoints from different sources to address different scenarios, such as on-premises to Azure cloud migration, IaaS to PaaS migration, disaster recovery to Azure, and so on.

- **Improved application scalability**   Traffic Manager can help organizations provide scaling capabilities to their applications by bursting to use Azure cloud capacity in the event of resource crunch issues in their primary hosting locations.

- **Reduced maintenance windows**   Traffic Manager can help reduce or eliminate maintenance windows for application upgrades or security updates by routing traffic to endpoints that are not under maintenance.

Design concepts and deployment considerations

The Traffic Manager service can be integrated into your environment in different ways, depending on your workloads, redundancy requirements, and routing requirements. To identify the right strategy for your workloads, it is important to understand the different components that make up the Traffic Manager service, as well as how they function. This will help you to identify all the different factors to consider when designing and deploying this service in your Azure environment.

Traffic Manager endpoints

Traffic Manager allows the use of different endpoint types for traffic distribution. Based on the routing method defined in the Traffic Manager profile, Traffic Manager assesses endpoint availability and applies the routing algorithm to determine which endpoint to route traffic to.

Traffic Manager supports three types of endpoints:

- **Azure endpoints**   These are services hosted inside Azure—for example, using App Services or virtual machines (VMs) running a public-facing application.

- **External endpoints**   These are referred to services hosted outside Azure, either on-premises or by another hosting provider (including other cloud providers). Traffic Manager refers to these using either their IPv4/IPv6 address or FQDN.

- **Nested endpoints**   These combine multiple Traffic Manager profiles to create more complex traffic routing configuration. This helps to address the requirements of larger deployments.

The following sections discuss each endpoint type in more detail.

Azure endpoints

Azure-hosted services are set up as Azure endpoints in Traffic Manager. A number of Azure services are supported for use with Traffic Manager, including the following:

- Web apps
- Web app slots
- VM-connected public IP addresses
- Load balancer–connected public IP addresses
- PaaS cloud services

The main benefit of using Azure endpoints is that Azure can detect the state of services, such as Azure Web Application service, to confirm whether it is running or stopped. Azure can then automatically stop billing for Traffic Manager while the back-end endpoint is stopped and resume once it's back online. This feature is not supported for public IP address–based endpoints, as no detection of the actual resource is possible in that instance.

External endpoints

External endpoints are services referenced only using public IPv4/IPv6 addresses or FQDNs, or hosted outside Azure. These include applications hosted in on-premises environments and in other hosted or non-Microsoft cloud environments. They also include applications hosted in Azure that must be published using only their IPv4/IPv6 addresses.

For some Azure services, such as Azure Web Application service, the Traffic Manager profile can reference only one endpoint per region as an Azure endpoint. However, if added as an external endpoint using the web app's FQDN, this limitation can be overcome.

With Azure endpoints, billing can be automatically turned off for offline or deactivated Azure-hosted services. The same does not apply to external endpoints, however. The only way to turn off billing for an external endpoint is to disable or delete the endpoint.

You can combine external and Azure endpoints in the same Traffic Manager profile. For example, an application's FQDN could be routed to endpoints hosted in an on-premises data-center and an Azure VM. This does not apply for endpoints that are specified using IPv4 or IPv6 addresses, however. These can only be set up individually as external endpoints.

When Azure and external endpoints are combined in a single Traffic Manager profile, various design scenarios become viable. These include the following:

- Increased resiliency through the provision of active-active or active-passive failover options for applications hosted between Azure and on-premises or Azure and other hosting provider–managed environments.
- Resource-burst capabilities for on-premises applications through the provision of capacity in the Azure cloud to scale as and when required.
- Improve application performance through the hosting of applications closer to the user's region and through the use of performance-based routing to make on-premises applications available with reduced latency.

Nested endpoints

Nested endpoints are a combination of multiple Traffic Manager profiles consisting of different endpoints. A "parent" profile is set up with an endpoint pointing to a "child" profile that contains different endpoints than the parent profile. Such a combination creates complex routing logic that can help provide global scale and redundancy for an application. The endpoints in the parent and child profile can be different and can even be other nested Traffic Manager profiles (discussed in the next section).

Nested Traffic Manager profiles

Nested Traffic Manager profiles combine multiple profiles to enable complex traffic-routing capabilities. This works well for larger application-deployment scenarios that call for a mixture of routing capabilities to address the complex needs of the organization.

In general, a single Traffic Manager profile can use a single traffic-routing method. With nested profiles, you can define a "child" Traffic Manager profile inside a "parent" profile to serve as an endpoint. This allows multiple profiles with different routing policies and endpoint types to work together in a single nested profile to address complex routing requirements.

Figure 7-1 shows how a parent profile is set up to use the performance-traffic routing method (discussed in a moment) and how one of its endpoints is a child profile set up to use the weighted-traffic routing method (again, discussed in a moment) and its own set of endpoints. This build allows for a small subset of traffic to be routed to the "trial" endpoint to test application upgrades or patches without affecting the majority of the environment.

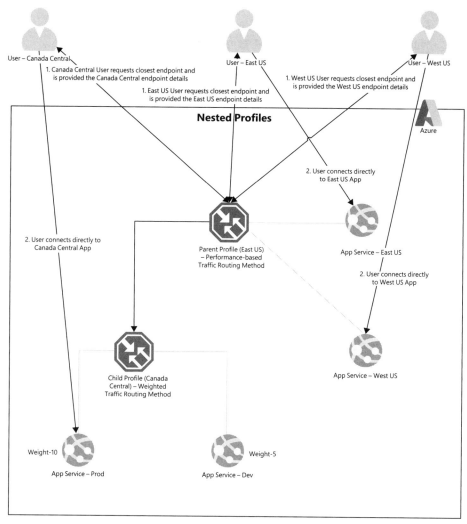

Parent Profile (East US)
– Performance-based
Traffic Routing Method

1. Canada Central User requests closest endpoint and
is provided the Canada Central endpoint details

1. East US User requests closest endpoint and
is provided the East US endpoint details

1. West US User requests closest endpoint and
is provided the West US endpoint details

User – Canada Central

User – East US

User – West US

Nested Profiles

Azure

2. User connects directly
to East US App

2. User connects directly to
Canada Central App

App Service – East US

2. User connects directly
to West US App

Child Profile (Canada
Central) – Weighted
Traffic Routing Method

App Service – West US

Weight-10

App Service – Prod

Weight-5

App Service – Dev

FIGURE 7-1   Azure Traffic Manager service overview.

Traffic routing methods

One of the most important aspects of Traffic Manager is to understand the different traffic-routing methods and algorithms it provides. There are various routing methods available, each with different capabilities, that can be used individually or combined in nested profiles to address various complex requirements. Four of these methods are as follows:

- Priority traffic routing
- Weighted traffic routing
- Performance traffic routing
- Geographic traffic routing

NOTE Each of these methods includes the capability to monitor and automatically failover to the next available endpoint per the profile configuration.

You can configure any of these traffic-routing methods as part of a Traffic Manager profile and apply it to a set of endpoints. The routing method you set up can be swapped out at any time and the changes applied with zero downtime. However, as mentioned, to address more complex scenarios, you can nest Traffic Manager profiles to apply multiple routing methods in combination. The following sections discuss these traffic-routing methods in more detail.

Multi-value and subnet-based traffic routing

In addition to priority, weighted, performance, and geographic traffic routing, Traffic Manager supports two other types: multi-value traffic routing and subnet-based traffic routing.

In scenarios in which all active endpoint addresses must be returned to the end client, you can use multi-value traffic routing to define all the different IPv4/IPv6 endpoints. By default, two active endpoints are returned as part of any reply, but this number can be increased if required. If an endpoint is dual-homed—that is, it uses both IPv4 and IPv6 addresses—multi-value traffic routing will provide both addresses to the end client, so the end client can decide which one to use when initiating the connection.

In contrast, subnet-based traffic routing maps different client subnets to different application endpoints. Requests originating from a specific subnet are then routed based on the endpoint map associated with that subnet.

Priority traffic routing

Suppose your organization has designed an application such that a single primary server runs the application and one or more backup servers handle application traffic in the event that the primary server fails. This might be because application limitations prevent it from supporting more than one active server at a time. Or it could be meant to address disaster-recovery scenarios in which the secondary endpoint cannot be used until the primary endpoint is offline.

In such instances, the most effective traffic-routing method is the priority method. Priority traffic routing defines the primary endpoint to route any client traffic to, and one or more backup endpoints, organized by priority, to failover to in case of a problem. The highest-priority endpoint receives traffic until it becomes unavailable, at which stage the traffic is redirected to the second-highest-priority endpoint. (See Figure 7-2.)

With this method, all endpoints have a unique priority; that is, no two endpoints can have the same priority. Unless an endpoint has been taken offline or disabled—for example, for maintenance purposes—or experiences an outage, it will automatically receive traffic if the endpoint that is prioritized immediately above it experiences a problem. If no priority has been defined for an endpoint, it is automatically assigned one based on the order in which it was added to the service.

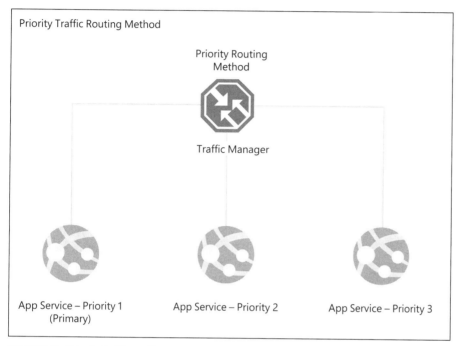

FIGURE 7-2 Priority traffic routing.

Weighted traffic routing

In scenarios in which traffic must be distributed evenly across a set of endpoints, weighted traffic routing is often the most suitable method. With this method, you can define a weight for each application endpoint; endpoints with higher weights receive more traffic. Put another way, the higher the endpoint's weight, the higher its priority. (See Figure 7-3.)

> **NOTE** If no weight is assigned to an endpoint, Traffic Manager assigns a weight of 1 by default.

You can assign the same weight to multiple endpoints to distribute traffic evenly across them. This approach is effective in scenarios in which traffic must be routed first to multiple active endpoints in a primary location and second to multiple active endpoints in a failback or disaster-recovery site.

Be aware that DNS responses are cached by end clients and by recursive DNS servers servicing those clients. This can result in traffic being distributed unevenly, as DNS caching behavior cannot be centrally controlled across all possible access points. You should take this into account when deciding whether this is the right routing method for your environment.

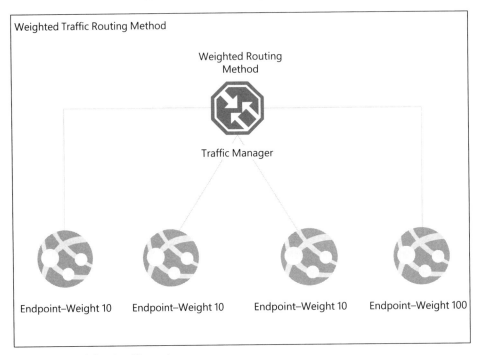

FIGURE 7-3 Weighted traffic routing.

Performance traffic routing

With performance traffic routing, Traffic Manager routes traffic based on which endpoint will provide the lowest latency. Sometimes this will be the endpoint that is closest to the client IP address, but not always. To determine whether another endpoint might offer lower latency, Traffic Manager refers to an internet latency table, which it generates and maintains by tracking round-trip times between source IP ranges and various Azure regions. (See Figure 7-4.) If the Azure region identified by Traffic Manager as offering the lowest latency contains multiple active endpoints, Traffic Manager automatically distributes traffic to that region evenly across all the available endpoints.

> **NOTE** Traffic Manager does not monitor the actual performance or availability of an endpoint itself to determine if it will offer the lowest latency. It assesses latency performance based only on the internet latency table. This latency table may be updated due to changes in the global internet routing infrastructure or performance, or new Azure regions coming online.

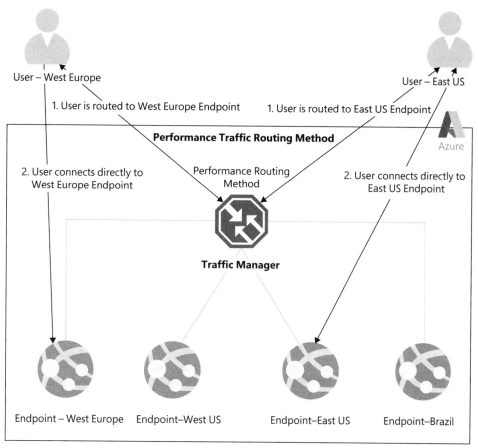

FIGURE 7-4 Performance traffic routing.

Performance traffic routing supports the use of external endpoints hosted outside Azure and of nested endpoints. In these cases, you must define the location of the endpoint by selecting the Azure region closest to that endpoint. If the endpoints in the closest Azure region are offline or degraded, Traffic Manager will move traffic to active endpoints in the next-closest Azure region.

The source IP of the endpoint performing the DNS query also helps gauge latency. In most cases, this will be a recursive DNS server; therefore, the Azure region returned in the DNS response will be the one closest to the DNS server. If an organization uses a centralized DNS server for all clients hosted in its datacenter, traveling employees may have to connect to the Azure region closest to the organization's datacenter, even if they themselves are connecting from the other side of the globe. You'll need to factor this in when choosing which traffic-routing method to use.

Geographic traffic routing

Geographic traffic routing defines the endpoints to which traffic should be routed based on the origin of the request. For example, you might route traffic from different locales to different endpoints based on data-sovereignty, content-localization, or compliance requirements.

You can define multiple endpoints to address traffic from different regions by redirecting them to specific external or nested endpoints hosted in Azure. You must assign each endpoint a set of geographic regions so that Traffic Manager understands how traffic must be routed after it determines the source geography of the DNS request. You can use different levels of granularity to define the geographic region:

- **World**   Any region.
- **Region**   A specific region—for example, Asia, Africa, North America, Australia/Pacific, and so on.
- **Country**   A specific country—for example, India, France, United States, Canada, and so on.
- **State/Province**   A specific state or province—for example, Australia-Victoria, Canada-Victoria, Canada-Ontario, USA-Florida, and so on (currently applicable only to Australia, Canada, and the US).

Depending on the regions associated with an endpoint, traffic is routed only to endpoints located in those regions. Routing occurs in the following order, based on the endpoint's configuration (see Figure 7-5):

1. State/Province
2. Country
3. Region
4. World

There are a few key points to note about this traffic-routing method:

- Each geographic region can be associated with only one endpoint.
- Traffic Manager does not check the health of the endpoint. It returns that endpoint as a response, even if the endpoint is in an unhealthy state.
- If a request matches the geographic mapping of multiple endpoints, the one that is defined with granularity closest to the request's region is returned.
- The use of nested endpoints is recommended to define a geographic mapping to cover unknown sources or scenarios in which endpoints are offline, as multiple endpoints can be defined in a nested endpoint.
- It's a best practice to use geographic traffic routing with nested Traffic Manager profiles so you can configure multiple endpoints to address all unknown traffic sources.
- Disabled endpoints are excluded from any response.

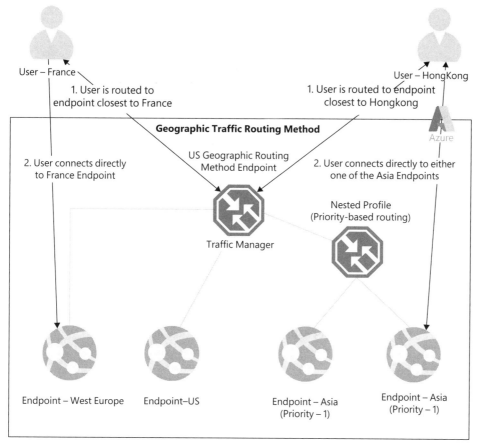

Geographic Traffic Routing Method

User – France

1. User is routed to endpoint closest to France

User – HongKong

1. User is routed to endpoint closest to Hongkong

Azure

2. User connects directly to France Endpoint

US Geographic Routing Method Endpoint

2. User connects directly to either one of the Asia Endpoints

Nested Profile (Priority-based routing)

Traffic Manager

Endpoint – West Europe

Endpoint–US

Endpoint – Asia (Priority – 1)

Endpoint – Asia (Priority – 1)

FIGURE 7-5   Geographic traffic routing.

Endpoint monitoring

One of the most important features of Traffic Manager is its ability to automatically failover traffic away from non-functional endpoints. This requires continuous monitoring to ensure that information about the health of every active endpoint is up to date. Any change in status that identifies an endpoint as offline, deactivated, or disabled leads to an action based on the routing method and endpoint configuration in place. Fortunately, Azure Traffic Manager has a built-in endpoint-monitoring feature that you can set up to monitor the health of endpoints and perform automated failover to other active or passive endpoints. This involves selecting a monitoring protocol and other critical settings. (You'll learn how to configure this feature in the next section.)

Endpoint failover and recovery

Traffic Manager periodically checks the health of every endpoint, including unhealthy endpoints. Traffic Manager detects when a previously unhealthy endpoint becomes healthy and brings it back into rotation. An endpoint is deemed unhealthy in the following scenarios:

- **If the monitoring protocol is HTTP or HTTPS** A non-200 response or a response that doesn't include the status range specified in the Expected Status Code Ranges setting is received. (This includes a different 2*XX*code or a 301/302 redirect.)

- **If the monitoring protocol is TCP** A response other than ACK or SYN-ACK is received in response to the SYN request sent by Traffic Manager to attempt to establish a connection.

- **Timeout** Any other connection issue results in the endpoint being not reachable.

When such a scenario occurs, traffic is failed over to remaining online endpoints based on the routing policies defined in the Traffic Manager profile.

Traffic Manager walkthrough

The following sections walk you through the process of setting up Azure Traffic Manager using the Azure Portal, Azure PowerShell, and the Azure CLI.

> **IMPORTANT** Before beginning this walkthrough, you should provision two VMs with public IPs in the Azure environment. Be sure to set up the DNS name for both VMs to enable them for use as Azure endpoints. You can set up IIS on both VMs so you can query each one while testing the Traffic Manager service. Book 1 in this series, *Microsoft Azure Compute: The Definitive Guide*, explains how to create VMs; see Chapter 1, "Azure virtual machines," for help.

USING THE AZURE PORTAL

To set up Traffic Manager using the Azure Portal, follow these steps:

1. Log in to the Azure Portal, type **Traffic Manager** in the search box to locate the service, and select it from the list that appears. (See Figure 7-6.)

2. Click **Create** or **Create Traffic Manager Profile** to start the Create a Traffic Manager wizard. (See Figure 7-7.)

FIGURE 7-6 Searching for the Traffic Manager service.

FIGURE 7-7 Click Create Traffic Manager Profile.

3. In the Create Traffic Manager Profile wizard (see Figure 7-8), enter the following information and click **Create**:

   ■ **Name** Type a unique name for the profile.

   ■ **Routing Method** Select the desired routing method—in this case, **Performance**.

   ■ **Subscription** Select the subscription to host the profile.

   ■ **Resource Group** Select the resource group you want to host the profile. Alternatively, click the **Create New** link and follow the prompts to create a new profile.

   ■ **Resource Group Location** This value is automatically populated based on the resource group you select.

FIGURE 7-8 Set up profile settings.

4. After the Traffic Manager profile is created, open its service configuration blade.

5. In the left pane, click **Endpoints**. Then click **Add**. (See Figure 7-9.)

FIGURE 7-9 Add a Traffic Manager endpoint.

6. The **Add Endpoint** wizard starts (see Figure 7-10). Enter the following information and click **Add**:

   ■ **Type**   Select the type of endpoint you want to use.

   ■ **Name**   Enter a unique name for the endpoint.

   ■ **Target Resource Type**   Select the type of resource you want to add—in this case, **Public IP address**.

   ■ **Public IP Address**   Select the public IP address you want to associate with the profile.

   ■ **Custom Header Settings**   Add the host header information using the tags **host:** and **customheader:**.

   ■ **Add as Disabled**   Select this check box if you want to add the endpoint now, but not make it live.

7. Repeat step 6 to add all necessary endpoints. Then verify they've been added correctly. (See Figure 7-11.)

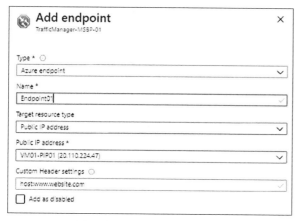

FIGURE 7-10 Add endpoint.

FIGURE 7-11 Endpoints in Traffic Manager.

8. In the left pane of the Traffic Manager profile's service configuration blade, click **Configuration**. Then enter the following configuration information in the right pane of the blade (see Figure 7-12):

- **Protocol**   Select the protocol you want to use (HTTP, HTTPS, or TCP) to monitor application health.

- **Port**   Specify the application port to be queried by Traffic Manager to verify endpoint health.

- **Path**   Specify a path to identify which endpoint should be monitored. This can be a relative path, such as a forward slash (/); a relative path, such as a forward slash (/) and the name of the web page; or a relative path, such as a forward slash (/) and the name of a file.

> **NOTE**   This setting applies only when HTTP or HTTPS is selected for the Protocol parameter.

- **Custom Header Settings** Set the custom HTTP header to use to connect to the endpoint. This header can be defined at a profile level (to apply to all endpoints) or at an individual endpoint level (to apply only to that endpoint). The header can also be applied at both the profile and endpoint level to accommodate custom endpoint requirements.

> **NOTE** The custom header can help in tagging traffic originating from Traffic Manager so it can be processed differently on the receiving application end.

- **Expected Status Code Ranges** Set the status codes to confirm successful connectivity. Success code responses appear in the format 200–299, 301–301.

> **NOTE** This setting is relevant only for the HTTP and HTTPS protocols and is set up only at the Traffic Manager profile level.

- **Probing Interval** Specify a probing interval to define how often an endpoint's health check should be performed. There are options: 30 (seconds), which is the default, and 10 (seconds), which is referred to as fast probing. (Note that additional service charges apply when you select the fast probing option.)
- **Tolerated Number of Failures** Specify the total number of failures to tolerate before initiating failover. This parameter can be set to any value between 0 and 9, with 0 implying that a single failure will result in the endpoint being moved out of service. (The default value is 3.)
- **Probe Timeout** Specify a response timeout value appropriate for your environment. This setting defines the total time the probing agent must wait for a response before assuming a health probe check has failed. This value depends on the Probing Interval setting. If Probing Interval is set to 30 (seconds), Probe Timeout must be set between 5 and 10 (seconds). (The default value is 10.) If Probing Interval is set to 10, Probe Timeout must be set between 5 and 9. (The default value is 9.)

9. Click the **Overview** tab and browse to the DNS name shown in the right pane to test whether you are connecting to one of the two VMs you provisioned as the endpoints. If so, turn off that Azure VM and repeat the process to validate that you are now connected to the other VM. (See Figure 7-13.)

myTMProfileKD - Configuration
Traffic Manager profile

Save   X Discard

Overview

Activity log

Access control (IAM)

Tags

Diagnose and solve problems

Settings

Configuration

Real user measurements

Traffic view

Endpoints

Properties

Locks

Automation script

Monitoring

Metrics (Preview)

Alerts

Support + troubleshooting

Resource health

New support request

Routing method
Performance

* DNS time to live (TTL)
60
seconds

Endpoint monitor settings
Protocol
HTTP

* Port
80

* Path
/

Custom Header settings
host.contoso.com

Expected Status Code Ranges (default: 200)
200-299

Fast endpoint failover settings
Probing interval
30

* Tolerated number of failures
3

* Probe timeout
10
seconds

FIGURE 7-12   Configure endpoint monitoring.

Overview
Activity log
Access control (IAM)
Tags
Diagnose and solve problems

^ Essentials

Resource group (change) : RG01
Status : Enabled
Subscription (change) : Pay-as-you-go
Subscription ID : 7719ec11-92dd-457c-b393-5a0c483e4c79
Tags (change) : Click here to add tags

DNS name : http://trafficmanager-msbp-01.trafficmanager.net
Monitor status : Unknown
Routing method : Performance

FIGURE 7-13   Traffic Manager Overview tab.

USING AZURE POWERSHELL

You can create a Traffic Manager profile using Azure PowerShell with the
`New-AzTrafficManagerProfile` command and various switches to set the profile's parameters.
The following code shows you how:

```
#Query Resource ID for the endpoints. Record these for use later in the script.
Get-AzResource -Name "VM01-PIP01" | select ResourceID
Get-AzResource -Name "VM02-PIP01" | select ResourceID
#Define required variables
$AzureRegion="EastUS2"
$RG="RG01"
$TrafficMgrprofile="TrafficManager-MSBP-01"
#Create Traffic Manager Profile
```

```
New-AzTrafficManagerProfile `
-Name $TrafficMgrProfile `
-ResourceGroupName $RG `
-TrafficRoutingMethod Performance `
-ProfileStatus Enabled `
-MonitorPath '/' `
-MonitorProtocol "HTTP" `
-RelativeDnsName $TrafficMgrProfile `
-Ttl 30 `
-MonitorPort 80
#Create Traffic Manager Endpoint-01
#Replace the value for TargetResourceID with the one you gathered earlier for "VM01-PIP01"
New-AzTrafficManagerEndpoint -Name "Endpoint01" `
-ResourceGroupName $RG `
-ProfileName "$TrafficMgrProfile" `
-Type AzureEndpoints `
-TargetResourceId /subscriptions/7719ec11-92dd-457c-b393-5adc483e4c79/resourceGroups/RG01/
providers/Microsoft.Network/publicIPAddresses/PublicIP-01 `
-EndpointStatus "Enabled"
#Create Traffic Manager Endpoint-02
#Replace the value for TargetResourceID with the one you gathered earlier for "VM02-PIP01"
New-AzTrafficManagerEndpoint -Name "Endpoint02" `
-ResourceGroupName $RG `
-ProfileName "$TrafficMgrProfile" `
-Type AzureEndpoints `
-TargetResourceId "/subscriptions/7719ec11-92dd-457c-b393-5adc483e4c79/resourceGroups/RG01/
providers/Microsoft.Network/publicIPAddresses/publicip-02" `
-EndpointStatus "Enabled"
```

USING THE AZURE CLI

You can create a Traffic Manager profile using the Azure CLI with the az network traffic-manager profile create command and various switches to set the profile's parameters. The following code shows you how:

```
#Query Resource ID for the endpoints. Record these for use later in the script.
az resource list --name "VM01-PIP01"
az resource list --name "VM02-PIP01"
#Define required variables
rg="RG01"
azureregion="eastus2"
trafficmgrprofile="TrafficManager-MSBP-02"
endpoint01name="endpoint01"
endpoint02name="endpoint02"
#Create Traffic Manager Profile
az network traffic-manager profile create \
                    --name $trafficmgrprofile \
```

```
                    --resource-group $rg \
                    --routing-method Performance \
                    --path "/" \
                    --protocol HTTP \
                    --unique-dns-name $trafficmgrprofile \
                    --ttl 30 \
                    --port 80
#Create Traffic Manager Endpoint-01
#Replace the value for TargetResourceID with the one you gathered earlier for "VM01-PIP01"
az network traffic-manager endpoint create \
    --name $endpoint01name \
    --resource-group $rg \
    --profile-name $trafficmgrprofile \
    --type azureEndpoints \
    --target-resource-id '/subscriptions/7719ec11-92dd-457c-b393-5adc483e4c79/resource-
Groups/RG01/providers/Microsoft.Network/publicIPAddresses/PublicIP-01' \
    --endpoint-status Enabled
#Create Traffic Manager Endpoint-02
#Replace the value for TargetResourceID with the one you gathered earlier for "VM02-PIP01"
az network traffic-manager endpoint create \
    --name $endpoint02name \
    --resource-group $rg \
    --profile-name $trafficmgrprofile \
    --type azureEndpoints \
    --target-resource-id '/subscriptions/7719ec11-92dd-457c-b393-5adc483e4c79/resource-
Groups/RG01/providers/Microsoft.Network/publicIPAddresses/PublicIP-02' \
    --endpoint-status Enabled
```

Best practices

Traffic Manager can be a critical component in your application design and is generally used for enabling complex application routing scenarios. It is recommended that you set up the service taking the following best practices into consideration:

- **Use RBAC to control access** Limit access to Traffic Manager to required administrators. Making unauthorized changes to the service can result in outages. Generally, Traffic Manager is used for applications that require high levels of redundancy and availability; hence it is imperative that you keep the access to the service restricted. You can add admins who require access to manage Traffic Manager configuration to the Traffic Manager Contributor role in Azure instead of providing them with Subscription Owner or other extended access. This role limits access to managing profiles.

- **Set up Real User Measurements** When using the performance-based routing algorithm, Traffic Manager must direct traffic based on the latency between the incoming client endpoint and the different Azure regions where the application is hosted and online. To achieve this, Traffic Manager maintains an internet latency table that monitors and records the latency between different client networks to active Azure regions for that application. You can obtain more accurate measurements at the application level to fine-tune this logic by enabling a feature called Real User Measurements. This feature embeds a piece of code in the application, which is used by end-user devices to test latency from those devices to the various active Azure regions hosting the application. This information is then shared with the web application, which forwards it to Traffic Manager. Because this information is collected over and over again, it helps Traffic Manager perform a deeper analysis of latency from those networks and redirect incoming traffic more accurately.

Enable Real User Measurements using the Azure Portal

1. Log in to the Azure Portal and browse to the Traffic Manager profile you created in the walkthrough earlier in this chapter.

2. In the left pane, click **Real User Measurements**. (See Figure 7-14.)

FIGURE 7-14   Real User Measurements.

3. In the right-pane, click **Generate Key** (see Figure 7-15) to create a unique key and measurement script to be embedded into the web application.

FIGURE 7-15   Generate a key.

4. Copy the measurement script and paste it into an HTML page that your end users consistently visit when accessing the web application—for example, the home page. (See Figure 7-16.)

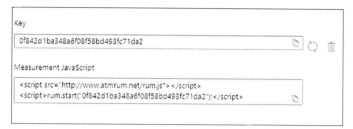

FIGURE 7-16   Real User Measurements key and JavaScript code.

- **Enable Traffic View**   Traffic View is an add-on service in Traffic Manager that enables you to monitor and gain deeper insights into the traffic to the Traffic Manager service. Using Traffic View, you can gain a better understanding of the following:

  - Where the source traffic for an application is generated from

  - The volume of traffic from different source client regions

  - Latency experienced by users in different source client regions

  - Traffic patterns between the source client regions and the Azure regions hosting their endpoints

These insights can help you make better decisions about which regions to scale in to address latency or performance issues, or in which to invest further for growth based on the volume of traffic currently being generated.

- **Use Azure Activity and Azure Monitor to centralize security logs**   Azure Activity log captures all information related to any operations performed on any Traffic Manager resources on the control plane level. You can monitor these logs in the Activity Log section of the service or ingest them into a central repository via Azure Monitor for data aggregation and analysis.

- **Enable threat detection**   All Traffic Manager logs can be forwarded and centralized using a SIEM such as Azure Sentinel or a third-party SIEM solution. You can use this to perform analysis and automate actions for any threats and breaches recorded in the logs.

- **Use Azure Policy to standardize configuration**   You can use Azure Policy to monitor the configuration of Traffic Manager resources to ensure they are in line with organizational standards. Azure Policy can detect whether Traffic Manager resource logging is enabled to ensure all operations on the control plane are recorded and centrally stored for security and compliance.

- **Enable monitoring and alerts using Azure Monitor**   Traffic Manager provides a couple of key service-specific metrics that can be monitored and can generate alerts using Azure Monitor:

- **Endpoint status by endpoint**   This metric monitors and confirms the health status of all endpoints in a Traffic Manager profile. It records whether an endpoint is up or down, and the value can be monitored by Azure Monitor to raise alerts as needed.

- **Queries by endpoint returned**   This metric monitors the load on different endpoints based on the number of queries received by the Traffic Manager profile and individual endpoints for a specific period of time. You can set up alerts to flag when there is an imbalance in query distribution, and you can address application capacity if alerts persist for a given period of time.

## Chapter 8

Azure Front Door

Overview

Azure Front Door is a fully managed scalable global service that provides a secure front end for any web application. It uses Microsoft's global edge network to improve speed of access and to provide better security and enhanced scalability for consumer-facing or internal web applications.

Organizations that have a global audience for their web applications can benefit from the proximity of the web application to the end user's region. To provide such an audience with a consistent experience, organizations can use content delivery networks (CDNs). The Azure Front Door service provides CDN capabilities along with security and routing features that are part of a Web Application Firewall (WAF) and Azure Traffic Manager services.

The Front Door service works on layer 7 (the application layer) of the OSI model. It uses the anycast protocol with split TCP; this provides the traditional CDN as well as security features such as distributed denial-of-service (DDoS) protection. The Front Door service's traffic-routing functionality provides global load balancing and automated failover capabilities to any public-facing services hosted in or external to Azure. Regional failure-handling capabilities are built into the service, ensuring it remains online in disaster scenarios.

Key features

Azure Front Door service provides a number of key features and benefits:

- **Improved application performance**   The Front Door service accelerates application performance using the split TCP–based anycast protocol.
- **Global scalability**   The Front Door service provides global scalability for web applications to allow access by users via edge locations closest to them.
- **Intelligent traffic routing**   The Front Door service can perform intelligent traffic routing to back-end services hosted inside or outside of Azure. Different routing algorithms support complex routing requirements.
- **Monitoring and automated failover**   Front Door provides health probes to monitor back-end resources and trigger automated failover actions.

- **WAF features** The Front Door service provides all the features provided by WAF, such as URL-based routing, URL rewrites, session affinity, SSL offloading, custom domain and certificate management, and application security.
- **Multiple website hosting** The Front Door service supports multiple websites at the same time, allowing for efficient use of the application infrastructure.
- **Native support for advanced features** The Front Door service natively supports dynamic site acceleration (DSA), TLS/SSL offloading, end-to-end IPv6 connectivity, and the HTTP/2 protocol.

Figure 8-1 shows how the Front Door service can support different scenarios, including the following:

- Failover between Azure regions
- Traffic routing–based URL paths
- Different back-end host types

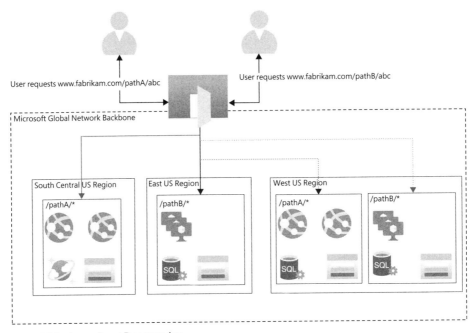

FIGURE 8-1 Azure Front Door service.

Design concepts and deployment considerations

Azure Front Door service provides different components and features that can be applied in combination to make full use of the service's CDN, WAF, and other security features. Before incorporating these features into your design, it helps to understand them in more detail so you can identify how best to apply them in any given environment to meet your organization's application, security, and compliance needs. The following sections review various components and features of Azure Front Door service.

Back ends

Back ends are web-based applications deployed inside or outside of Azure. Back end refers to the server or service hosting the application front end. Front Door service supports applications hosted on any on-premises infrastructure or hosting or cloud infrastructure provider. Back ends can be referenced using their host name or public IP address.

Front Door service supports a variety of Azure services for use as back ends, including the following:

- App Service
- Cloud Service
- Azure Storage
- Public IP address

For any other Azure or non-Azure services, custom hosts can be defined.

A back end can contain multiple instances of the same web application hosted in the same or different Azure regions or in a hybrid setup. You can assign priorities and weight to the different back-end endpoints to define which ones should be used as the primary endpoints and which should be used as backup.

Back-end pools

Multiple back-end endpoints can be combined into a back-end pool, which receives traffic for the web application. These endpoints can serve a web application hosted in the same or different Azure regions or in a hybrid setup between on-premises, Azure, and other cloud-hosting services.

A back-end pool in the Front Door service describes the set of back ends that receive similar traffic for an app. In other words, it's a logical grouping of app instances across the world that receive the same traffic and respond with expected behavior. These back ends are deployed across different regions or within the same region. All back ends can be in Active/Active Deployment mode or in Active/Passive configuration.

> **NOTE** You configure monitoring and load balancing for the back-end endpoint on the back-end pool.

Health probes

The Front Door service can monitor the health of back-end endpoints using health probes. Health probes help the Front Door service identify the back ends that are currently available to handle incoming client requests. A health probe is a synthetic request from the Front Door service to each of the back ends over HTTP/HTTPS, defined during the configuration phase. The response from the endpoints helps the Front Door service determine the best back end to route the incoming traffic.

The service takes into account different parameters to determine the back end that is best-suited for a given request. This includes the following:

- Identifying enabled endpoints and ignoring disabled ones
- Identifying endpoints that have no existing health probe errors and ignoring endpoints that do
- Accounting for the latency for each healthy back end in its calculations

> **NOTE** If the Front Door service determines that all back ends are offline, it assumes they are all healthy and continuously routes traffic between all of them until at least one healthy back end is back online.

Load balancing

The back-end pool holds the configuration for a web application's load-balancing policies. These settings define how the health probe responses are evaluated to determine whether a back end is healthy or not, based on the following parameters:

- **Sample size** This establishes how many samples of health probes should be considered for health evaluation.
- **Successful sample size** This defines how many successful samples out of the collected samples based on the sample size qualify an endpoint to be deemed healthy.
- **Latency sensitivity** This defines how the endpoints' latency will be considered when making routing decisions.

Traffic routing

The Front Door service supports different traffic-routing algorithms that define how to identify the most appropriate back-end endpoint for incoming application traffic. When the Front Door service receives HTTP/HTTPS traffic matching a host header, the traffic-routing algorithm helps identify the most appropriate back-end endpoint to connect to based on the active endpoints associated with it. All methods support automated monitoring and failover to active endpoints, but the basis of endpoint selection changes for each.

The four different traffic routing methods are as follows:

- **Latency-based routing** This method identifies the endpoint with the least latency to the end user and routes traffic to that endpoint if it is available for use.

- **Priority-based routing** This method identifies the primary endpoint that should receive application traffic and backup endpoints in case the primary is offline.
- **Weight-based routing** This method identifies the different weights for each endpoint for traffic distribution. Traffic is evenly distributed among all endpoints that share the highest weight. If those back ends are unavailable, traffic is automatically routed to the next set of endpoints. Based on the acceptable latency range defined for the pool, traffic is evenly distributed when the endpoint is deemed to be within acceptable limits.
- **Session affinity** This method ensures that incoming client requests from the same end client are sent to the same back-end instance. This is useful for applications that require session affinity to function correctly.

> **NOTE** You can combine multiple routing methods to address complex routing requirements and achieve faster and more efficient failovers.

URL rewrite

URL rewrite enables you to set up custom forwarding rules when constructing the URL request to route the request to the back end. This helps in scenarios in which traffic must be routed to a custom path for specific incoming requests due to page changes or masking.

> **NOTE** If you do not define a custom forwarding path for an application, traffic is always routed to the path defined in the incoming request.

In the example shown in Figure 8-2, a request to /path1 is forwarded to the custom path /path2 with a wildcard at the end to denote that it applies to all segments below that path. This results in all incoming requests for path1 being redirected to path2.

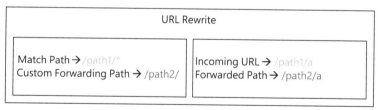

FIGURE 8-2 Set up URL rewrite.

URL redirect

The Front Door service supports URL redirect. This allows rules to be defined for traffic redirection based on protocol, app hostname, app path, and query string. Because this redirection is granular and works even on the path level, it can be configured for individual microservices as well as global redirections, thereby optimizing service usage.

Figure 8-3 shows the parameters in the Azure Portal for URL redirection. These include the following settings:

- **Route Type** Set this to Redirect to make the redirection configuration options available.

- **Redirect Type** This indicates the purpose of the redirect, which helps end clients correctly interpret the response from the service.

- **Redirect Protocol** This indicates whether traffic is to be allowed only over HTTP or HTTPS or retained as is.

- **Destination host** Destination host indicates whether the traffic must be redirected to a different hostname instead of the one indicated in the incoming request. This can help to redirect traffic to internal URLs. For example, traffic for https://www.fabrikam.com/* can be set to redirect to https://www.contoso.com/*.

- **Destination Path** Set this to Replace if the path segment of a URL must be replaced with a different path. For example, traffic to *https://www.fabrikam.com/** can be set to redirect to *https://www.fabrikam.com/redirected-path*.

- **Query String** Set this to Replace to replace query string parameters in the redirected URL.

- **Destination Fragment** This indicates a fragment of a URL to redirect to. This fragment is part of the URL after # character that helps a browser land on a specific section of a web page. You can use this setting to set up the redirected URL to use destination fragments.

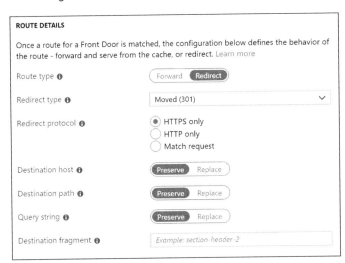

FIGURE 8-3 Set up URL redirect.

Wildcard domains

The Front Door service supports the use of wildcard domains for mapping front-end endpoints in a profile. Using wildcard domains provides multiple benefits, such as the following:

- It reduces the need to set up individual child domains in the Front Door service profile and facilitates HTTPS certificate binding for each domain.

- You can simplify traffic-routing behavior for multiple subdomains using a single routing rule. For example, a single rule for *.domain.com can be used to define routing policies for subdomain1.domain.com, subdomain2.domain.com, subdomain3.domain.com, and so on.

- You can easily bring new subdomains online without requiring changes to the Front Door service configuration. Policies that have already been defined are automatically applied to the new subdomain.

Rules Engine

The Rules Engines provided with the Front Door service give you the ability to define rules and control how incoming HTTP and HTTPS requests are handled at the edge. You can use this feature to address various requirements such as the following:

- Enforce HTTP-to-HTTPS redirection so that all end-user traffic occurs only over a secure connection.

- Prevent exploitation of browser-based vulnerabilities in HTTP Strict-Transport-Security (HSTS), X-XSS-Protection, Content-Security-Policy, X-Frame-Options, and Access-Control-Allow-Origin headers for Cross-Origin Resource Sharing (CORS) scenarios. You can also define security-based attributes with cookies.

- Route requests to mobile or desktop versions of the application based on patterns in request header contents, cookies, or query strings.

- Use redirect capabilities to return 301, 302, 307, and 308 redirects to the client to direct to new hostnames, paths, or protocols.

- Dynamically modify the caching configuration of your route based on incoming requests.

- Rewrite the request URL path and forward the request to the appropriate back end in your configured back-end pool.

Caching

The Front Door service has caching capabilities similar to those provided by CDNs, except the Front Door service also provides dynamic site acceleration and load-balancing features. The caching functionality helps to reduce the load on the back ends—for example, due to high demand for the service or to traffic generated by a DDoS attack. In these cases, caching results in the Front Door service edge nodes responding to client requests to prevent the attack or to prevent the requests from reaching the back-end nodes.

Cache-related features available in the Front Door service include the following:

- **Support for large file chunking**   The Front Door service can cache and deliver large files by splitting them into smaller (8 MB) chunks during ingestion from the back end. As one chunk is cached and delivered to the user, the Front Door service immediately initiates the retrieval of the next chunk. That way, it is available for delivery when the delivery of the previous chunk is complete. This continues until either the entire file is delivered or the client connection is terminated.

NOTE   The back end must support byte-range requests for large file chunking to work.

- **Dynamic content compression**   The Front Door service supports dynamic content compression on edge nodes to reduce file sizes. This results in faster delivery to end clients. Content must be of specific supported MIME types for compression to work, and the file sizes currently supported range from 1 KB to 8 MB. Compression is carried out using either Brotli- or gzip-based compression methods, with Brotli preferred over gzip if both are supported.
- **Query string behavior**   The Front Door service can manage caching behavior based on the query string contained in a web request. A query string is the section of the web request that comes after the question mark (?) in the request string. Management options are as follows:
  - **Ignore query strings**   This ensures that the Front Door service passes any query strings in an initial request to the back end and caches the content that is retrieved. In subsequent requests, the query string is ignored, and cached content is returned to the requestor until that content expires.
  - **Cache every unique URL**   In this case, the Front Door service caches the content associated with every unique URL—including the query string. All content is retained in cache and returned when requested until expiry.
- **Purging the cache**   Any files cached on the Front Door service edge nodes have an associated time-to-live (TTL) value. This value indicates when the file expires, after which the Front Door service removes it from its cache. If the Front Door service receives any subsequent requests for that file or content, it will retrieve it again from the back end and cache it with a new TTL value. Depending on the content served and the frequency of refresh required, files or content can be published with version numbers and as new URLs to force updates at the time of the next request. You can purge all cached content as well, if you have a need to do so.
- **Cache expiration**   You can set the expiration period for cached files using the response headers for a request. Specifically, you can set Cache-Control response headers to indicate how long the content should be stored in the cache. If this header is missing, the content is randomly cached between 1 to 3 days.
- **Request headers**   When caching is enabled, there are two request headers—Content-Length and Transfer-Encoding—that are not forwarded to a back-end node.

- **Cache duration**   This is the minimum amount of time content will be kept in cache. This can be set using Front Door Designer or a Rules Engine. If you set the cache duration using Front Door Designer, the minimum cache duration is defined on the global level. Unless a cache control header contains a higher cache duration, this will be the minimum TTL value. However, if you set the cache duration using the Rules Engine, that is accepted as the true cache value, regardless of it being higher or lower than the value in a cache control header.

Network and security

The Front Door service has a number of built-in security features as well as integrations with other Azure services to provide high levels of security and prevent large-scale DDoS attacks that can disrupt applications. Some of these features are unique to the Front Door service, while others overlap with services such as WAF. The following sections discuss these security features in more detail.

Azure DDoS Protection Basic

The Front Door service is integrated with Azure DDoS Protection Basic by default, meaning the service is automatically protected from commonly occurring DDoS attacks such as layer 3 and layer 4 attacks on public endpoints with high traffic volume and layer 7 attacks that involve overloading DNS with massive numbers of queries. Microsoft uses Azure Front Door to protect several of their public-facing consumer services, such as Office365, Dynamics365, and so on, proving the strength of this service against such attacks.

> **NOTE**   Azure DDoS Protection Basic is provided free of charge for all Front Door service users.

Protection against unwanted protocols

The Front Door service accepts traffic only on HTTP and HTTPS for requests with known host headers. This helps prevent a number of known DDoS attack types, such as DNS amplification attacks, TCP poisoning attacks, and volumetric attacks. Because this is a built-in feature of the Front Door service, no additional configuration is required to achieve this level of security.

Handling large volumes of traffic

As mentioned, Microsoft uses the Front Door service for its consumer-facing cloud services, which handle traffic from millions of clients globally. The global scaling, caching, and security capabilities built into the Front Door service help it handle large volumes of traffic and attacks without issues.

WAF security features

The Front Door service has a number of security features that overlap with the Azure WAF service. These provide a number of key benefits, such as the following:

- You can filter or redirect traffic based on the source geographic region using geo-filtering. This helps restrict traffic from unwanted locales to the application.
- You can prevent known malicious public IP addresses and IP ranges from connecting.
- You can define rule sets to protect against common and known attack vectors.
- You can prevent DDoS attacks by applying rate limits to the number of connections allowed from each IP address.

Front Door service walkthrough

The following sections walk you through the process of setting up a Front Door service using the Azure Portal, Azure PowerShell, and the Azure CLI. If you are following along, provision two web apps in the Azure environment, to be used during the setup process.

USING THE AZURE PORTAL

To set up Front Door using the Azure Portal, follow these steps:

1. Log in to the Azure Portal, type **Front Door** in the search box to locate the service, and select it from the list that appears. (See Figure 8-4.)

FIGURE 8-4 Searching for the Front Door service.

2. Click the **Create** or **Create Front Door** button to start the Create a Front Door wizard. (See Figure 8-5.)

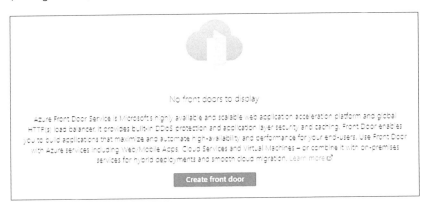

FIGURE 8-5 Click Create Front Door.

3. In the **Basics** tab of the Create a Front Door wizard (see Figure 8-6), enter the following information and click **Next**:

- **Subscription** Select the subscription to host the Front Door service.

- **Resource Group** Select the resource group you want to host the Front Door service. Alternatively, click the **Create New** link and follow the prompts to create a new resource group.

- **Resource Group Location** This box is automatically populated based on the resource group you select.

FIGURE 8-6 The Basics tab of the Create a Front Door wizard.

4. In the **Configuration** tab of the Create a Front Door wizard (see Figure 8-7), under **Frontend/Domains**, click the **Add a Frontend Host** button (marked with a plus sign).

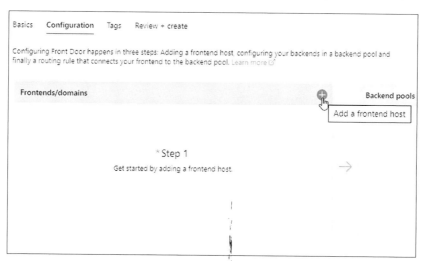

FIGURE 8-7 The Configuration tab of the Create a Front Door wizard.

5. In the **Add a Frontend Host** settings (see Figure 8-8), enter the following information and click **Add**:

- **Host Name**   Type a unique host name for the front-end host.
- **Session Affinity Status**   Specify whether session affinity should be enabled or disabled.
- **Web Application Firewall Status**   Specify whether WAF should be enabled or disabled.

FIGURE 8-8   Add a frontend host.

6. In the **Configuration** pane of the Create a Front Door wizard (see Figure 8-9), under **Backend Pools**, click the **Add a Backend Pool** button (marked with a plus sign).

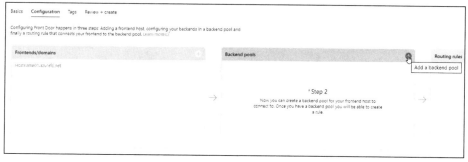

FIGURE 8-9 Add a backend pool.

7. In the **Add a Backend Pool** settings, in the **Name** box, type a unique name for the back-end pool. (See Figure 8-10.)

FIGURE 8-10 Add a backend pool.

8. Click the **Add a Backend** link.

9. In the **Add a Backend** settings (see Figure 8-11), enter the following information and click **Add**:

- **Backend Host Type** Select **Custom Host** to set up web applications hosted outside Azure as back-end hosts.

- **Backend Host Name** Enter the host name associated with the back-end host. (I typed **mbsp-webapp-01.azurewebsites.net**.)

- **Backend Host Header** Enter the host header associated with the back-end host. (Again, I typed **mbsp-webapp-01.azurewebsites.net**.)

- **HTTP Port** Enter the HTTP port associated with the back-end host—here, **80**.

- **HTTPS Port** Enter the HTTPS port associated with the back-end host—in this case, **443**.

- **Priority** Enter the priority for this back-end host. (I entered **1**.)

- **Weight** Assign a weight to this back-end host. (I entered **50**.)

- **Status** Specify whether the host is enabled or disabled—in this case, **Enabled**.

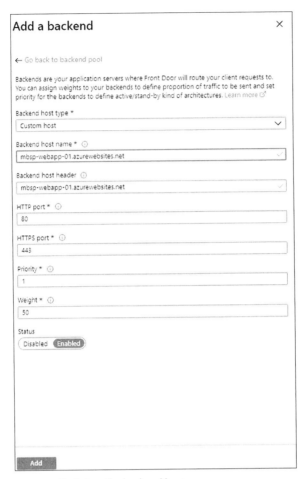

FIGURE 8-11 Set up the backend host.

10. Repeat steps 8 and 9 to add another custom back-end host, named mbsp-webapp-02.azurewebsites.net. Figure 8-12 shows the result.

FIGURE 8-12 Summary of backend pools.

11. Let's create a health probe for the back-end pool. In the **Add a Backend Pool** settings, under **Health Probes** (see Figure 8-13), enter the following information:

- **Path**   Enter the path you want the health probe to check.
- **Protocol**   Choose either **HTTP** or **HTTPS** based on your application setup.
- **Probe Method**   Choose either **HEAD** or **GET**.
- **Interval (Seconds)**   Specify how frequently, in seconds, you want the probe to perform health checks. The default is set to **30** (seconds).

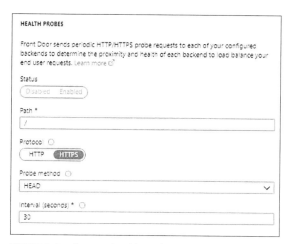

FIGURE 8-13   Create a health probe.

12. Next, enter the load-balancing settings. In the **Add a Backend Pool** settings, under **Load Balancing** (see Figure 8-14), enter the following information. Then click **Add**:

- **Sample Size**   Set the sample size to take into consideration—for example, **4**.
- **Successful Samples Required**   Set the minimum successful samples required to consider a host to be healthy—in this case, **2**.
- **Latency Sensitivity**   Set the expected latency for a response from a healthy endpoint—here, **0**.

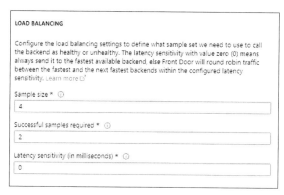

FIGURE 8-14   Set up load balancing.

13. In the **Configuration** pane of the Create a Front Door wizard (see Figure 8-15), under **Routing Rules**, click the **Add a Rule** button (marked with a plus sign).

FIGURE 8-15 Set up routing rules.

14. In the **Add a Rule** settings (see Figure 8-20), enter the following information:

- **Name**   Enter a unique name for the routing rule that reflects the rule's purpose. I typed **ForwardingRule**.
- **Accepted Protocol**   Select the protocol the rule will support, especially if you want to enforce the use of HTTP/HTTPS. I chose **HTTPS Only**.
- **Frontends/Domains**   Specify the front ends or domains you want to associate with the rule. In this case, choose the front end you created earlier (**Frontend-MBPS-01. azurefd.net**).

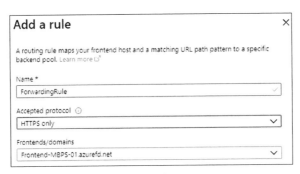

FIGURE 8-16 Adding a routing rule.

15. In the **Add a Rule** settings, under **Patterns to Match** (look ahead to Figure 8-17), enter the pattern that incoming requests must match to trigger the rule—in this case, **/path**.

16. In the **Add a Rule** settings, under **Route Details** (see Figure 8-17), enter the following information. Then click **Next**:

- **Route Type**   Specify the route type—in this example, **Forward**.
- **Backend pool**   Select the back-end pool to associate the rule with—here, **Backend-01**.
- **Forwarding Protocol**   Select the protocol to use when forwarding the request to the back-end pool. I chose **HTTPS Only**.

- **URL Rewrite** Specify whether URL rewrite should be enabled or disabled. I chose **Disabled**.

- **Caching** Specify whether caching should be enabled or disabled. I chose **Disabled**.

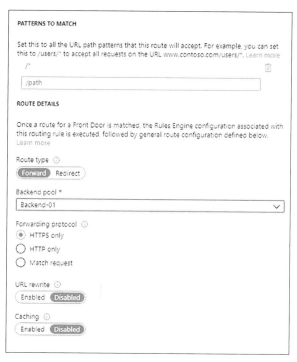

FIGURE 8-17 Set up a routing rule.

17. In the **Tags** tab, enter any tags required for the Front Door service or leave the fields blank (see Figure 8-18). Then click **Next**.

FIGURE 8-18 The Tags tab of the Create a Front Door wizard.

18. In the **Review + Create** tab of the Create a Front Door wizard (see Figure 8-19), review your settings and click **Create**.

Validation passed

Basics   Configuration   Tags   Review + create

Basics

Subscription   Pay-As-You-Go
Resource group   RG01
Region   East US 2
Front Door name   Frontend-MBPS-01
Host name   Frontend-MBPS-01.azurefd.net

Tags

None

FIGURE 8-19 The Review + Create tab of the Create a Front Door wizard.

USING AZURE POWERSHELL

You can create a Front Door service using Azure PowerShell with the `New-AzFrontDoor` command and various switches to set its parameters. The following code shows you how. Use this snippet to create the same Front Door service as you did in the Azure Portal. Be sure you delete the service you created earlier or modify its variables as appropriate before you use the following code before testing:

```
#Define required variables
$Azureregion1="EastUS2"
$Azureregion2="EastUS"
$RG="RG01"
$AppServicePlan01="MBSP-ASP-01"
$AppServicePlan02="MBSP-ASP-02"
$frontend="MBSP-Frontend-01"
$BackendPool="MBSP-Backendpool-01"
$frontdoorname="MBSP-Frontdoor-01"
# Create first web app in East US 2 region.
$app01 = New-AzWebApp -Name "WebApp-MBSP-01" `
-Location $azureregion1 `
-ResourceGroupName $RG `
-AppServicePlan $AppServicePlan01
# Create second web app in East US region.
$app02 = New-AzWebApp -Name "WebApp-MBSP-02" `
-Location $azureregion2 `
-ResourceGroupName $RG `
-AppServicePlan $AppServicePlan02
#Create the front-end object
$FrontendObject01 = New-AzFrontDoorFrontendEndpointObject -Name $frontend -HostName
$frontdoorname".azurefd.net"
```

```
# Create back-end objects that point to the hostname of the web apps
$backend01 = New-AzFrontDoorBackendObject -Address $app01.DefaultHostName
$backend02 = New-AzFrontDoorBackendObject -Address $app02.DefaultHostName
# Create a health probe
$HealthProbe = New-AzFrontDoorHealthProbeSettingObject -Name "HealthProbe"
# Create load balancing settings
$LoadBalancing = New-AzFrontDoorLoadBalancingSettingObject -Name "Loadbalancing" `
-SampleSize "4" `
-SuccessfulSamplesRequired "2" `
-AdditionalLatencyInMilliseconds "0"
# Create a back-end pool
$BackendPool01 = New-AzFrontDoorBackendPoolObject -Name "$BackendPool" `
-FrontDoorName $frontdoorname `
-ResourceGroupName $RG `
-Backend $backend01,$backend02 `
-HealthProbeSettingsName "HealthProbe" `
-LoadBalancingSettingsName "Loadbalancing"
# Create Routing rule connecting the front end to the back-end pool
$RoutingRule = New-AzFrontDoorRoutingRuleObject `
-Name RoutingRule `
-FrontDoorName $frontdoorname `
-ResourceGroupName $RG `
-FrontendEndpointName $frontend `
-BackendPoolName $BackendPool `
-PatternToMatch "/*"
# Creates Azure Front Door
New-AzFrontDoor `
-Name $frontdoorname `
-ResourceGroupName $RG `
-RoutingRule $RoutingRule `
-BackendPool $BackendPool01 `
-FrontendEndpoint $FrontendObject01 `
-LoadBalancingSetting $LoadBalancing `
-HealthProbeSetting $HealthProbe
```

USING THE AZURE CLI

You can create a Front Door service using the Azure CLI with the az network front-door
create command and various switches to set its parameters. The preceding Front Door
configuration can be created using the following PowerShell script in Azure CLI. The following
code shows you how. Use this snippet to create the same Front Door service as you did earlier.
Be sure you delete the service you created earlier or modify its variables as appropriate before
you use this code before testing:

```
#Define required variables
azureregion1="EastUS2"
azureregion2="EastUS"
```

```
rg="RG01"
appserviceplan01="MBSP-ASP-01"
appserviceplan02="MBSP-ASP-02"
frontend="MBSP-Frontend-01"
backendpool="MBSP-Backendpool-01"
frontdoorname="MBSP-Frontdoor-01"
app01="WebApp-MBSP-01"
app01="WebApp-MBSP-02"
#Create test app service plans and webapps in different regions
az appservice plan create \
--name $appserviceplan01 \
--resource-group $rg \
--location $azureregion1
az appservice plan create \
--name $appserviceplan02 \
--resource-group $rg \
--location $azureregion2
az webapp create \
--name MBSP-WebApp-03 \
--resource-group $rg \
--plan $appserviceplan01
az webapp create \
--name MBSP-WebApp-04 \
--resource-group $rg \
--plan $appserviceplan02
#Create Azure Front Door Service
az network front-door create --backend-address $app01.azurewebsites.net\
                                           --name $frontdoorname \
                                           --resource-group $rg

#Create Front Door Health Probe
az network front-door probe create --front-door-name  $frontdoorname \
                                           --interval 30 \
                                           --name "Healthprobe" \
                                           --resource-group $rg \
                                           --path "/"

#Create Load Balancing Rule
az network front-door load-balancing create --resource-group $rg \
                                           --front-door-name $frontdoorname \
                                           --name "LoadBalancingSetting" \
                                           --sample-size 4 \
                                           --successful-samples-required 2 \
                                           --additional-latency 0

#Create Back-end Pool
az network front-door backend-pool create --address $app01.azurewebsites.net \
                                           --front-door-name $frontdoorname \
                                           --load-balancing "LoadBalancing
                                             Setting" \
```

```
                                           --name $backendpool \
                                           --probe "HealthProbe" \
                                           --resource-group $rg
az network front-door backend-pool backend add --resource-group $rg \
                                           --front-door-name $frontdoorname \
                                           --pool-name $backendpool \
                                           --address $app02.azurewebsites.net \
                                           --disabled false
#Create Routing Rule
az network front-door routing-rule create --front-door-name  $frontdoorname \
                                           --frontend-endpoints  $frontend \
                                           --name RoutingRule \
                                           --resource-group $rg \
                                           --route-type Forward \
                                           --backend-pool $backendpool \
                                            --accepted-protocols "HTTPSOnly"
```

Best practices

Following are some best practices associated with the Azure Front Door service:

- **Use Azure Monitor to monitor and alert**   You can integrate the Azure Front Door service with Azure Monitor to monitor key Front Door metrics. These include Front Door performance counters such as the following:
  - RequestCount
  - RequestSize
  - ResponseSize
  - TotalLatency
  - BackendRequestCount
  - BackendRequestLatency
  - BackendHealthPercentage
  - WebApplicationFirewallRequestCount
- **Use activity and diagnostic logs**   You can use activity logs to identify, monitor, and alert on any administrative actions performed on the Front Door service. You can use diagnostic logs to monitor, analyze, and alert on operations performed by the Front Door service.
- **Use geo-filtering when applicable**   With geo-filtering, you can allow traffic only from specified regions or block traffic from unwanted regions. If applicable, use geo-filtering for a client environment based on its location and on the countries from which you expect it to be used to limit the application's attack surface.

- **Use virtual network service tags** Virtual network service tags define network access controls on network security groups (NSGs) applied to back-end resources. It's easier to use, manage, and maintain these service tags than to use specific IP addresses in security rules.

- **Restrict administrative access** You can use Azure role-based access control (RBAC) to restrict access to the Front Door service only to required administrative accounts. Ensure that this access is restricted as needed and reviewed on a regular basis to prevent unwanted access as early as possible.

- **Encrypt sensitive information in transit** The Front Door service supports TLS and HTTPS protocols for communication between services and back ends. Use encryption where possible to limit the risk of traffic snooping on that environment.

- **Use Azure Policy to restrict Azure service usage** Azure Policy helps audit and restrict the usage of Azure services in an environment. Use Azure Policy to restrict the deployment of the Front Door service only to required administrators. You can use Azure Monitor to trigger alerts when a deviation is detected.

- **Enable network traffic logging** You can set up network flow logs to monitor network traffic passing through the Front Door service. You can retain these logs in an Azure storage account based on the organization's long-term retention and auditing requirements.

- **Restrict access to back ends only via Front Door** You can set up back-end resources to accept traffic only from the Front Door service, thereby limiting the attack surface on these services. You can also set up rules on back-end services to monitor for the X-Azure-FDID header value in incoming traffic to identify traffic originating from the Front Door service.

- **Use HTTPS as the forwarding protocol** Connections between the Front Door service and the back end happen over public IP. Therefore, it's a good idea to configure the Front Door service to use HTTPS only to forward traffic to back ends. This will restrict malicious activity if traffic is intercepted.

## Chapter 9

Azure Bastion

Overview

Azure Bastion is a fully managed platform as a service (PaaS) provided by Microsoft that helps users securely access Windows and Linux virtual machines (VMs) hosted in Azure with any HTML5-based web browser. As a fully managed secure service, Azure Bastion eliminates the need for public exposure of any VMs in Azure.

Azure Bastion provides secure access directly from the Azure Portal over TLS via RDP or SSH protocols to VMs hosted in Azure. The VMs do not require the installation of any agents or custom software for RDP/SSH access to work.

Setting up and using Azure Bastion is extremely easy. Doing so can reduce the direct public exposure of critical infrastructure components—that is, VMs—and thereby improve overall network security.

Azure Bastion features

Some key features and benefits of using Azure Bastion are as follows:

- **Direct RDP/SSH access via the Azure Portal**   Azure Bastion enables access to Windows and Linux VMs using the Azure Portal directly within an HTML5-based web browser without requiring those VMs to be publicly exposed.

- **Reduced public exposure of Azure VMs**   Azure Bastion enables you to remove public IPs from VMs set up for remote access. The service provides the required RDP/SSH connectivity for administrative purposes over the VM's internal IP, making it the sole entry point to the network for management.

- **Compatible with most networks**   Azure Bastion works securely over port 443, making it accessible over most corporate firewalls. It eliminates the need to redirect RDP/SSH sessions to custom ports to provide additional security and expose additional ports on the network firewalls for secure access.

- **No file data transfer from VMs**   Azure Bastion prevents files from being copied or transferred from the VMs over the RDP/SSH session. Only copying and pasting of text is supported. This removes the risk of unwanted data loss.

- **Customer data management**   Azure Bastion ensures that no client data is stored or moved out of the region in which the service is deployed, providing additional data security for organizations that must adhere to strict data-localization rules.

- **No special software or agent for access**   Azure Bastion does not require the installation of agents or custom software, or custom configuration on either the VM or the client end.

- **Works with any HTML5-based browser**   Azure Bastion supports the use of HTML5-based web browsers such as Microsoft Edge and Google Chrome for access via any operating system, including Windows and macOS.

- **Removes the need for complex NSGs**   By eliminating the need for public exposure of VMs for administrative purposes, Azure Bastion also eliminates the need for complex NSGs to gain secure access to VMs from specific IP ranges, over custom ports, and so on. Azure Bastion only needs RDP/SSH access from its subnet to be open and available.

- **Reduced network exposure**   Because VMs are not exposed directly to the internet, attackers cannot perform malicious activities such as port scanning from external networks to identify ports open for administrative purposes.

- **Reduced exposure to zero-day attacks**   As a fully managed PaaS, Bastion provides perimeter security. Microsoft secures back-end components through service-hardening and patching to keep them up-to-date.

- **Works across the virtual network and peered networks**   Azure Bastion provides secure access to all VMs hosted by the virtual network on which it is deployed. It also provides secure access into any peered virtual networks, removing the need to create multiple instances of the service for different networks.

- **Ideal for remote IT management scenarios**   Azure Bastion gives IT administrators secure access to Azure-based VMs from anywhere, making secure remote administration possible. It also allows remote access without having to procure licensing for Remote Desktop Services as long as the access is for administrative purposes only.

Azure Bastion limitations

Now that we have covered some key features and benefits of Azure Bastion, let's address some of the service's limitations:

- You cannot copy files to and from VMs. Depending on your organization's requirements, this can be both a benefit and a limitation of the service, as it's not a configurable setting.

- Azure Bastion is not supported for VMs that are Azure AD–joined.

- The Azure Bastion subnet does not support user-defined routing.

- Azure Bastion does not currently support the use of IPv6.

- The subnet that hosts the Azure Bastion service cannot be used for the deployment of any other service.

- Even though Azure Bastion provides RDP to the VM in Azure, the redirection of the time zone supported over RDP is not supported over Azure Bastion. The time zone will be set to the one defined on the VM.

- Azure Bastion VMs support only the US English QWERTY keyboard layout. (Support for other locales is ongoing.)

Design concepts and deployment considerations

The following sections cover design concepts and deployment considerations, starting with the architecture of the Azure Bastion service. You'll want to account for these when deploying to ensure Azure Bastion is a highly available redundant service.

Architecture

In most environments, remote management activities require the use of management networks, jump servers, and/or publicly exposed VMs. This exposes the network to unnecessary risks and malicious attacks. As a result, exposed VMs must be patched regularly and hardened to reduce the attack surface. As the number of VMs in the environment increases and more virtual networks are interconnected, the complexity of the network architecture and the time required to securely maintain and manage it increases.

Azure Bastion reduces the complexity of the VM management network architecture by allowing for the deployment of a secure, centralized managed service layer. This layer provides RDP/SSH connectivity to the VMs while ensuring that the underlying layer is hardened by default and kept secure and up to date.

Using Azure Bastion to access VMs across peered networks in Azure simplifies the design of the management network layer, reducing the attack surface while also allowing for redundancy to manage outages in an Azure region. Figure 9-1 shows how client sessions via the Azure Portal using the Azure Bastion service enables VM access.

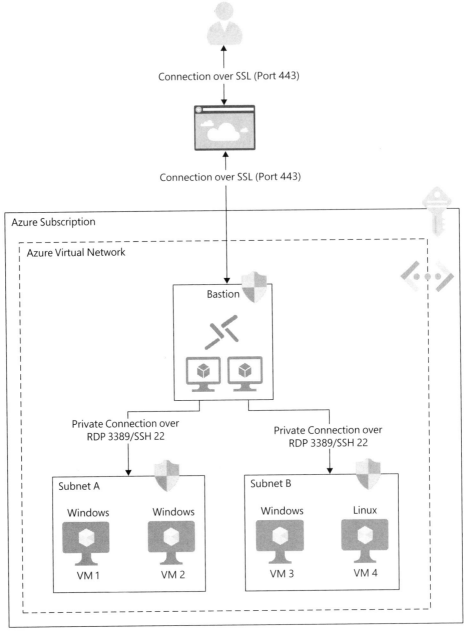

Connection over SSL (Port 443)

Connection over SSL (Port 443)

Azure Subscription

Azure Virtual Network

Bastion

Private Connection over RDP 3389/SSH 22

Private Connection over RDP 3389/SSH 22

Subnet A

Windows

Windows

VM 1

VM 2

Subnet B

Windows

Linux

VM 3

VM 4

FIGURE 9-1 Azure Bastion client access.

SKUs

Azure Bastion provides two SKUs: Basic and Standard. Both currently provide the same functionality, except that the Basic SKU supports only two hosts (discussed next). The Standard SKU is currently in preview; hence, it is not covered in detail in this book.

High-availability hosts

By default, when provisioned, Azure Bastion creates two secure instances that provide redundancy in case of an instance failure. Each Azure Bastion instance supports between 10 and 12 concurrent RDP/SSH connections, depending on the overall load generated by a connection. Scaling beyond two hosts is supported with the Standard SKU. (As mentioned, the Standard SKU is currently in preview, and thus is not covered in detail in this book.)

Virtual network peering

If different virtual networks are peered together, you can deploy Azure Bastion in only one of them to access VMs across different virtual networks. For this to work, the user or administrator needs reader permissions on the virtual network (at a minimum).

Azure Bastion supports two types of peering, as follows:

- **Regional peering** This allows Azure Bastion hosts in one of the peered virtual networks to connect to VMs in all peered networks in the same Azure region.
- **Global peering** This allows Azure Bastion hosts in one of the peered virtual networks to connect to VMs in all globally peered networks.

Disaster recovery

You must manage disaster recovery for the Azure Bastion service. Although Azure Bastion is redundantly deployed in the Azure region in which it is created, if there is an outage in that region, the service will be unavailable for use.

There are two ways to address this:

- **Deploy Azure Bastion in advance on one other virtual network in another Azure region where VMs resources are running** Because Azure Bastion supports a full-mesh design, you can divert to the Azure Bastion host in the closest available Azure region if the primary region experiences an outage.
- **Deploy Azure Bastion in another Azure region after the failure of the Azure Bastion service in the primary region** Setting up Azure Bastion does not take long—meaning you can do it quickly in a different region after the primary region experiences an outage. This approach is the more cost-effective, as you need not run an additional Azure Bastion host at all times.

Service requirements

There are a few service requirements you need to consider before setting up the Azure Bastion service. These requirements are as follows:

- **Dedicated subnet to host the Azure Bastion service** You must set up a dedicated subnet before deploying the Azure Bastion service on a virtual network. This subnet must meet the following requirements:

  - The subnet should be in the same resource group and virtual network as your Azure Bastion deployment.

  - The subnet should be named AzureBastionSubnet; otherwise, it will not be recognized by the Create a Bastion wizard when you create the Azure Bastion service.

  - The subnet octet must be /27 or larger (/26, /25, etc.).

  - The subnet must be used exclusively to host Azure Bastion. It cannot host any other resources.

- **Public IP address** A dedicated public IP address must be assigned to the Azure Bastion service. This public IP address must meet the following requirements:

  - The public IP address must be set to static allocation (not dynamic allocation).

  - The public IP address must be the Standard SKU.

  You can use any existing unused public IP that meets these criteria when you create the Azure Bastion service.

- **Access permissions** Users or administrators who use the Azure Bastion service to connect to a VM must have the following permissions in the Azure environment (at minimum):

  - Reader role on the VM

  - Reader role on the NIC with the VM's private IP

  - Reader role on the Azure Bastion resource

  - Reader role on the virtual network if that virtual network is peered

Azure Bastion walkthrough

The following sections walk you through the process of creating an Azure Bastion service using the Azure Portal, Azure PowerShell, and the Azure CLI.

USING THE AZURE PORTAL

To create an Azure Bastion service using the Azure Portal, follow these steps:

1. Log in to the Azure Portal, type **bastion** in the search box to locate the Azure Bastion service, and select **Bastions** in the list that appears. (See Figure 9-2.)

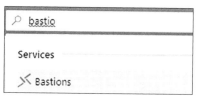

FIGURE 9-2 Search for the Azure Bastion service.

2. Click the **Create Bastion** button to start the Create a Bastion wizard. (See Figure 9-3.)

FIGURE 9-3 Create an Azure Bastion service.

3. In **Basics** tab of the Create a Bastion wizard, in the Project Details and Instance Details sections, enter the following information (see Figure 9-4):

   ▪ **Subscription**   Select the subscription that will host the Azure Bastion service.

   ▪ **Resource Group**   Select the resource group you want to use to host the Azure Bastion service. Alternatively, to create a new resource group, click the **Create New** link and follow the prompts.

   ▪ **Name**   Type a unique name for the service.

   ▪ **Region**   Select the Azure region in which you want to host the Azure Bastion service.

   ▪ **Tier**   Select **Basic**.

   ▪ **Instance Count**   Because you selected the Basic tier, this is automatically set to 2 and grayed out. (Recall that the Basic SKU supports only two instances.)

4. Still in the **Basics** tab of the Create a Bastion wizard, in the **Configure Virtual Networks** section (see Figure 9-5), open the **Virtual Network** drop-down list and select the virtual network on which you want to create the Azure Bastion service.

5. Under the **Subnet** drop-down list, click the **Manage Subnet Configuration** link to create a new subnet.

6. In the Add Subnet dialog box, in the **Name** box, type **AzureBastionSubnet**. (The subnet must have exactly this name.)

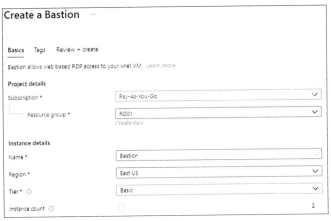

FIGURE 9-4 The Basics tab of the Create a Bastion wizard.

FIGURE 9-5 Configure virtual networks.

7. In the **Subnet Address Range** box, enter an address range for the subnet. (Recall that the subnet must be **/27** or larger.) Leave the other settings in this dialog box as is and click **Save**. (See Figure 9-6.)

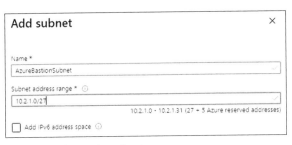

FIGURE 9-6 Set up the subnet.

8. Back in the **Basics** tab of the Create a Bastion wizard, in the Configure Virtual Networks section, open the Subnet drop-down list and choose the subnet you just created (**AzureBastionSubnet**).

9. Still in the **Basics** tab, in the **Public IP address** section, enter the following information (see Figure 9-7). Then click **Next**:

   ■ **Public IP Address** Select the **Use Existing** option button if a public IP address has already been created for the Azure Bastion service. Alternatively, you can select **Create New** and follow the prompts. In this case, select **Create New**.

- **Public IP Address Name** Type a unique name for the public IP address.
- **Public IP Address SKU**   By default, this will be set to Standard and grayed out.
- **Assignment**   By default, this will be set to Static and grayed out.

FIGURE 9-7 Set up a public IP for the Azure Bastion service.

10. In the **Tags** tab, enter any tags required for the Azure Bastion service or leave the fields
    blank (see Figure 9-8), and click **Next**.

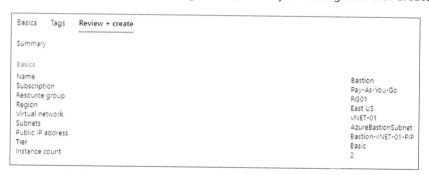

FIGURE 9-8 Set up tags.

11. In the **Review + Create** tab (see Figure 9-9), review your settings and click **Create**.

```
Basics    Tags    Review + create

Summary

Basics
Name                                                    Bastion
Subscription                                            Pay-As-You-Go
Resource group                                          RG01
Region                                                  East US
Virtual network                                         vNET-01
Subnets                                                 AzureBastionSubnet
Public IP address                                       Bastion-vNET-01-PIP
Tier                                                    Basic
Instance count                                          2
```

FIGURE 9-9 Review and create the Azure Bastion service.

USING AZURE POWERSHELL

You can create an Azure Bastion service with Azure PowerShell using the `New-AzBastion`
command with various switches to set the service's parameters. For example, to create the
same Azure Bastion service as you did in the preceding section, you use the following code:

```
#Define required variables
$subnetName = "AzureBastionSubnet"
```

```
$rg = "RG01"
$location = "eastus"
#Create subnet and public IP for Azure Bastion
$subnet = New-AzVirtualNetworkSubnetConfig -Name $subnetName -AddressPrefix 10.2.1.0/27
$vnet = New-AzVirtualNetwork -Name "vNET-01" -ResourceGroupName "RG01" -Location
$location -AddressPrefix 10.2.0.0/16 -Subnet $subnet
$bastionpublicip = New-AzPublicIpAddress -ResourceGroupName $rg -name "Bastion-
vNET01-PIP" -location $location -AllocationMethod Static -Sku Standard
#Create Bastion service
New-AzBastion -ResourceGroupName $rg -Name "Bastion" -PublicIpAddress $bastionpublicip
-VirtualNetwork $vnet
```

USING THE AZURE CLI

You can create an Azure Bastion service with the Azure CLI using the `az network bastion` command with various switches to set the service's parameters. The following script shows you how to set up the same Azure Bastion service you created in the preceding sections with the Azure CLI:

```
#Define required variables
vnet="vNET-01"
resourcegroup="RG01"
location="eastus"
publicip="Bastion-vNET01-PIP"
#Create Azure Bastion service
az network bastion create --location $location --name Bastion --public-ip-address
$publicip --resource-group $resourcegroup --vnet-name $vnet
```

Connect to a VM walkthrough

The following section walks you through using Azure Bastion to connect to Windows and Linux VMs via the Azure Portal.

USING THE AZURE PORTAL

To use Azure Bastion to connect to Windows or Linux VMs using the Azure Portal, follow these steps:

1. Log in to the Azure Portal and navigate to the configuration page for the Windows or Linux VM that you want to access using Azure Bastion.

2. In the left pane of the VM's configuration page, under **Settings**, click **Connect**.

   The pane on the right displays three tabs, one for each connection type: RDP, SSH, and Bastion. (See Figure 9-10.)

3. Click the **Bastion** tab.

4. In the **Bastion** tab, click the **Use Bastion** button. (See Figure 9-11.)

FIGURE 9-10 Connect to VM.

FIGURE 9-11 Connect to the VM using the Azure Bastion service.

5. In the Connect Using Azure Bastion dialog box, do one of the following, depending on whether you are using Windows or Linux:

   - **Windows VM** Type the username and password required to log in to the VM and click **Connect**. (See Figure 9-12.)

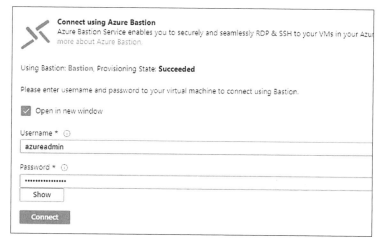

FIGURE 9-12 Log in to the Windows VM.

- **Linux VM** Enter the username. Then enter the password, SSH private key, SSH private key from local file, or SSH private key from Azure Key Vault (depending on what option button you select under **Authentication Type**) and click **Connect**. (See Figure 9-13.)

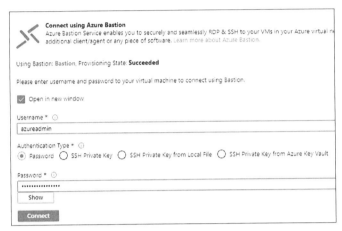

FIGURE 9-13 Log in to the Linux VM.

6. A new tab opens in your web browser, showing the main page for the Windows VM (see Figure 9-14) or Linux VM (see Figure 9-15).

NOTE If a new tab does not open, disable the setting you use to block pop-ups, and try again.

FIGURE 9-14 Windows Server console.

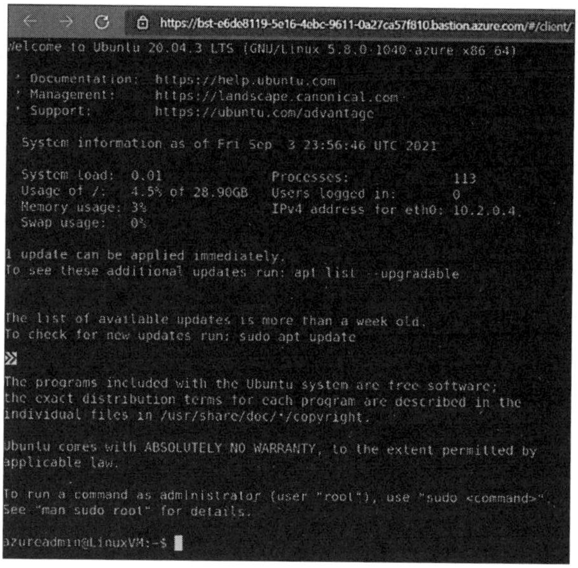

FIGURE 9-15 Linux Server console.

Best practices

Following are a few best practices related to deploying, securing, monitoring, and managing the Azure Bastion service. This is not an exhaustive list, but it provides a good starting point for most organizations using this service:

- **Allow only for required network ports**   Azure Bastion requires a limited number of ports to allow ingress and egress traffic from end-users to VMs hosted in Azure. The port requirements are as follows:

  - **Ingress traffic from clients/administrators**   Only port 443 is required from the internet to the Azure Bastion public IP. No other ports are needed.

  - **Egress traffic to Azure VMs**   Only ports for RDP (3389) and SSH (22) are required between the Azure Bastion subnet and the subnets hosting the VMs.

  - **Egress traffic to other Azure services**   Azure Bastion uses port 443 to connect to other Azure services, such as Azure Storage for storing logs. Enable outbound access to port 443 for the AzureCloud service tag to allow this to work correctly across all Azure resources from Azure Bastion.

- **Use Azure Active Directory for access authentication and authorization**   Azure Active Directory (AD) is the default identity and access-management service in Azure. By default, Azure Bastion is integrated with Azure AD, and you can use Azure AD to control user access to the Azure Bastion service. Limiting access either in Azure AD on the user level, or using Azure AD on the resource level, can help restrict access to resources.

- **Use Key Vault to store SSH keys**   Consider storing SSH keys as Key Vault secrets and allowing access to these secrets only for required administrators to log in to VMs using Azure Bastion. This can help centralize the storing, management, and sharing of these SSH keys.

- **Use multi-factor authentication**   Access to the Azure Portal is integrated with Azure AD. To add another layer of security to protect logins to the Azure Portal, you can enable multi-factor authentication (MFA). You should do this as soon as possible to increase security for user logins.

- **Set up monitoring and alerting**   Use diagnostic logging to monitor remote sessions and keep track of user logins. You can configure alerts based on criteria related to time of access, location of access, etc., to implement additional restrictions to limit access from approved networks or certain timeframes based on suspicious access patterns.

- **Use conditional access policies**   Conditional access policies allow you to put restrictions in place to allow access to the Azure Portal only from specific networks, specific countries, using MFA, and other criteria. Depending on your organization's security requirements, you can also use conditional access policies for suspicious logins and monitoring alerts for additional security.

- **Restrict administrative access to business-critical systems**   Azure Bastion uses Azure role-based access control (Azure RBAC) to specify which accounts should be granted access to VMs that host business-critical systems. You should adhere to the principle of least privilege to ensure that users have only the permissions they need to perform their specific tasks. Also be sure to restrict access to the management, identity, and security tools that have administrative access to your business-critical systems, such as Active Directory Domain Controllers (DCs), security tools, and system-management tools. Attackers who compromise these security systems can easily weaponize them to compromise critical business assets!

- **Regularly review user access**   Implement processes to extract, review, and eliminate unwanted access in Azure AD and on the resource level to ensure that only required administrators have access to the Azure Bastion service to connect to VMs.

- **Use Azure Privileged Identity Management**   This can alert you if too many administrator accounts have been created in the environment and can identify and monitor unused administrator accounts for cleanup.

- **Use privileged access workstations**   Privileged access workstations (PAWs) are isolated workstations that are hardened to protect against breaches on devices. These are then set up as the only devices to access the Azure Portal and other sensitive resources. Consider using PAWs to prevent access from unsecured and untrusted devices to the Azure environment for management purposes.

- **Use Azure Policy** Azure Policy audits, detects, and restricts unwanted deployments of Azure Bastion resources, and monitors the service's network configuration. This can prevent unwanted deployments from enabling additional entry points in the Azure network.

- **Remove access once not required** It is a good practice to remove access to a particular VM if a specific administrator no longer needs it. Implement processes to automate this removal when a change in permission requirements is detected.

- **Enable long-term logging for Azure network activities** You can set up Azure Bastion to store diagnostic service logs in a storage account for monitoring, alerting, and review. Consider setting up retention configuration for logs, taking into account any compliance requirements for your organization.

## Chapter 10

Azure Private Link

Overview

Azure Private Link supports secure private connectivity for access to Azure PaaS Services such as Azure Storage, Azure App Services, and Azure SQL Database, among others. A private endpoint provides connectivity between the PaaS and the client's Azure virtual network.

With Azure Private Link, all network traffic traverses the Microsoft Azure global backbone that connects its massive enterprise and consumer services. This eliminates the need for exposure of PaaS services to the public internet for user consumption, keeping access private and easier to control.

You can use Azure Private Link for your internal users or for partners, customers, or clients to provide access to Azure-hosted services.

Azure Private Link features

Azure Private Link provides the following features and benefits:

- **Enhanced security** By enabling private access to Azure PaaS offerings, Private Link enhances the security posture on the access layer for services hosted in Azure.

- **Improved routing** Private Link enables better routing to Azure-hosted services, as the traffic traverses the Microsoft backbone instead of the public internet (which can be unreliable).

- **Secure access from on-premises or peered networks** Access can be from resources on-premises or in peered virtual networks. You can set up ExpressRoute and VPN tunnels with on-premises environments to provide connectivity to Azure.

- **Restricted access** You can connect private endpoints to specific PaaS resources to allow users access to just those resources instead of the entire Azure back end. This reduces the risk of exposure for other services hosted in Azure not exposed via Private Link or the public internet.

- **Global interconnectivity** You can use Private Link to connect to Azure services hosted in any Azure region, regardless of the source region requiring private access.

- **Secure access for multiple customers**   Private Link enables customers to access Azure-hosted services privately. Customers can set up a private endpoint in their own virtual network and use that to connect to services.

- **Consistent experience**   Whether a service is an Azure PaaS, customer-owned, or partner-owned, using Azure Private Link provides a consistent end-user access experience.

Design concepts and deployment considerations

The following sections cover key considerations when planning the design and deployment of Azure Private Link.

Private endpoints

A *private endpoint* is a network interface connected to an Azure virtual network and is assigned a private IP address from that virtual network. Private endpoints allow private and secure access to the following services:

- **Azure PaaS offerings**   You can associate a private endpoint with an Azure PaaS such as Azure Storage. This effectively enables access over the private IP address assigned to the private endpoint.

- **Customer-owned services**   You can associate a private endpoint with a standard Azure load balancer to provide secure internal access to customer-hosted workloads.

Integration with Azure PaaS offerings

An Azure PaaS offering that is the destination target of a private endpoint is called a *Private Link resource*. Table 10-1 contains examples of Azure PaaS offerings that can currently act as Private Link resources.

TABLE 10-1   Examples of Private Link resources

Azure Application Insights	Azure Database for MySQL	Azure Log Analytics
Azure App Service	Azure Database for PostgreSQL – Single Server	Azure Machine Learning
Azure Backup	Azure Managed Disks	Azure Monitor
Azure Batch	Azure Event Grid	Azure Search
Azure Container Registry	Azure Event Hub	Azure Service Bus
Azure Cosmos DB	Azure IoT Hub	Azure SQL Database
Azure Data Factory	Azure Key Vault	Azure Storage (Blob, File, Queue, and Table)
Azure Database for MariaDB	Azure Kubernetes Service	Azure Synapse Analytics

> **NOTE**   This list is constantly evolving, as more services are either under preview or under development for integration with Azure Private Link.

Integration with customer-owned services

Azure Private Link can be connected with a standard Azure load balancer. Using an internal Azure load balancer, access can be provided to a service or application hosted on other services, such as Azure virtual machines.

Private endpoint features

Here are a few key features of private endpoints that you should take into consideration:

- **Connectivity across different networks**   Private endpoints allow access to connected virtual networks, peered virtual networks, and on-premises networks connected using ExpressRoute or VPN.
- **Integration across Azure regions**   You can host Private Link resources in one Azure region and integrate with a private endpoint hosted in another Azure region.
- **Read-only private IP**   Every private endpoint has an associated read-only network interface that is configured and managed by the service. The network interface is assigned an IP address based on the private virtual network and subnet assigned during service creation. This IP stays with the network interface until the private endpoint is deleted.
- **Integration with Azure private DNS**   You can integrate private endpoints with Azure private DNS for automatic DNS record registration and management.
- **Support for multi-endpoint interconnects**   You can associate a single Private Link resource with multiple private endpoints. This allows for connection to the resource over different IP networks if such segregation is required—for example, in multi-tenant scenarios.
- **Support for multiple private endpoints on the same virtual network**   Every virtual network and subnet can support multiple private endpoints. Currently, as many as 1,000 private endpoints are supported per virtual network.
- **No dedicated subnet required**   Private endpoints do not require a dedicated subnet in the virtual network. Any subnet can be selected to host some or all private endpoints.

Private endpoint limitations

Here are a few limitations or requirements to keep in mind when designing and deploying private endpoints:

- All connections to the private endpoint must be incoming—that is, clients must connect to the private endpoint to access a resource. Outgoing connections from an Azure resource to on-premises or endpoint-connected resources are not supported.
- You must deploy a private endpoint using the same region and subscription as the virtual network. Using a different Azure region or subscription is not currently supported.
- Employing user-defined routing for a private endpoint can result in asymmetric routing. It is best to set up a SourceNAT (SNAT) for such traffic at the network virtual appliance to ensure symmetric routing takes place.

- The subscription hosting the Private Link resource must be registered with the Microsoft.Network resource provider for the integration to work.

Enhanced network security

A private endpoint maps to a single Private Link resource and provides access only to that resource. This ensures that you can securely control and manage network communication. If users require access to multiple resources, you will need to deploy multiple private endpoints. You can restrict or curtail access to public endpoints for Azure resources to ensure access to only the private endpoint.

DNS configuration

To access a resource over Private Link using the resource's fully qualified domain name (FQDN), you need to keep two points in mind:

- You should update the DNS record(s) for the private endpoint to reflect the correct private IP address.
- You should set up the DNS services employed to connect to the private endpoint to use the private DNS records. Otherwise, connectivity will continue over the public endpoint. (These can be DNS services referenced in Azure virtual networks or customer-managed DNS services used by on-premises resources.)

There are different ways to set up DNS for accessing resources over private endpoints:

- **Using HOSTS files** You can manually set up HOSTS files to contain a reference for the private endpoint. This approach is suitable during testing. However, using it on a large scale would be impractical, especially when rolling out or changing the configuration— for example, if the IP changes in a disaster-recovery scenario.
- **Using an Azure private DNS zone** You can integrate an Azure private DNS zone to manage the DNS name resolution for private endpoints. All virtual networks that need to connect using the private endpoint can then be set up to use the private DNS zone for custom name resolution.
- **Using customer-managed DNS forwarders** You can set up DNS forwarders to route requests for the private endpoint domain to DNS servers that have the private IP reference for the service.

Disaster recovery

By default, private endpoints come with 99.99% SLA. However, in the event of a regional outage, services would be unavailable. To handle such a scenario, it's recommended that you do the following:

- Set up multiple private endpoints that point to the same Private Link resource in different Azure regions.
- Set up redundancy for the Private Link resource if it is in the same region as the private endpoint and account for resource failover in your disaster-recovery plan.

This approach will provide redundancy in the event of a large disaster in any Azure region impacting customer workloads that use private endpoints.

Private endpoint walkthrough

The following sections walk you through the process of setting up a private endpoint using the Azure Portal, Azure PowerShell, and the Azure CLI.

Before you proceed with the walkthrough, you need to complete these prerequisites:

- Set up an Azure web app using the App Service Plan – Premium_v2.
- Set up or identify the virtual network and subnet where the private endpoint will be hosted.

USING THE AZURE PORTAL

To create a private endpoint using the Azure Portal, follow these steps:

1. Log in to the Azure Portal, type **Private Link** in the search box to locate the service, and select it from the list that appears. (See Figure 10-1.)

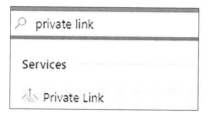

FIGURE 10-1 Search for the Private Link service.

2. Click the **Create Private Endpoint** button to start the Create a Private Endpoint wizard. (See Figure 10-2.)

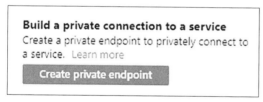

FIGURE 10-2 Create a private endpoint.

3. In the **Basics** tab of the Create a Private Endpoint wizard, enter the following informa-tion (see Figure 10-3) and click **Next**:
   - **Subscription** Select the subscription that will host the private endpoint.
   - **Resource Group** Select the resource group you want to use to host the private endpoint. Alternatively, to create a new resource group, click the **Create New** link and follow the prompts.
   - **Name** Type a unique name for the private endpoint.
   - **Region** Choose the Azure region in which you want to host the private endpoint.

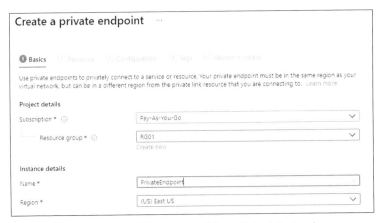

FIGURE 10-3   The Basic tab of the Create a Private Endpoint wizard.

4. In the **Resource** tab, enter the following information (see Figure 10-4) and click **Next**:
   - **Connection Method**   Specify what connection method to use to identify the Azure resource to connect the private endpoint.
   - **Subscription**   Select the subscription in which the Azure resource is located.
   - **Resource Type**   Select the type of Azure resource you want to connect the private endpoint to.
   - **Resource**   Select the specific resource from your subscription to connect the private endpoint to.
   - **Target Sub-Resource**   Select the resource sub-type to connect. The options here will automatically change based on the resource type and resource you selected earlier.

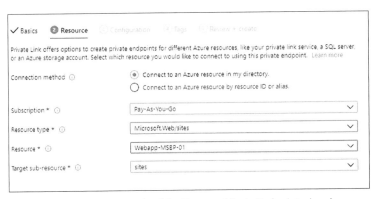

FIGURE 10-4   The Resource tab of the Create a Private Endpoint wizard.

5. In the **Configuration** tab, enter the following information (see Figure 10-5) and click **Next**:
   - **Virtual Network**   Select the virtual network on which you want to create the private endpoint.

- **Subnet** Select the subnet to associate with the private endpoint. The endpoint NIC will pick up an IP address based on this subnet IP range.
- **Integrate with Private DNS Zone** Specify whether the private endpoint should integrate with a private DNS zone.
- **Private DNS Zone Configuration** If you enable integration, specify what private DNS zone you want to integrate with the private endpoint.

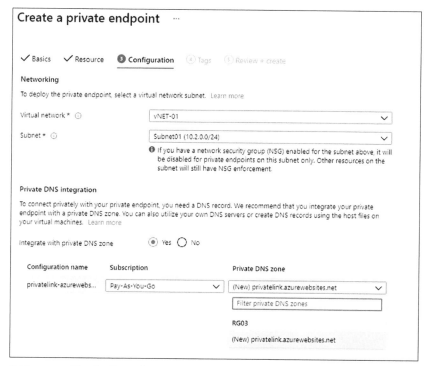

FIGURE 10-5 The Configuration tab of the Create a Private Endpoint wizard.

6. In the **Tags** tab, enter any tags required for the private endpoint service or leave the fields blank (see Figure 10-6), and click **Next**.

FIGURE 10-6 The Tags tab of the Create a Private Endpoint wizard.

7. In the **Review + Create** tab (see Figure 10-7), review your settings and click **Create**.

FIGURE 10-7 Review and create a private endpoint.

USING AZURE POWERSHELL

You can create a private endpoint with Azure PowerShell using the `New-AzVirtualNetworkLink` command with various switches to set its parameters. For example, to create the same private endpoint as you did in the preceding section, you use the following code:

```
#Define required variables
$rg = "RG01"
$vnet = "vNET-01"
$subnetName = "Subnet01"
$webapp = "WebApp-MBSP-01"
$endpointname = "PrivateEndpoint"
$location = "East US"
#Configure the private endpoint
$PrivEndPointConn = New-AzPrivateLinkServiceConnection -Name "myPrivateEndpointconnec-
tion" -PrivateLinkServiceID $webApp.Id -GroupId sites
```

```
$privateEndpoint = New-AzPrivateEndpoint -Name "myPrivateEndpoint" `
-ResourceGroupName $resourcegroupname `
-Location $location `
-Subnet $subnet `
-PrivateLinkServiceConnection $privEndPointConn
#Create the private DNS zone
$PrivdnsZone = New-AzPrivateDnsZone -Name "privatelink.azurewebsites.net"
-ResourceGroupName $rg
#Create the private DNS link
$dnsLink = New-AzPrivateDnsVirtualNetworkLink -Name "privateendpointlink" `
-ResourceGroupName $rg `
-ZoneName "privatelink.azurewebsites.net" `
-VirtualNetworkId $vnet.Id
#Create the private DNS config
$dnsConfig = New-AzPrivateDnsZoneConfig -Name "privatelink.azurewebsites.net" `
-PrivateDnsZoneId $privdnsZone.ResourceId
$dnsZoneGroup = New-AzPrivateDnsZoneGroup -Name "PrivDNSZoneGroup" `
-ResourceGroupName $rg `
-PrivateEndpointName $privateEndpoint.Name `
-PrivateDnsZoneConfig $dnsConfig
```

USING THE AZURE CLI

You can create a private endpoint with the Azure CLI using the `az network private-endpoint create` command with various switches to set its parameters. For example, to create the same private endpoint as you did in the preceding sections, you use the following code:

```
#Define required variables
rg="RG01"
vnet="vNET-01"
subnetName="Subnet01"
webapp="WebApp-MBSP-01"
endpointname="PrivateEndpoint"
location="East US"
#Find the web app resource ID
id=$(az webapp list \
    --resource-group $rg \
    --query '[].[id]' \
    --output tsv)
#Create and configure the private endpoint
az network private-endpoint create \
    --name PrivateEndpoint \
    --resource-group $rg \
    --vnet-name $vnet --subnet $subnet \
    --private-connection-resource-id $id \
```

```
    --group-id sites \
    --connection-name PrivEndpointConnection
#Create the private DNS zone
az network private-dns zone create \
    --resource-group $rg \
    --name "privatelink.azurewebsites.net"
#Create the private DNS link
az network private-dns link vnet create \
    --resource-group $rg \
    --zone-name "privatelink.azurewebsites.net" \
    --name privateendpointlink \
    --virtual-network $vnet \
    --registration-enabled false
#Create the private DNS config
az network private-endpoint dns-zone-group create \
    --resource-group $rg \
    --endpoint-name PrivateEndpoint \
    --name PrivDNSZoneGroup \
    --private-dns-zone "privatelink.azurewebsites.net" \
    --zone-name webapp
```

Azure Private Link service

If a service provider needs to provide its customers with secure private connectivity to Azure-hosted services, they can do so using the Azure Private Link service. The Azure Private Link service provides a reference to service provider–hosted services that customers can connect to using Azure Private Link.

For this to work, customers need to create a private endpoint inside their Azure virtual network and map it to the Azure Private Link service alias or a resource URI provided by the service provider. Once this mapping is complete on the customer end, the service provider can either auto-approve or manually approve the connection request before traffic is allowed over the Microsoft backbone. Figure 10-8 shows how such an integration can be performed.

Notice the following points in Figure 10-8:

- A customer has created a private endpoint in their Azure virtual network and associated it with the Private Link service.

- The Private Link service is mapped to a standard Azure load balancer that front-ends all traffic to the back-end service resources hosted on virtual machines and virtual machine scale sets.

- The customer has connected their on-premises network to the Azure environment using ExpressRoute. This allows traffic from on-premises and Azure-hosted virtual machines to securely and privately route to the service provider's Azure tenant over the Microsoft backbone.

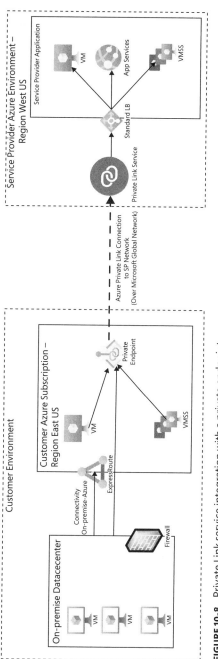

FIGURE 10-8 Private Link service integration with a private endpoint.

Private Link service does not require a dedicated subnet. It can be deployed in any subnet in the same Azure virtual network where the Private Link resource is deployed.

> **NOTE** Each individual Private Link service can receive connections from multiple private endpoints. However, a private endpoint can only connect to one Private Link service.

Connect to the Private Link resource

Azure allows you to map to a Private Link service using two methods:

- **Resource URI** The resource URI is a unique reference to the Azure Private Link service hosted in the service provider tenant. The format of this is quite complex and unique. For example:

```
/subscriptions/<Subscriptionid>/resourceGroups/<resourcegroupname>/providers/
Microsoft.Network/privateLinkServices/{serviceName}
```

- **Service alias** When a Private Link service is created, a unique alias is generated automatically for the service. This alias can be used by customers instead of the resource URI to connect to the Private Link service. The alias consists of multiple parts:

  - **Prefix** This is provided by the service provider when the Private Link service is created.
  - **GUID** This is a unique GUID provided by Azure.
  - **Region** This is the Azure region in which the Private Link service was created.
  - **Azure.privatelinkservice Suffix** This is an automated standardized suffix that is added to the alias.

Once combined, the complete alias would be as follows, making it unique across the entire global Azure network:

```
-Prefix.{GUID}.region.azure.privatelinkservice
```

Service visibility

There are three visibility options to control the exposure of the Private Link service. Each setting controls how customers can connect to the service:

- **Role-Based Access Control Only (None)** RBAC helps control service visibility across virtual networks sharing the same Azure AD tenant. Although you can set up cross-tenant visibility, it is not the ideal method and can result in excessive permission delegation if performed incorrectly.
- **Subscription Restriction (Restrictive)** You can define trusted subscriptions to provide access to and set up auto-approvals for connection requests received from the private endpoints hosted in trusted subscriptions.

- **Anyone with Service Alias (All)** For services that are designed for public consumption, you choose this visibility option so anyone can request to connect. Manual approvals would still be required to approve the connection request.

Service access approvals

You can control access to the Private Link service in one of two ways:

- **Automated approval** When the service provider predefines a set of trusted subscriptions or is hosting the private endpoint, any connection requests are automatically approved.
- **Manual approval** In cases where the service provider wants to control access to the Private Link service before traffic is allowed through, manual approval can be set up. In this scenario, connection requests are kept in a pending state until the manual approval is performed.

High availability

Private Link service supports up to eight IPs per service. This can be used to provide high availability in case connectivity issues occur over a single IP. In addition, you can add multiple Private Link services standard load balancers to provide redundancy in case of service failure. Currently, each standard load balancer supports up to eight Private Link services.

Limitations

The Private Link service has a few limitations that you should consider when deciding on its use:

- Private Link service requires the use of a standard load balancer. The basic load balancer is not supported.
- The back-end pool on the standard load balancer should be configured to point to VMs or a VMSS.
- Private Link supports IPv4 TCP and UDP traffic only.

Private Link service walkthrough

The following sections walk you through the process of setting up an Azure Private Link service using the Azure Portal, Azure PowerShell, and the Azure CLI.

Before you proceed with the walkthrough, you need to complete these prerequisites:

- Set up an Azure standard load balancer and assign at least one VM to the back-end pool.
- Set up or identify the virtual network and subnet where the Private Link service will be created.

USING THE AZURE PORTAL

To create a Private Link service using the Azure Portal, follow these steps:

1. Log in to the Azure Portal, type **Private Link** in the search box to locate the service, and select it from the list that appears. (See Figure 10-9.)

FIGURE 10-9   Search for the Private Link service.

2. Click the **Create Private Link Service** button to start the **Create Private Link Service** wizard. (See Figure 10-10.)

FIGURE 10-10   Create a Private Link service.

3. In the **Basics** tab of the Create Private Link Service wizard, enter the following information (see Figure 10-11) and click **Next**:

- **Subscription**   Select the subscription that will host the Private Link service.
- **Resource Group**   Select the resource group you want to use to host the Private Link Service. Alternatively, to create a new resource group, click the **Create New** link and follow the prompts.
- **Name**   Type a unique name for the Private Link service.
- **Region**   Choose the Azure region in which you want to host the Private Link service.

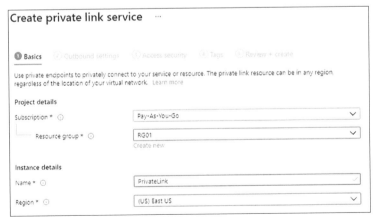

FIGURE 10-11   The Basics tab of the Create Private Link Service wizard.

4. In the **Outbound settings** tab, enter the following information (see Figure 10-12) and click **Next**:

- **Load Balancer** Select the load balancer to associate with the Private Link service.

- **Load Balancer Frontend IP Address** Select the front-end IP address to use for the load balancer.

- **Source NAT Virtual Network** This is set automatically based on the load balancer's virtual network.

- **Source NAT Subnet** Select the subnet to associate with the Private Link service.

- **Enable TCP Proxy V2** Specify whether TCP proxy V2 should be enabled. Leave this at the default value of **No** unless required.

- **Private IP Address Settings** Specify whether the private IP address should be dynamic or static. Leave this at the default value of **Dynamic**.

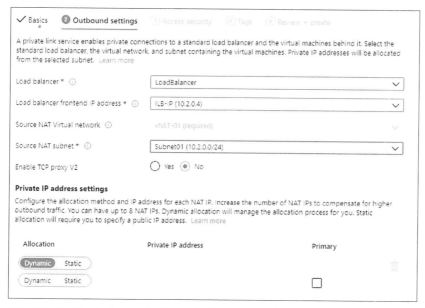

FIGURE 10-12 The Outbound Settings tab of the Create Private Link Service wizard.

5. In the **Access Security** tab, next to Who Can Request Access to Your Service, select the **Role-Based Access Control Only** option button and click **Next**. (See Figure 10-13.)

6. In the **Tags** tab, enter any tags required for the Private Link service or leave the fields blank (see Figure 10-14), and click **Next**.

7. In the **Review + Create** tab (see Figure 10-15), review your settings and click **Create**.

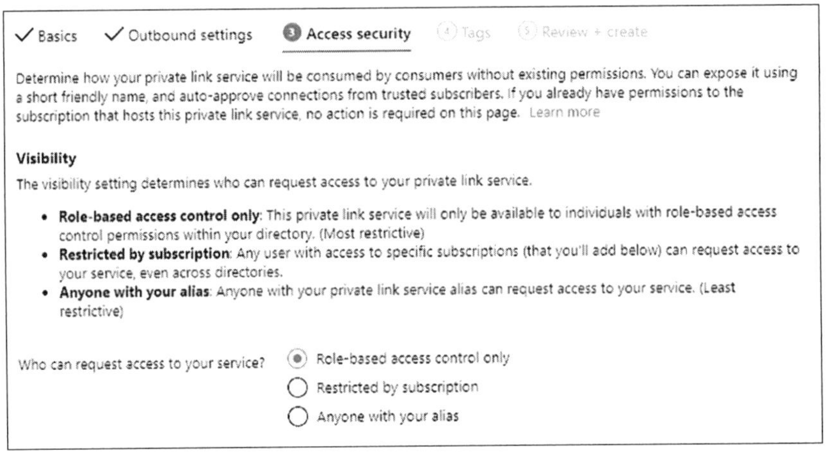

FIGURE 10-13   The Access Security tab of the Create Private Link Service wizard.

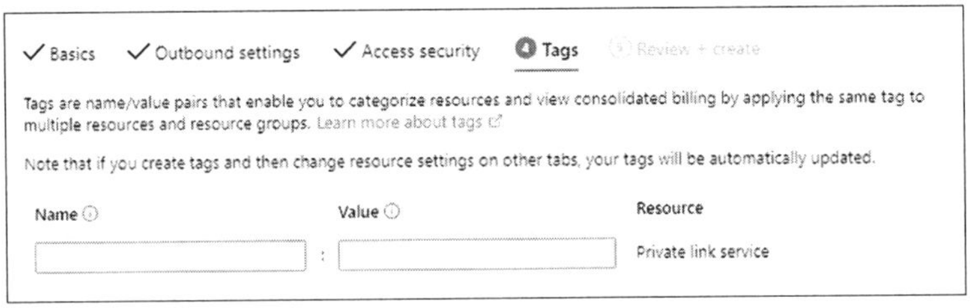

FIGURE 10-14   The Tags tab of the Create Private Link Service wizard.

FIGURE 10-15   Review and create a Private Link service.

USING AZURE POWERSHELL

You can create a Private Link service with Azure PowerShell using the New-AzVirtualNetworkLink command with various switches to set its parameters. For example, to create the same Private Link service as you did in the preceding section, you use the following code:

```
#Define required variables
$rg = "RG01"
$vnet = "vNET-01"
$subnet = "Subnet01"
$loadbalancer = "LoadBalancer"
$lb-ip = "lb-frontend-ip"
$location = "East US"
#Create Private Link private IP
$IPConf = New-AzPrivateLinkServiceIpConfig -Name 'PrivLink-IPConfig' -Subnet $subnet
-PrivateIpAddress '10.2.0.5'
#Create Private Link service
New-AzPrivateLinkService -Name 'PrivateLinkService' -ResourceGroupName = $rg -Location =
$location -LoadBalancerFrontendIpConfiguration $lb-ip -IpConfiguration $IPConf
```

USING THE AZURE CLI

You can create a Private Link endpoint with the Azure CLI using the az network private-endpoint create command with various switches to set its parameters. For example, to create the same Private Link service as you did in the preceding sections, you use the following code:

```
#Define required variables
rg="RG01"
vnet="vNET-01"
subnetName="Subnet01"
loadbalancer="LoadBalancer"
lb-ip="lb-frontend-ip"
location="eastus"
#Create Private Link service
az network private-link-service create \
    --resource-group $rg \
    --name PrivateLinkService \
    --vnet-name $vnet \
    --subnet $subnetname \
    --lb-name $loadbalancer \
    --lb-frontend-ip-configs $lb-ip \
    --location $location
```

Best practices

Following are some best practices for private endpoint and Private Link service setup, management, monitoring, and security. Although this list is not exhaustive, it is a great starting point, and covers most of the important areas to consider:

- **Control access using custom groups**   If you must delegate permissions for deploying Private Link resources, use custom roles to granularly define the required permissions instead of providing access to built-in role groups such as Owner, Contributor, or Network Contributor. Microsoft provides detailed templates for role permissions to create custom role groups to limit access.

- **Use one private endpoint for a shared DNS**   You can create multiple private endpoints for every Private Link resource. However, if the DNS service is common across all the endpoints, it's best to deploy a single private endpoint to avoid DNS record duplication or conflicts resulting in service outages.

- **Use activity logs and alerts**   Use Azure activity logs to monitor changes to Private Link resources. Set up alerts for unwanted activities so you can take effective rollback actions in a timely manner.

- **Use Azure Monitor**   To monitor logs generated by Private Link resources in a centralized manner, ingest them into Azure Monitor for easier analysis. You can also use Log Analytics workspaces to analyze the data, derive actionable insights, and set up effective alerts related to activity logs and security logs generated by the service.

- **Configure long-term log retention**   If organizational compliance demands the storage of activity and security logs for extended periods of time, set up retention policies on the log analytics storage to ensure data is stored for the required period.

- **Perform regular service backups**   Azure Private Link does not integrate with Azure Backup for service backups. However, Azure provides the ability to export the Private Link service configuration as a template, which you can use to restore Private Link endpoints and related resources. In addition, you should perform regular backups using Azure Automation and REST APIs.

Index

freedom

DISCOVER DISCIPLESHIP
WORKBOOK 2: DISCOVER FREEDOM

Jay Morgan

table of contents

getting the most from this study

We are glad that you have chosen to pursue this course of study and hope that you are looking forward to beginning. Before you dig in, there are three important things to take into account:

SMALL DAILY INVESTMENT

To get the maximum benefit from this course of study, a 10-15 minute investment to complete a lesson each day is recommended. Small choices we make each day create the lives we live. Your commitment to spending a few minutes every day to think, journal, study and learn, is a commitment to planting and watering seeds of change.

By doing this, you are creating a harvest of good fruit in your life for yourself and for others to benefit from over time. Even if you do not continue this study, forming the habit of taking time for daily personal growth will benefit you for the rest of your life.

WEEKLY DISCUSSION WITH OTHERS

Each journey that you take in life, whether physical or spiritual, is more enjoyable when you have companions. Someone may see something that you missed or have an idea that is different than your own. Travel is almost always safer in groups.

Likewise, we encourage you to meet regularly with another person or a group of people to discuss thoughts. Spend time with someone who is further down the spiritual road so that you can learn from and lean on them as you progress along your own path. This road is too serious for you to travel upon alone.

MORE THAN A STUDY

This workbook is the second in a series of six. You will find that the six core discoveries as put forth in this series will serve you well beyond this study. These core discoveries are to be used as guides for your spiritual journey, and the workbooks will serve as reference guides throughout your lifetime. This content doesn't end with the course.

Also, keep in mind that each of the six workbooks in this series builds upon each other. It is imperative that you study them in order – and completely – to get the most from this study.

May God bless you as you increase in your knowledge of Him.

Pastor Jay Morgan

For ongoing support and conversations around the topics contained in the *Discover Discipleship Course,* join our online discussion by searching "Discover Discipleship Tribe" on Facebook.

group guidelines

If you are completing this study in a group setting, the following guidelines will help keep meetings safe, focused and productive:

GROUP LOGISTICS

Appropriate group size. Ideally a group should consist of 4-6 people: a group leader and apprentice leader who have both previously completed the *Discover Discipleship Course,* and 3-4 new participants. If a group is larger, consider discussing key concepts from the lessons together, and then forming smaller break-out groups to discuss the questions.

Meet consistently. During the first meeting the group should agree upon a day/time each week for the meeting. Weekly meetings are ideal. Avoid routinely canceling meetings.

Plan the material. Decide each week how many days/lessons you will want to work on at the next meeting. It is recommended that you cover 3-5 lessons at each weekly group meeting.

Be prepared. Both the leader and participants should fully engage with each week's planned material, and answer all questions *before* the group meeting.

MEETING LOGISTICS

Meeting agenda. Begin each meeting by briefly connecting with everyone. Read the meeting ground rules (on the next page) and pray. Summarize lesson points, one lesson at a time, and allow ample time to discuss the lesson questions. The questions are key to the effectiveness of this study.

Group Prayer. End each group meeting with a time of extended prayer when possible. Worship together a few minutes and then pray for each other's needs. These times of prayer will most likely develop more after *Workbook 3: Discover Growth.*

Meeting length. Weekly meetings should typically last 1 to 1 1/2 hours. Make sure to always start and *end* the meeting on time. People might want to stay longer than originally planned, however, be mindful that members might have other obligations after the scheduled meeting time.

MEETING GROUND RULES

To help keep meetings focused, safe and productive, begin every meeting by reading these ground rules aloud.

1. **I will commit to make group meetings and this study a priority by being prepared and being on time.** The group meeting is not the time to work on answers to questions. I understand the group meeting will be unproductive if I have not read the lessons and answered the questions before the group meeting.

2. **I will maintain confidentiality.** What is said in the group stays in the group unless someone threatens to hurt themselves or others. In that case, appropriate people will be notified to ensure the safety of all parties involved.

3. **I will refrain from gossiping about others during the group meeting.** I will keep my focus on my experiences and not on other people. I will leave others' names anonymous when sharing my negative personal experiences in the group setting.

4. **I will be honest.** The purpose of this study is to give honest answers and work toward the study of God's truth. Everyone is here to discover God's truth together. We cannot discover truth until we ask questions and seek answers.

5. **I will respect the other members of the group.** I will refrain from being on electronic devices, interrupting others and/or having side conversations.

6. **I understand that my role is not to "save" or "fix" anyone else.** Together, our role is to continue to point each other toward Jesus and the truth of His teachings.

Go to the *Church Leader Resources* section of **www.discoverdiscipleship. com** for additional resources to assist with leading a productive group meeting.

introduction to freedom

> We have to present the liberty of Christ, and we cannot do it if we are not free ourselves. There is only one liberty, the liberty of Jesus Christ at work in my conscience, enabling me to do what is right. **— OSWALD CHAMBERS**

discovering freedom

Congratulations on making it to the second core decision of your spiritual journey.

We are glad you have chosen to continue this study, and hope you look forward to discovering more spiritual truths.

REVIEW

In *Workbook 1: Discover Identity,* we learned that God created everything for His purpose.

> … all things have been created through him and
> for him. — **Colossians 1:16b**

Man was created in the image of God—as a son of God. God created us to be His children, His family (Genesis 1:26; Luke 3:38). Initially, in the Garden of Eden, God and man enjoyed a close, intimate relationship. This was destroyed when Adam and Eve left God and instead pursued sin. Fear and mistrust of God separated mankind from the relationship they shared with Him (Genesis 3:9-10).

Since that time, we have continued to search for security, worth and fulfillment apart from God. Having lost our identity as children of God, we derive *substitute identities* from other people or things, or from our own self-perception. *Substitute identities* promise much, but deliver little. They lead to more sin, leaving us empty and separated from God. Sin results in spiritual death. Spiritual death results in eternal death—separation from God in hell.

> ...for all have sinned and fall short of the glory
> of God... — **Romans 3:23**

We are dead in sin and cannot restore ourselves to our place as God's children, yet many people sense their need for God. When we know we need Him, but fail to understand or accept His plan to restore us to our place as His children, we try to make Him happy by doing good deeds or by being what we consider a good person. Our efforts can only fail. Only spiritual rebirth can accomplish our restoration.

> As for you, you were dead in your transgressions and sins...But because of his great love for us, God, who is rich in mercy, made us alive with Christ even when we were dead in transgressions—it is by grace you have been saved...For it is by grace you have been saved, through faith—and this is not from yourselves, it is the gift of God—not by works, so that no one can boast. — **Ephesians 2:1-9**

It is only through Jesus that we can be brought back to life and experience a relationship with God as His children.

> And all of this is a gift from God, who brought us back to himself through Christ. And God has given us this task of reconciling people to him. — **II Corinthians 5:18 NLT**

> Yet to all who did receive him, to those who believed in his name, he gave the right to become children of God—children born not of natural descent, nor of human decision or a husband's will, but born of God. — **John 1:12-13**

In *Workbook 1: Discover Identity*, you made the decision to live in your created identity as a child of God by surrendering to the Lordship of Jesus. Through faith in Jesus, you were spiritually reborn. Remember, as a spiritually reborn child of God, you have new desires.

As a child of God you will desire the following:

- More of God and less of sin. (Galatians 5:17)

- Intimacy with the Father and the nourishment of the Word of God. (Romans 8:15 16, 1 Peter 2:2)

- The community of God's family. (Ephesians 2:19)

- To bear the image of God in the world and do the works you were created to do. (Ephesians 2:8-10, Matthew 28:18-20)

- To honor God with all of your life and resources. (1 Corinthians 6:19-20)

The purpose of the *Discover Discipleship Course* is to help you develop these desires that God placed in you. You must cooperate with God and allow these desires to mature and grow. Living in your identity as God's child and allowing these desires to grow will help you to discover lasting security, worth and fulfillment.

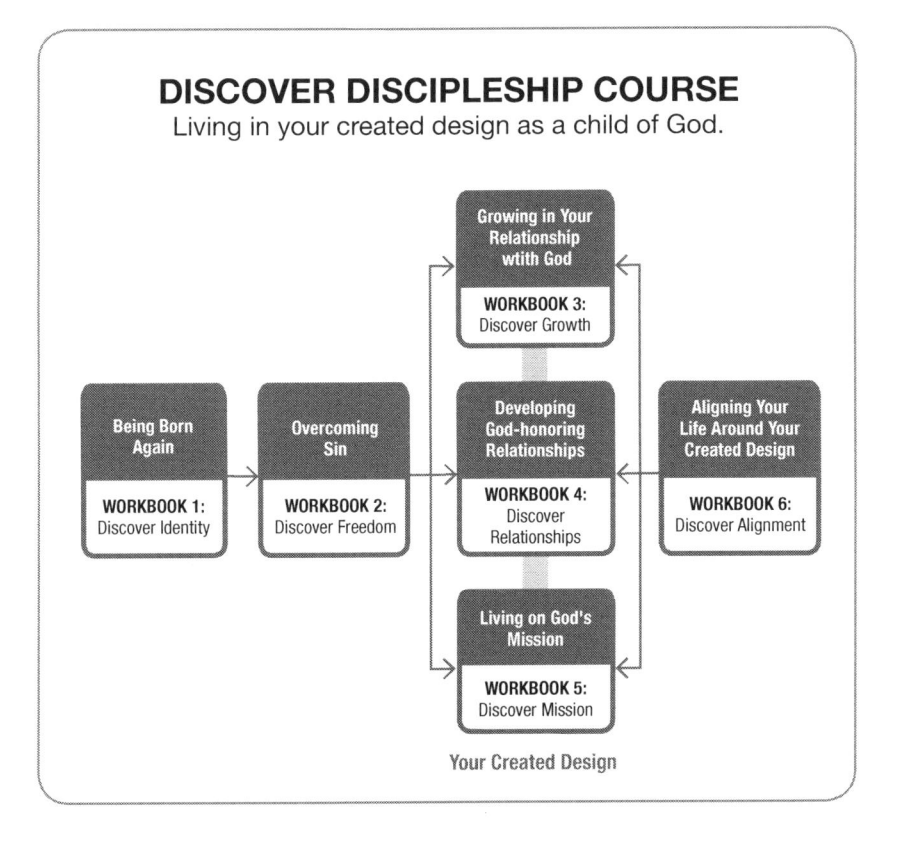

THE FREEDOM DECISION

When you surrendered to Jesus and were spiritually reborn, He put your old life to death. But you still have old desires and habits left from your old life that must be destroyed.

> Set your minds on things above, not on earthly things. For you died, and your life is now hidden with Christ in God. When Christ, who is your life, appears, then you also will appear with him in glory. Put to death, therefore, whatever belongs to your earthly nature: sexual immorality, impurity, lust, evil desires and greed, which is idolatry. — **Colossians 3:2-5**

Before you can fully live out God's purposes for your life, you must confront and find freedom from these old, sinful habits. *The child of God in you desires more of God and less of sin.* Failure to overcome patterns of sin in your life will keep you spiritually immature, limit your Kingdom effectiveness and eventually destroy your life.

In this workbook, you will explore why and how to live in spiritual freedom as you learn to make the next core decision of your spiritual journey.

The Freedom Decision:
I choose to live in freedom from sinful habits by: taking *personal responsibility* for my change; relying on the strength of God's *power* to change me; finding *partners* to support my change; developing a *plan* for change.

understanding the gospel

Let's review the message of the Gospel of Jesus:

Creation: God created the world as it should be. All things were created by Jesus, for Jesus (Colossians 1:16). His desire for creating humans was to have a family to share for eternity.

- Mankind was created to "Glorify God and enjoy Him forever."[1]

- Mankind was given the mission to rule—bring the Kingdom of God to earth (Genesis 1:28).

- Mankind was given the gift of human relationships as God created Eve and gave them the shared job of ruling over the earth (Genesis 2:18).

Separation: Mankind separated themselves from a relationship with God by listening to the lies of Satan and pursuing their own desires (Genesis 3).

- Each one of us were born into this separated state of sin (Romans 5:12).

- Beginning with Adam and Eve, each of us have gone our own way, away from God (Isaiah 53:6; Romans 3:23).

- Sin not only separates us from God, it brings death and destruction (Romans 6:23).

- Separated from God, we will share Satan's fate—Hell (Matthew 25:41).

Redemption: God saw man in the fallen state he was in and through Jesus, He took on flesh and made a way for man to be reunited with Him (John 1; Romans 5:8).

- Jesus' life taught us the will of God—how to live as children of God (Hebrews 1:1-2).

- Jesus' death paid our death penalty (Romans 6:23; I John 2:2).

- Jesus' resurrection gives us the power to live a new life as a child of God (Romans 6:4-6).

Decision: Jesus did everything necessary to bring us to God, everything except force us to trust and love God. We must each decide who we will follow. Will you continue to live life your own way, or will you surrender to Jesus' Lordship and be reunited with God (Romans 10:9-10)?

- We must repent—turn—from our way and turn toward Jesus and follow His way (Acts 2:38). Remember, it is turning toward our own way that separates us from God to begin with. Salvation comes from turning back to Him. For "you were like sheep going astray," but now you have returned to the Shepherd and Overseer of your souls. (1 Peter 2:25).

- When we surrender to Jesus' Lordship, we are saved from our sins and spiritually reborn (Romans 10:9-19; John 3:3).

- The Holy Spirit will enter into us and give us a new heart and will teach us how to follow God's ways (Ezekiel 36:26-27).

- We will then spend the rest of our lives living as Jesus' disciples—learning, obeying and teaching others what Jesus desires (Matthew 28:19-20).

We previously learned the identity of being a child of God is offered to everyone. However, to receive it, you must turn from your old life of sin and surrender to the Lordship of Jesus.

Many Christians believe that leaving their old life is optional. In other words, Jesus will save them from Hell even if they do not turn from their sinful lifestyles and fully obey Him. Some will even say that they have accepted Jesus as their Savior but have not accepted Him as their Lord. This idea is simply not taught in Scripture. Remember, salvation comes through repentance—turning from our way—and surrendering to Jesus' Lordship.

REPENTANCE

Jesus said that He came to call sinners to repentance. Repentance means *having a change of mind or turning around.*[2]

> I have not come to call the righteous, but sinners to repentance. — **Luke 5:32**

Jesus' point when He made this statement to religious leaders wasn't that they did not need to repent—change direction—but that they were sinners, too. Only sinners who admit they are sinners can repent. Scripture is clear that we have all sinned and we have all gone our own way, apart from God. When we repent, we turn from our old way back to God's way.

1. Why is it hard to learn a new way of doing something while refusing to admit you need to change?

The Apostles taught that repentance and surrendering to the Lordship of Jesus was the way of salvation.

"Therefore let all Israel be assured of this: God has made this Jesus, whom you crucified, both Lord and Messiah." When the people heard this, they were cut to the heart and said to Peter and the other apostles, "Brothers, what shall we do?" Peter replied, "Repent and be baptized, every one of you, in the name of Jesus Christ for the forgiveness of your sins. And you will receive the gift of the Holy Spirit. With many other words he warned them; and he pleaded with them, "Save yourselves from this corrupt generation." — **Acts 2:36-38, 40**

Notice that Apostle Peter preached that Jesus was Lord and Messiah. Then He preached that in order to be saved, people must repent—turn from their way and the way of their corrupt culture—to Jesus' way. In other words, they were to turn from sin and give Jesus control of their life.

2. **What does it mean to turn from your way to Jesus' way?**

confessing Jesus as Lord

Apostle Paul reiterated that surrender to Jesus' Lordship was necessary for salvation.

> that if you confess with your mouth Jesus as Lord, and believe in your heart that God raised Him from the dead, you will be saved;
> — **Romans 10:9 NASB**

Confessing, or agreeing, that Jesus is Lord involves more than just saying the words. Notice the above Scripture teaches that we must not only confess Jesus with our mouth, but that we must also believe in our heart that He is Lord of all things, including death.

Your heart is the center of your will. To truly believe in your heart that Christ is Lord involves a surrender of your life and will to His authority. It means you live in obedience to His will and desires.

> Why do you call me, "Lord, Lord," and do not do what I say? — **Luke 6:46**

Remember that many people have false assurances of salvation. Believing in God and that Jesus is the Son of God is not enough to save you; even demons believe this. Sensing the Presence of God, performing miracles, saying a prayer or being baptized also are not complete indications of salvation[3] (Review *Workbook 1: Discover Identity, Day 17: Incomplete Belief* for further teaching on this.)

While these things are *important*, they are, at best, a verbal acknowledgment or a mental agreement with spiritual concepts—that is not enough to save you. You must believe *in your heart* in order to be saved.

Although self-sufficient people might acknowledge or agree with who Jesus is, they—along with Satan and his demons—will never submit to Jesus' Lordship. They will not trust Jesus enough to surrender their will and desires—the control of their life—to Him.

1. **What is the difference between mentally or verbally agreeing that Jesus is Lord and actually surrendering the control of your life to Him?**

Being born again results in a changed life. Jesus said that many will stand before Him and call Him Lord and will claim to have performed many miracles and good deeds in His name. However, He will declare that He does not know them. He said that only those who actually *do the will of God* will enter into heaven.

> "Not everyone who says to me, 'Lord, Lord,'
> will enter the kingdom of heaven, but only the
> one who does the will of my Father who is in
> heaven. Many will say to me on that day, 'Lord,
> Lord, did we not prophesy in your name and
> in your name drive out demons and, in your
> name, perform many miracles?' Then I will tell
> them plainly, 'I never knew you. Away from
> me, you evildoers!' — **Matthew 7:21-23**

Let's be clear, doing the will of God does not save you. That would mean your works could save you. However, if you are saved, you do the will of the Father. You have turned from your desires and will and have surrendered to the Father's desires and will. This turning—repentance—is *evident* in your words and in your actions. If you have surrendered to Jesus, you will live life with Jesus as your Lord.

> "Beware of false prophets who come disguised
> as harmless sheep but are really vicious wolves.

You can identify them by their fruit, that is, by
the way they act...

Yes, just as you can identify a tree by its fruit, so
you can identify people by their actions."
— Matthew 7:15-16, 20 NLT

2. What does this warning from Jesus mean to those who confess Him as Lord yet refuse to do the will of God?

The following passage of Scripture reaffirms that our good works will not save us, however, if we are saved, we will do the good works which God created us to do. In other words, doing the will of God is not an effort on your part to *earn* salvation; it is a *result* of salvation.

For it is by grace you have been saved, through
faith—and this is not from yourselves, it is the
gift of God—not by works, so that no one can
boast. For we are God's handiwork, created
in Christ Jesus to do good works, which God
prepared in advance for us to do.
— Ephesians 2:8-10

3. What is the difference between doing the right thing because you are saved and doing the right thing to earn your salvation?

relearning life

In the last lesson, we read where Jesus stated that only those who do the will of the Father will enter into the kingdom of heaven. So, how do we really know the will of the Father?

HOW DO WE KNOW THE WILL OF THE FATHER?

Jesus answers this by saying that His words and His teachings are from God and will lead to life.

> For I did not speak on my own, but the Father who sent me commanded me to say all that I have spoken. — **John 12:49**

> The Spirit gives life; the flesh counts for nothing. The words I have spoken to you—they are full of the Spirit and life. — **John 6:63**

Scripture explains that God has spoken to us through Jesus.

> In the past God spoke to our ancestors through the prophets at many times and in various ways, but in these last days he has spoken to us by his Son, whom he appointed heir of all things, and through whom also he made the universe. — **Hebrews 1:1-2**

God Himself spoke from heaven and affirmed Who Jesus was, and instructed the disciples to listen to Him.

> A voice came from the cloud, saying, "This is my Son, whom I have chosen; listen to him."
> — Luke 9:35

Scripture is clear, if you want to know and do the will of God, you must learn and live the teachings of Jesus. The Father's will, as stated through Jesus' teachings, compels us to leave our old ways of thinking and acting and to learn new ways of thinking and acting. When we surrender our lives to the Lordship of Jesus, we start life over and relearn everything with Him as our teacher. Jesus referred to this when He said that we are to be born again and become like a child.

> Jesus replied, "Very truly I tell you, no one can see the kingdom of God unless they are born again." — John 3:3

> And he said: "Truly I tell you, unless you change and become like little children, you will never enter the kingdom of heaven."
> — Matthew 18:3

This becomes clearer once we understand the Biblical meaning of the word *disciple*. The practice of making disciples is rooted in Hebrew rabbinic tradition where students not only memorized their rabbi's words; they also learned to *emulate* the rabbi's ministry, life, and character. Disciples in Jesus' day followed their rabbi wherever He went, learning from his teachings and training to live as the rabbi lived.[4] Jesus trained His first disciples in this manner. And before He returned to heaven, He commanded them to go make new disciples and teach these new disciples to obey everything He commanded as well (Mathew 28:18-20).

The first disciples of Jesus were called "Followers of the Way" (Acts 9:2; 22:4). They were called this because they lived following Jesus' way of life, based on His teachings. They were His

disciples. A Christian is someone who has surrendered their life to the Lordship of Jesus, been spiritually reborn and now lives as a disciple of Jesus.

1. What does it mean to relearn life with Jesus as our Lord and train to live as He did?

FOLLOWING JESUS' TEACHINGS

To truly confess Jesus as Lord and become His disciple, means that you admit you have been wrong. You admit that your ways and desires have not honored God. Even actions that seem normal or natural to us, if condemned in Scripture, are sinful and must be changed.

> For the flesh desires what is contrary to the Spirit, and the Spirit what is contrary to the flesh. They are in conflict with each other, so that you are not to do whatever you want.
> — Galatians 5:17

2. Why is it hard to admit that you are wrong?

When you confess Jesus as Lord, you decide in advance that He is right. Right about what? *Everything!* You decide that you will no longer live as you desire, but as He desires. You probably do not understand all that Jesus asks or wants of you at this point in your spiritual journey, but as a disciple of Jesus, you will spend your life learning what He desires and doing what He desires.

> You must have the same attitude that Christ Jesus had. — **Philippians 2:5 NLT**

3. **What does it mean to decide in advance that Jesus is right?**

The life of a disciple is one of relearning and change. Relearning life, with Jesus as your teacher, means you will begin doing new things that might be difficult at first but actually lead to life, and you will stop doing things that you may think benefit you but actually lead to death.

> If you cling to your life, you will lose it; but if you give up your life for me, you will find it. — **Matthew 10:39 NLT**

Jesus would not have told us to deny ourselves, take up our cross daily and follow Him if following Him did not involve making difficult decisions.

> Then he said to them all: "Whoever wants to be my disciple must deny themselves and take up their cross daily and follow me." — **Luke 9:23**

As your Lord, Jesus will teach you the will of the Father. However, you must submit to it and obey Him. You will not be perfect. But as a Christian, a disciple of Jesus, you will spend the rest of your life learning and surrendering to what He desires.

> Why do you call me, "Lord, Lord," and do not do what I say? — **Luke 6:46**

4. **According to the previous verse, can you truthfully claim Jesus as your Lord and yet consistently refuse to obey Him? Why or why not?**

Simply put, discipleship is learning to be like Jesus. The Christian life and faith are firmly centered on the teachings and life of Christ Himself. Discipleship is not merely *learning* what Christ taught; one must learn to *obey* what He taught.

> Then Jesus came to them and said, "All authority in heaven and on earth has been given to me. Therefore go and make disciples of all nations, baptizing them in the name of the Father and of the Son and of the Holy Spirit, and *teaching them to obey everything I have commanded you.* And surely I am with you always, to the very end of the age."
> — **Matthew 28:18-20** *(emphasis added)*

Discipleship is an active response to this directive—to be a disciple who lives as Jesus did, and then make new disciples of Jesus and teach them to obey everything He taught as well.

turning away from sin

Scripture teaches that Jesus did not just come to save us from hell. He also came to save us from the *sins* that will send us to hell.

> She will give birth to a son, and you are to give him the name Jesus, because he will save his people from their sins. — **Matthew 1:21**

Doing our own thing apart from God's will is sin. Scripture teaches that sin is of the devil and that Jesus came to destroy the devil's influence and work in the world. This means that Jesus will not leave us in our sin.

> The one who does what is sinful is of the devil, because the devil has been sinning from the beginning. The reason the Son of God appeared was to destroy the devil's work. — **I John 3:8**

As previously noted, Scripture repeatedly teaches that Christians are people who leave their old way of living—a life of sin that is influenced by Satan—and learn a new way of living with Jesus in charge.

Many people try to exempt themselves from living as Christ did. They want to continue to live their lives doing what they want, but still have assurance of salvation. Or put another way: they want to live like criminals, but be assured pardon for their crimes.

People like this want to continue to pursue their old *substitute identities*—seeking security, worth and fulfillment through themselves, people and things—and still have the assurance of salvation when they die.

Scripture does not support this belief. Only surrender to the Lordship of Christ brings salvation. If you surrender to His Lordship, you will live as He lived. How can anyone claim to have surrendered to Christ and not obey His teachings?

> Whoever says, "I know him," but does not
> do what he commands is a liar, and the truth
> is not in that person. But if anyone obeys his
> word, love for God is truly made complete
> in them. This is how we know we are in
> him: Whoever claims to live in him must live as
> Jesus did. — **1 John 2:4-6**

Remember, a Christian is not someone who simply believes in Jesus. A Christian is born again. Who you were is gone. You have been raised to new life. This means a Christian is someone who lives like Jesus, through the power of Jesus. Christians become like Christ.

> So, all of us who have had that veil removed
> can see and reflect the glory of the Lord. And
> the Lord—who is the Spirit—makes us more
> and more like him as we are changed into his
> glorious image. — **II Corinthians 3:18 NLT**

This is where the word Christian is derived from. The suffix, "-ian", means *adhering to, following or resembling*.[5] A Christian adheres to, follows, and resembles Christ. They have placed Him in charge of their lives, and they live as Jesus lived (I John 2:6). Jesus lived holy—pure, free from sin.[6] So, if we are to live as Jesus did, we too must live free from the power of sin.

> But just as he who called you is holy, so be holy
> in all you do; for it is written: "Be holy, because
> I am holy." — **I Peter 1:15-16**

The Apostles understood it was illogical to claim Christ's salvation from sin without leaving sin. How can you be saved—rescued— from something, yet remain in it?

What then? Shall we sin because we are not under the law but under grace? By no means! Don't you know that when you offer yourselves to someone as obedient slaves, you are slaves of the one you obey—whether you are slaves to sin, which leads to death, or to obedience, which leads to righteousness? But thanks be to God that, though you used to be slaves to sin, you have come to obey from your heart the pattern of teaching that has now claimed your allegiance. You have been set free from sin and have become slaves to righteousness.
— **Romans 6:15-18**

Come back to your senses as you ought and stop sinning; for there are some who are ignorant of God—I say this to your shame.
— **1 Corinthians 15:34**

As for you, you were dead in your transgressions and sins, in which you used to live when you followed the ways of this world and of the ruler of the kingdom of the air, the spirit who is now at work in those who are disobedient. All of us also lived among them at one time, gratifying the cravings of our flesh and following its desires and thoughts. Like the rest, we were by nature deserving of wrath.
— **Ephesians 2:1-3**

For God did not call us to be impure, but to live a holy life. — **1 Thessalonians 4:7**

Dear friends, I urge you, as foreigners and exiles, to abstain from sinful desires, which wage war against your soul. — **1 Peter 2:11**

I say this because some ungodly people have
wormed their way into your churches, saying
that God's marvelous grace allows us to live
immoral lives. The condemnation of such
people was recorded long ago, for they have
denied our only Master and Lord, Jesus Christ.

— Jude 1:4 NLT

1. After reading these verses, do you think that Scripture
teaches that it is optional for Christians to stop
sinning? Why or why not?

becoming like Christ

Many argue that one can be saved—justified—without being changed—sanctified. This is an illogical argument. It is like asking if one can be born, remain alive, and not ever grow. If you have genuinely been spiritually reborn, you have become a child of God; and that child of God has new desires. Remember, the child of God in you desires more of God and less of sin.

Living free from sin is not just about your will power. When we surrender to Jesus, the Holy Spirit enters us and gives us a new heart. That is spiritual rebirth. His Spirit then lives in us, and empowers us to keep the commands of God.

> I will give you a new heart and put a new spirit in you; I will remove from you your heart of stone and give you a heart of flesh. And I will put my Spirit in you and move you to follow my decrees and be careful to keep my laws.
> — **Ezekiel 36:26-27**

Many assume that after they surrender to Christ they are still the same person they were before—only now, they are forgiven. That is not what Scripture teaches. Scripture makes it clear that through salvation and baptism, who you once *were* is gone—buried. God has resurrected your spirit to *new life!* The old has gone, the new has come. You are not the same person as before—you have been born again.

> For we died and were buried with Christ by baptism. And just as Christ was raised from the dead by the glorious power of the Father, now we also may live new lives. — **Romans 6:4 NLT**

Before coming to Christ, our normal inclination is toward sinful desires. We were sinners. After surrendering to Christ and being spiritually reborn, Christ changes our normal inclination to His desires—loving God and loving others. As you mature and become spiritually stronger, the new desires of a child of God in you will become stronger. Those desires might be weak at first, but they are present, and you have to nurture them and allow them to grow.

Being changed and spiritually growing up does not mean you will no longer have old, sinful desires. However, it does mean you learn how to "walk in the Spirit so that you do not fulfill the desires of the flesh" (Galatians 5:16).

You are now a citizen of the Kingdom of God and live in the world as His ambassador. An ambassador of Jesus represents the values of the King and His kingdom.

> For he has rescued us from the dominion of darkness and brought us into the kingdom of the Son he loves. — **Colossians 1:13**

> We are therefore Christ's ambassadors, as though God were making his appeal through us. We implore you on Christ's behalf: Be reconciled to God. — **II Corinthians 5:20**

1. **What do you think it means to represent the values of Christ?**

CHANGE IS GOD'S PLAN FOR YOU

God desires to conform us into the image of His son—Jesus. We cannot have true Christianity without moving toward Christ-likeness.

> For those whom He foreknew, He also predestined to become conformed to the image of His Son, so that He would be the firstborn among many brethren. — **Romans 8:29 NASB**

Being conformed to Christ means that you take on His character— you become like Him (Review 1 John 2:4-6).

Many people read Christ's commands and teachings and believe that it is acceptable to simply say, *"I do not feel 'called' to do that."* Or, *"I don't have time for that."* Or, *"That's too difficult for me to do."* Or, *"I know I'm not following Christ's commands, but I'm okay with God."*

These assumptions are dangerous. Remember that there are many false assurances of salvation. As we have read, Jesus stated, "Not everyone who says to me, 'Lord, Lord,' will enter the kingdom of heaven, but only the one who does the will of my Father who is in heaven" (Matthew 7:21).

Again, let's be clear—simply doing the will of God does not save you. That would mean your works can save you. However, if you are genuinely saved, Christ lives in you and does the will of God through you. Christ will not live through us in a way that is different from how He lived while on earth.

Being transformed and conformed to the character of Christ is referred to in different ways, including:

- Sanctification

- Holiness

- Discipleship

- Spiritual Growth/Maturity

- Becoming like Christ

All of these terms refer to laying down old ways of thinking and acting and taking on new ways. Remember the word "repent" means *to turn or have a change of mind.* It is not merely asking forgiveness for your behavior. It is a decision to turn from your sinful behavior.

2. **How is seeking to be changed by God different from asking for forgiveness from God?**

A CAUTION

It is cause for great concern if you profess faith in Christ and willfully continue in patterns of sin without sorrow and change—repentance.

> Godly sorrow brings repentance that leads to salvation and leaves no regret, but worldly sorrow brings death. — **II Corinthians 7:10**

Continued resistance against the Word of God and the work of the Holy Spirit to change your life highlights some serious issues. Either you have not truly been born again and the Spirit of Christ does not live in you; or you are born again, but live in rebellion against God. Either of these concerns should sober you.

Have you been born again? You can be deceived into thinking you are born again when you are not. Remember, there are many false assurances of salvation (Review *Workbook 1: Discover Identity, Day 17: Incomplete Belief* for further teaching on this). Did you truly give up the control of your life to Jesus? Remember, it is not enough to just say, "Jesus is Lord." You must believe it in your heart. If you believe it in your heart, you will turn from your way and surrender your will to His. Which points to the second concern:

Are you living in rebellion against God's commands? A Christian still has the capacity to sin, but if they do sin, they will experience Godly sorrow and the discipline of God, which will guide them back to the right path. The ability to continue in sin without feeling Godly sorrow and experiencing the discipline of the Lord indicates that you have never been saved.

> In your struggle against sin, you have not yet resisted to the point of shedding your blood. And have you completely forgotten this word of encouragement that addresses you as a father addresses his son? It says,
>
> "My son, do not make light of the Lord's discipline, and do not lose heart when he rebukes you, because the Lord disciplines the one he loves, and he chastens everyone he accepts as his son."
>
> Endure hardship as discipline; God is treating you as his children. For what children are not disciplined by their father? If you are not disciplined—and everyone undergoes discipline—then you are not legitimate, not true sons and daughters at all. — **Hebrews 12:4-8**

The question is not, *"Are you still tempted by sin?"* Earlier in today's lesson, we learned that Christians can be tempted to sin and can still fall into sin's trap. The question is, *"Are new desires for righteousness present in me?"* And, *"When I do sin, do I experience the discipline of the Lord? Does He correct me?"*

3. **What do think it means to experience the discipline of the Lord?**

why would you want to remain in sin?

Some people argue in an attempt to justify their right to continue in sinful behavior, and refuse to cooperate with the Holy Spirit to overcome it. A bigger question to ask yourself is, *"Why would I want to remain in sin?"*

Sin destroys you. True: sin is pleasurable for a while. But it will destroy you. Why would you want to keep sinning rather than seek freedom from it?

> For the wages of sin is death, but the gift of God
> is eternal life in Christ Jesus our Lord.
> — **Romans 6:23**

Remember, Jesus' words lead to life. Surrendering to His Lordship should not be viewed as a miserable task. His love for us motivates His commands. Surrendering to His way—although sometimes uncomfortable—ultimately leads to a free and overflowing life.

> The Spirit gives life; the flesh counts for
> nothing. The words I have spoken to you—they
> are full of the Spirit and life. — **John 6:63**

1. **How will the choice to focus on what you receive by changing, rather than focusing on what you are giving up, affect your attitude toward change?**

Your sin hurts others. Not only does your sin hurt you, but it also hurts others. Each of us have been hurt by someone else's sin. We have also sinned in response to hurt or followed an example and sinned in the same way. In fact, God's Old Testament Law can be understood through the two greatest commandments:

> Jesus replied: "'Love the Lord your God with all your heart and with all your soul and with all your mind.' This is the first and greatest commandment. And the second is like it: 'Love your neighbor as yourself.'"
> — **Matthew 22:37-39 NLT**

2. **How does acknowledging how other people's sin has hurt you, help you understand how your sin hurts others?**

Sin offends God. Not only does your sin hurt you and others, it hurts God. It offends Him. God is holy and perfectly good. Sin is the opposite of holy. Even if you do not feel immediate sorrow for certain sins, you should turn from those sins and ask God to forgive you because sin offends Him. You should pray for Godly sorrow.

> Godly sorrow brings repentance that leads to salvation and leaves no regret, but worldly sorrow brings death. — **II Corinthians 7:10**

> And do not grieve the Holy Spirit of God, with whom you were sealed for the day of redemption. — **Ephesians 4:30**

3. How does understanding that your sin offends God change your view of sinful choices?

FULL DEVOTION IS THE NATURAL RESPONSE

When you realize how destructive sin is and how much it hurts and offends God, you understand what a gift you have been given by God's grace—undeserved favor[7]—and His willingness to forgive you. God's extravagant love overwhelms you. Your only logical response is to extravagantly love Him in return. You love Him more than sin, more than fleshly desires, more than any other attachment—more than anything. *All of me for all of You* is the natural response to Jesus' love.

> Either way, Christ's love controls us. Since we believe that Christ died for all, we also believe that we have all died to our old life. He died for everyone so that those who receive his new life will no longer live for themselves. Instead, they will live for Christ, who died and was raised for them. — **II Corinthians 5:14-15 NLT**

4. Take some time to think about God's extravagant love. Write your reaction to it.

change motivated by love

It comes down to answering these questions: *"What means the most to me? Living a life focused on myself, which leads to sin and separation from God, or living a life that honors God because of my love for Him?"* Does love motivate your obedience to Christ?

Many Christians seem to see how much sin they can get away with, as if their attitude is, *"What is the least amount I have to give up and still be a Christian?"* Jesus' response to this is: the least amount is everything.

> You cannot be my disciple, unless you love me more than you love your father and mother, your wife and children, and your brothers and sisters. You cannot follow me unless you love me more than you love your own life.
> — **Luke 14:26 CEV**

Surrendering to Jesus begins with giving Him your full allegiance and love. Notice that Jesus said that if you do not love Him more than anything, you cannot be His disciple. He means that you will not *have the ability* to be His disciple if you do not love Him more than anything—including your own life.

In the verse above (Luke 14:26) Jesus points out that life demands a decision. Whatever you love most will be what you pursue. Christ calls you to live your life centered upon loving God, loving others, and spreading His kingdom. This runs opposite to your natural desire to live for yourself and worldly attachments. There will be conflict. You will have to make a choice. Your love and devotion to Jesus must be stronger than your worldly attachments and the sins that they produce.

1. What does it mean to say, "Whatever you love most will be what you pursue?"

Many of the first disciples and early Christians faced the severity of this choice. Many encountered betrayal by their own family, and were killed for proclaiming their faith in Jesus. Throughout the centuries, Christians in various parts of the world have faced persecution, and it continues today. But they love Jesus more than their comfort and physical safety. They love Him more than anything this world has to offer.

This means that being a Christian involves more than going to church, trying to be a "good person," and avoiding a handful of "taboo" sins. The change goes much deeper than that.

Your love for Him will change your desires, ambitions, and motives. Your attachment to Jesus will become stronger than any other attachment or desire in the world. You will desire to honor Him with all of your life.

You will discover security, worth, and fulfillment through Jesus. You will find meaning through your real identity as a child of God rather than through *substitute identities*.

Love for Jesus—not obligation, guilt, or fear—will motivate your change.

"If you love me, keep my commands."

"Whoever has my commands and keeps them is the one who loves me. The one who loves me will be loved by my Father, and I too will love them and show myself to them."

Jesus replied, "Anyone who loves me will obey my teaching. My Father will love them, and we will come to them and make our home with them. — **John 14:15, 21, 23**

2. **Do you think love is a more powerful motivator than guilt, obligation, or fear? Why or why not?**

understanding how Satan works

> "...in order that Satan might not outwit us. For we are not unaware of his schemes."
> —II CORINTHIANS 2:11

it's a war

Once you have surrendered your life to the Lordship of Jesus, doing the right thing will not always come easily. When confronted with the desire to sin after salvation, Christians often assume two different stances:

- Some dismiss sin as a part of life, assuming Christ's forgiveness grants them the option to continue in sin. This attitude is refuted all throughout Scripture. (Reference *Day 5: Turning From Sin.*)

- Some assume that if they struggle with any temptation or desire to sin, then they have not truly been born-again.

Apostle Paul described doing the right thing as a battle or struggle inside of him. Even after salvation, there are still some old desires in you that oppose your new desires. You must overcome those old desires and put them to death.

> Set your minds on things above, not on earthly things. For you died, and your life is now hidden with Christ in God. When Christ, who is your life, appears, then you also will appear with him in glory. Put to death, therefore, whatever belongs to your earthly nature: sexual immorality, impurity, lust, evil desires and greed, which is idolatry. — **Colossians 3:2-5**

> But there is another power within me that is at war with my mind. This power makes me a slave to the sin that is still within me.
> — **Romans 7:23 NLT**

This struggle is actually a sign that Christ is in you. As a disciple of Jesus, you don't just automatically "let yourself of the hook" and keep sinning. In other words, you know what the right thing is— even if you want to resist it. You do not make excuses. You state it for what it is. You may even think, *"I know Jesus is right. I know I should change, but it's hard."* That is why you must rely on the power of the Holy Spirit to give you His power to live a new life.

> For we died and were buried with Christ by baptism. And just as Christ was raised from the dead by the glorious power of the Father, now we also may live new lives. — **Romans 6:4 NLT**

1. **What does it mean to "let yourself off the hook" and keep sinning?**

Satan opposes your changes. The Bible teaches that you have a real enemy at work in the world. He seeks your destruction and will oppose your changes.

> For our struggle is not against flesh and blood, but against the rulers, against the authorities, against the powers of this dark world and against the spiritual forces of evil in the heavenly realms. — **Ephesians 6:12**

Your biggest battle with Satan is fought in your mind. Overcoming Satan is a struggle. The biggest battlefield you will fight him on will be in your mind, in your thoughts.

For though we live in the world, we do not
wage war as the world does. The weapons we
fight with are not the weapons of the world.
On the contrary, they have divine power to
demolish strongholds. We demolish arguments
and every pretension that sets itself up against
the knowledge of God, and we take captive
every thought to make it obedient to Christ.
— II Corinthians 10:3-5

SPIRITUAL STRONGHOLDS

Satan has established "spiritual strongholds" in your mind. Stronghold is an old military term that refers to a place in which an army has established a "strong hold." It is well-protected, and therefore difficult for an enemy to penetrate. Think of a fort or castle.[8]

Spiritual strongholds are *protected attitudes, mindsets or patterns of thinking that produce sin in your life.* When you come to Christ, you still have these old ways deeply ingrained in the way that you think. As you have just read, Scripture teaches that you are to war against those arguments and thoughts and make them submissive to Christ.

2. What does it mean to "protect" an attitude, mindset or pattern of thinking?

spiritual maturity

Overcoming Satan causes you to spiritually mature. As you learn to confront and overcome Satan's work in your life, you will grow from a spiritual child to a mature Christian.

> I write to you, dear children, because you know the Father. I write to you, fathers, because you know him who is from the beginning. I write to you, young men, because you are strong, and the word of God lives in you, and you have overcome the evil one. — **1 John 2:14**

In this passage, John is not referring to biological age. He is describing three phases of spiritual growth in the life of a believer:[9]

- Spiritual children have their sins forgiven.

- Spiritual young men are overcoming the evil one (sin) in their lives.

- Spiritual fathers have a long history with God.

When you see a believer, who has been saved for many years and yet still acts in spiritually immature ways, it is a clear sign there are still spiritual strongholds in their life. They have not learned to overcome the evil one's work in their life.

We must seek to be free from our old sinful ways of acting and reacting. Failure to overcome patterns of sin your life will keep you spiritually immature, limit your Kingdom effectiveness and will eventually destroy your life.

1. What is the difference between having your sins forgiven and overcoming Satan?

Overcoming Satan is a process. This battle to overcome sin in your life will not be won overnight. Some things go quickly, others hang on and must be battled. However, your life should show movement toward full cooperation with Jesus' Lordship.

> I have discovered this principle of life—that when I want to do what is right, I inevitably do what is wrong. I love God's law with all my heart. But there is another power within me that is at war with my mind. This power makes me a slave to the sin that is still within me. Oh, what a miserable person I am! Who will free me from this life that is dominated by sin and death? Thank God! The answer is in Jesus Christ our Lord. — **Romans 7:21-25a NLT**

> Therefore, I urge you, brothers and sisters, in view of God's mercy, to offer your bodies as a living sacrifice, holy and pleasing to God—this is your true and proper worship.
> — **Romans 12:1**

2. What are some indications that your life is showing movement toward full cooperation with Jesus' Lordship?

Having a new nature does not mean you will never sin again.
True salvation involves turning from yourself and surrendering to Christ. Then—and only then—will His Spirit enter you. If His Spirit is alive in you, He will show Himself through you. If you have surrendered your will to Christ, you will *let* Him show Himself through your life.

This does not mean that a Christian can never sin. We still have the capacity to sin and our bodies have been trained to sin. As we learned in *Day 6: Becoming Like Christ,* if you are truly God's child and you turn from Him to pursue sin, He will discipline you and bring you back onto the right path. If you sin and do not experience remorse and the correction of God, then you should consider if you are truly His child and have honestly given your heart to Him.

> If God doesn't discipline you as he does all of his children, it means that you are illegitimate and are not really his children at all. For our earthly fathers disciplined us for a few years, doing the best they knew how. But God's discipline is always good for us, so that we might share in his holiness.
> — **Hebrews 12:8,10 NLT**

3. **Review what you think it means for God to discipline you and bring you back onto the right path.**

how thoughts influence actions

When attempting to overcome sin, people usually just try to correct their bad behavior. However, Scripture teaches that you should first change your thinking and then your behavior will line up.

> Don't copy the behavior and customs of this world, but let God transform you into a new person by *changing the way you think*. Then you will learn to know God's will for you, which is good and pleasing and perfect.
> — **Romans 12:2 NLT** *(Emphasis added)*

Jesus emphasized this concept when He taught that you should focus on your heart and motives and not just on your actions.

> You have heard that it was said to the people long ago, "You shall not murder, and anyone who murders will be subject to judgment." But I tell you that anyone who is angry with a brother or sister will be subject to judgment. You have heard that it was said, "You shall not commit adultery." But I tell you that anyone who looks at a woman lustfully has already committed adultery with her in his heart.
> — **Matthew 5:21-22a, 27-28**

Let's examine how what you think and believe, influences your actions and forms habits —patterns of behavior—in your life.

HOW YOU FORM HABITS

You seek a desired *result*. Based on *input* through your senses and/or experience, you develop a *belief* that a particular *action* will produce the desired result. Sometimes you are conscious of this belief; sometimes you are not.

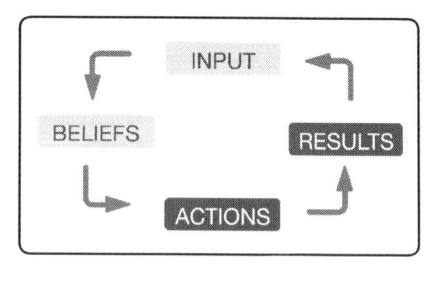

When you try the action and it produces the desired result, the belief is reinforced in your mind.

After repeated reinforcement, the action turns into a pattern, or habit. Your unconscious mind maintains it without you giving it conscious thought.[10] Here's why:

When you learn something new, neurons in your brain are connected in a new way. As you recall and repeat the action, the pathway is reinforced. Repeating behaviors strengthens the connection and deepens the pathway. These form habits. Basically, your habits are ruts— deeply ingrained pathways— in your mind. Once formed, they can be very difficult to maneuver out of.[11]

Example of a behavior learned through observation: When you were a toddler, you were contained in rooms for your own safety. Your desired *result* was to be able to leave the room like everyone else.

Through the *input* of your senses you observed how people would approach certain sections in the wall (doors), twist a shiny object (doorknob), and pass through the wall to the other side. You unconsciously developed a *belief* that the *action* of twisting a doorknob would open the door for you, too.

Without any formal training, your desire for freedom prompted you to try to reach one of those shiny objects and twist it until you gained your freedom. It may not have worked for you at first. But because you knew it worked for others you kept trying until it worked for you. After it worked, your belief that twisting a doorknob would grant your freedom was reinforced.

By now, you have been opening doors for yourself as long as you can remember. When you want to leave a room, you walk to a door, twist the knob, the door opens and you leave. You do this dozens of times a day without even thinking about it. Usually the only time you consciously think about it again is when there is a problem (ie: the door won't open). Your conscious mind then begins to determine what you should do next.

You may not remember when you learned to use doorknobs. But you probably remember when you learned to drive. Think of all the things you had to concentrate on when you first learned. Now you can drive for 30 minutes and not even remember where you have been. That may not be safe, but it happens because your unconscious mind has developed a pattern and maintains it so that your conscious mind can focus upon other things.

1. What is one thing you do without thinking because you have been doing it for so long?

how spiritual strongholds form

Our mind develops patterns for all types of things we do. Some patterns you may not have wanted to learn. For example, if you were raised with an angry, explosive parent you may have vowed you would not be like that. However, you sometimes find yourself reacting the way your parent did. The behavior is almost involuntary, because you learned it unconsciously. Let's examine what influences this.

DESIRED RESULTS—MEETING OF CORE NEEDS

We learned in *Workbook 1: Discover Identity,* that each of us have basic, core needs for security, worth and fulfillment. When we are separated from a relationship with God, these desires are not fulfilled, but we still have them.

The need for security. We all have a core instinct for survival. Security is the confidence that your present and future needs are met. It is confidence that you can survive in this world.

The need for worth. Because we were created in the image of God and crowned with glory and honor, we have a need to feel that our lives matter—that we have worth. This is often expressed as a desire for respect or love.

The need for fulfillment. As image bearers of God, we desire to have purpose. This is often expressed as a desire to be happy or feel satisfied. We know that we were created for more than just existence, and we remain restless until we discover our created design.

FALSE INPUT—FALSE BELIEFS—FALSE SUBSTITUTE IDENTITIES

Satan fills our world with his lies and falsely promises that our desired results of security, worth and fulfillment can be obtained through assuming a *substitute identity,* rather than through our true identity as children of God.

Note the following list of *substitute identities*–ways we are defined rather than through our relationship with God.[12] Notice how each of these are associated with finding a sense of security, worth or fulfillment, through ourselves, other people or things, rather than from God. (We explored these concepts in more detail in *Workbook 1: Discover Identity.*)

ACCOMPLISHMENTS	I am defined by what I can do or by what I know.
ABILITIES	I am defined by a skill or ability that I have.
POSSESSIONS	I am defined by what I own.
APPEARANCE	I am defined by how I look.
APPROVAL	I am defined by who accepts me.
ATTENTION	I am defined by being noticed for positive or negative behavior, or by getting sympathy from others.
POWER	I am defined by being in control.
AFFECTION	I am defined by who loves me.

(continued on pg. 45)

APPETITES	I am defined by my desires. These can be natural desires such as those of food or sex, or acquired desires such as those for drugs or alcohol.
PLEASURE	I am defined by feeling good.

Reference *Appendix 1: Substitute Identities and Scriptures* for this list with Scriptures

We receive a constant stream of *input* from our culture that models how to obtain security, worth and fulfillment through these *substitute identities*. Consciously or unconsciously, we form *beliefs* that our core needs will be found in these substitutes.

For example, power will give me security. I have worth because of what I can do or achieve, or by who gives me attention or affection. Fulfillment comes through pleasure.

Some of these things that become *substitute identities* are not in and of themselves wrong. For example, you may own possessions, receive and give affection, accomplish things, or have great abilities. However, allowing them to define who you are, or pursuing them apart from God, will lead you into sin.

SINFUL ACTIONS

Pursuit of our core needs through these *substitute identities* produces sinful *actions*, called "acts of the flesh."

> The acts of the flesh are obvious: sexual immorality, impurity and debauchery; idolatry and witchcraft; hatred, discord, jealousy, fits of rage, selfish ambition, dissensions, factions and envy; drunkenness, orgies, and the like. I warn you, as I did before, that those who live like this will not inherit the kingdom of God.
> — **Galatians 5:19-21**

These sinful actions give us short-term benefits and create the illusion of fulfilling our needs—which reinforces the lie in our minds. In reality, these acts of the flesh produce death. We will learn about sin in more detail on *Day 22: Identifying Sinful Actions.*

For the wages of sin is death, — **Romans 6:23a**

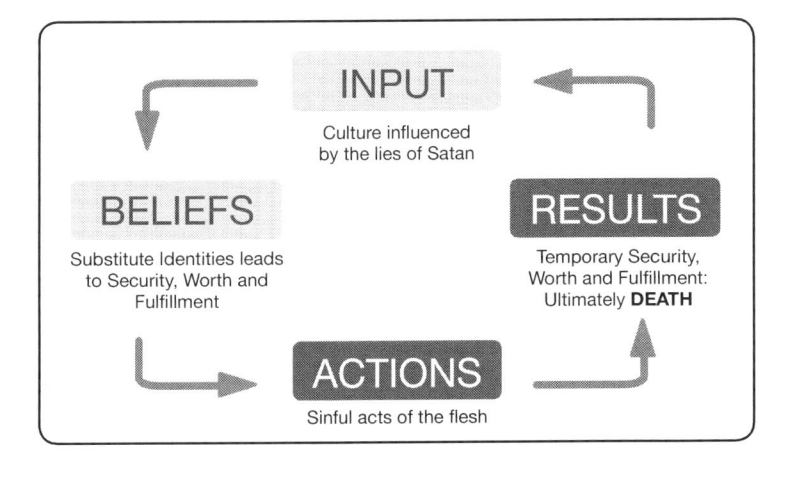

As we repeat these actions, and they give us the temporary illusion of meeting our needs for security, worth and fulfillment, we develop habitual, sinful patterns of thinking and reacting that do not require much conscious thought. These are called spiritual strongholds.

Remember that spiritual strongholds are *protected attitudes, mindsets or patterns of thinking that produce sin in your life.* When you come to Christ, you still have these old ways deeply ingrained in the way that you think.

WHY SPIRITUAL STRONGHOLDS PERSIST

Attempting to change sinful acts without identifying the false beliefs that fuel them will leave you frustrated and in bondage. This is why Scripture teaches us to take our thoughts captive and change how we think. Recognize your false beliefs for what they are—lies from Satan— your enemy.

> Don't copy the behavior and customs of this
> world, but let God transform you into a new
> person by changing the way you think. Then
> you will learn to know God's will for you,
> which is good and pleasing and perfect.
> — **Romans 12:2 NLT**

This is why many people come to Christ and remain bound to patterns of sin. They have not confronted the lies fed to them through the input of the customs and behaviors of the world. They fail to recognize they have formed false beliefs in their thoughts concerning their true identity. Rather than finding validation through their identity as a child of God, they continue to seek it through these *substitute identities*, which produces sin.

Note the following examples of persisting strongholds:

A young woman is convinced that her *worth* (core need) is based on getting *affection* (substitute identity) from the right guy. This desire for affection led her into a series of relationships, which in turn led to *sexual immorality* (sin). Even after giving her life to Christ, she finds it difficult to maintain sexual integrity. Rather than accepting the true worth she has as a child of God, she continues to seek worth by getting affection from men.

A man who spent his life finding *fulfillment* (core need) from his abilities and *accomplishments* (substitute identities) would get *prideful and jealous* (sins). After coming to Christ, he uses his abilities in ministry but continues to seek validation in what he can do and in recognized accomplishments. He tries to do more than everyone around him and is jealous of others. Rather than being fulfilled in his identity as a child of God, he is still defined by what he can do.

Another man has found *security* (core need) through *power* (substitute identity). He manipulates, deceives and gets *angry* (sins) when he does not get his way. Even after coming to Christ, he continues to seek power and will do whatever he thinks he must—both in church and in business—to maintain it. Rather than being secure in God's provision, he still finds security in his power and control.

1. Discuss your reaction to the previous three examples. What stands out to you from each of these? Explain:

conflicting natures

OUR SIN NATURE

To be clear, we are not suggesting that we only desire to sin, because we have seen sin modeled to us. Scripture teaches that because of the original sin of Adam and Eve, everyone is born into a world where death and sin are realities. Like Adam and Eve, we have a desire to pursue sin.

> Therefore, just as sin entered the world through one man, and death through sin, and in this way death came to all people, *because all sinned*
> —**Romans 5:12** *(Emphasis added)*

We sin because we believe the lies of Satan and consequently do not look to our heavenly Father to adequately provide what we need—our security, worth and fulfillment.

> But each one is tempted when he is carried away and enticed by his own lust. Then when lust has conceived, it gives birth to sin; and when sin is accomplished, it brings forth death.
> — **James 1:14-15 NASB**

In this passage, the word lust literally means a *desire or craving*.[13] The desire to sin will usually be very strong and can feel very natural to us. This is because sin is a result of our "flesh nature" (Galatians 5:19-21). When Scripture refers to our "flesh" it is referring to our natural tendency to live contrary to God. Sin is a natural desire of our flesh nature and can feel "normal" to us. This means, simply because we desire something, does not mean we should do it.

We are all tempted to sin because of a desire to pursue life apart from God. This desire then becomes rooted in our thoughts, or as the Scripture above states "lust is conceived" and gives birth to sin in our actions. Sin then brings death. Our desire is not death, but we are tempted to believe that what we need can be achieved apart from God. This leads to sin, which leads to death.

The culture around us feeds our sin nature—our flesh—with the lies that life can be found apart from God. As a child of God, we have been given a new heart or nature—the nature of Jesus. We must align our thinking with the nature of Jesus in us. We must refuse to conform to the world around us and we must change what we believe by renewing our mind.[14]

> His divine power has given us everything we need for a godly life through our knowledge of him who called us by his own glory and goodness. Through these he has given us his very great and precious promises, so that through them you may participate in the divine nature, having escaped the corruption in the world caused by evil desires. — **II Peter 1:3-4**

The desire for Christ must replace the desire for sin. As His nature grows in us, we will turn from evil desires. The desire for sin might present itself, but we must keep the desire from conceiving in our thoughts and forming false beliefs which lead to sin. Filling our minds with Christ is the solution. The rest of this workbook will teach us how to take on the nature of Christ and leave our old nature behind.

1. **How is the nature of Christ different from your flesh or old nature?**

LIFE FLOWING FROM GOD

When you come to Christ and live in your identity as His child, life begins to look different.

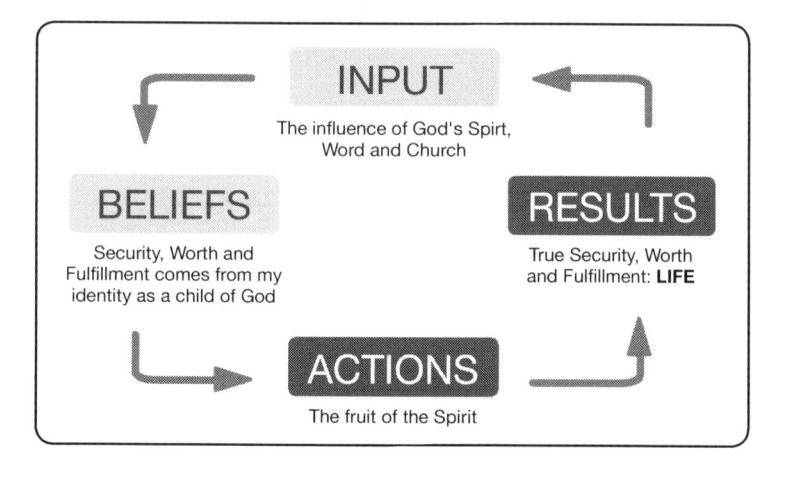

Through Godly *input,* you believe your desired *result* for security, worth and fulfillment is found in being a child of God and living for His purposes. This *belief* begins to produce new actions called the fruit of the Spirit in your life.

> But the fruit of the Spirit is love, joy, peace, patience, kindness, goodness, faithfulness, gentleness, self-control; against such things there is no law. — **Galatians 5:22-23 NASB**

2. **How do the fruit of the Spirit differ from the sinful desires of our flesh? (Reference Galatians 5:19-21)**

TURNING FROM SUBSTITUTE IDENTITIES

SUBSTITUTE IDENTITIES
Accomplishments
Abilities
Possessions
Appearance
Approval
Attention
Power
Affection
Appetites
Pleasure

Remember that living life apart from God has caused us to be defined by *substitute identities*. These substitutes have become a replacement for God and our identity as His child.

As noted before, some of these things that become *substitute identities* are not in and of themselves wrong. For example, you may own possessions, receive and give affection, accomplish things, or have great abilities. However, allowing them to define who you are, or pursuing them apart from God, will lead you into sin.

Rather than understanding that attachments to these things can pull their devotion away from Jesus, countless people try to use Him as a means to get more. While you follow Jesus, He may bring some of these things into your life. But if they go away, will you still love Him?

3. **How have you or others you know attempted to use Jesus as a means to attain any of these substitute identities?**

4. **Review the *Substitute Identities List*. Identify the top three that you struggle with being attached to. For detailed descriptions of these Substitute identities along with helpful Scripture, see *Appendix 1: Substitute Identities and Scriptures.***

Sometimes these *substitute identities* are outright sin or lead to sin, and you must walk away from them altogether. There may also come a time as you follow Jesus that He will ask you to set aside your "rights," or sacrifice something for the good of others and His mission. When you truly love Him, you are no longer concerned about your rights. You are concerned about honoring Him regardless of the cost to you.

The Apostle Paul knew what it was to have everything that people count as valuable. He had status, money, power, and heritage. Yet when following Jesus demanded a choice, he walked away from all of it. His devotion to Jesus was greater than anything the world could offer.

> But whatever were gains to me I now consider loss for the sake of Christ. What is more, I consider everything a loss because of the surpassing worth of knowing Christ Jesus my Lord, for whose sake I have lost all things. I consider them garbage, that I may gain Christ.
> — Philippians 3:7-8

As stated before, it comes down to answering these questions: *What means the most to me? Living a life focused on myself, which leads to sin and separation from God, or living a life that honors God because of my love for Him?"*

5. How does living for God's purposes—loving Him and others—differ from living for substitute identities?

FREEDOM FACTORS

The rest of this workbook will focus on four critical factors that will help you overcome spiritual strongholds in your life.

Power. Breaking spiritual strongholds and overcoming Satan's work in your life will not always be easy. Your own power and strength are no match against Satan. However, Jesus defeated him, and Satan is no match against the power of Jesus!

Personal Responsibility. Before you will change, you must assume responsibility for change. You cannot change in your own power, but until you see the need to change and take responsibility for seeking help, you will most likely resist change in your life. To overcome, you must learn to confess your sin and cooperate with the Holy Spirit's power.

Partners. No one can walk the journey of change for you; however, you do not have to walk it alone. Scripture teaches that others can bring power and strength when we are weak.

Plan. Earthly armies do not go into battle without a plan, and neither should you. You must be intentional in waging war and have a strategy to demolish spiritual strongholds in your life.

the power factor

> For God is working in you, giving you the desire and the power to do what pleases him. — **PHILIPPIANS 2:13 (NLT)**

DAILY POWER CONFESSION

Jesus, you are Lord of my thoughts.
You have power to change and heal my mind.

My thinking will be transformed.

Old thought patterns and habits will be broken, and new ones will take their place.

Jesus, you are Lord of my feelings.
You have power over my emotions.

Worry, stress, anxiety, anger and depression will be subject to You as I walk in Your kingdom seeking Your purposes.

I will walk by faith in your Word today, not by what I see or feel.

Jesus, you are Lord of my body.
You have power over my natural desires.

My body will not be used for sin.

Any substance (food, drink, drug, medication or chemical) I put into my body will honor You.

My physical fitness and health will honor You.

Jesus, you are Lord of my behavior.
You have power over my attitude and actions.

I will think and act like Christ.

I will be proactive today, not reactive.

Guide my steps today. I will seek and seize kingdom opportunities.

I am your child, made in your image. True security, worth and fulfillment are found only in You.

the power of Jesus

Breaking spiritual strongholds and overcoming Satan's work in your life will not be easy. Your own power and strength are no match against Satan. However, Jesus defeated him.

> Because he himself suffered when he was tempted, he is able to help those who are being tempted. — **Hebrews 2:18**

God placed Jesus above every power in the world. As a result, through His power and Name—His power and Name only—you can overcome Satan.

> Therefore God exalted him to the highest place and gave him the name that is above every name, that at the name of Jesus every knee should bow, in heaven and on earth and under the earth, and every tongue acknowledge that Jesus Christ is Lord, to the glory of God the Father. — **Philippians 2:9-11**

> For God is working in you, giving you the desire and the power to do what pleases him.
> — **Philippians 2:13 NLT**

> And if the Spirit of him who raised Jesus from the dead is living in you, he who raised Christ from the dead will also give life to your mortal bodies because of his Spirit who lives in you.
> — **Romans 8:11**

HOW JESUS OVERCAME TEMPTATION

> This High Priest of ours understands our
> weaknesses, for he faced all of the same testings
> we do, yet he did not sin.
> — Hebrews 4:15 NLT

Scripture teaches us that Adam and Eve fell victim to sin. They listened to the lies of Satan and turned away from God to pursue temptation. (Genesis 3:1-10).

In contrast, when Jesus came to the world, He resisted Satan. After Jesus was baptized, the Holy Spirit led him into the wilderness alone to fast and pray. While there, Scripture says He was tempted by the devil (Matthew 4:1-11). Scripture says He was tempted in every way that we were, but He did not sin (Hebrews 4:15).

Satan tempted Jesus' appetites, questioned the authority of God, and challenged Jesus to prove who He was. He challenged His identity. This is very similar to the temptation in the garden of Eden. Satan tempted their appetites and questioned the authority of God. It's interesting to note Jesus' response to Satan.[15]

Jesus' response of, *"Man shall not live by bread alone, but by every word that proceeds from the mouth of God"*[16] reveals what Jesus valued. He valued the Word of God.

A few days before this temptation, after Jesus was baptized, God spoke over Him and declared, "This is My beloved Son, in whom I am well-pleased." (Matthew 3:17). Fast forward to the temptation and note Satan began challenging Jesus' identity: *"If you are the son of God..."*[17] But Jesus did not feel the need to "prove" anything. He was validated by the approval of His Heavenly Father, and this was more important than even His need for food.

In contrast to Adam and Eve, while being tempted, Jesus was not swayed by His natural appetite, the need to prove who He was, or by any power offered to Him separate from the authority that God had already given Him. He rested in who He was — the Son of God.

1. **What stands out to you in the contrast between Jesus' response to temptation and Adam and Eve's response to temptation?**

LIVING IN YOUR IDENTITY AS A CHILD OF GOD.

Remember the following concepts from *Workbook 1: Discover Identity:*

Security: As a child of God I understand that I do not need to look to others or myself to "fix" everything. I can relax and be secure in my role as His child. My responsibilities, as God's child, are to listen to Him, obey Him and trust Him with the outcomes.

Worth: As a child of God, I understand that I was created to have a relationship with Him. If I have Him, I have unsurpassed worth. What others think of me no longer defines me because my worth is found in God's love.

Fulfillment: As a child of God, I understand that His love fills and fulfills me. I am free from the drive to pursue empty, *substitute identities*. I can "drink" from His love and purpose and be satisfied.

2. **Reflect on these statements. How will your life change as you live these statements out?**

the power over sin

Our power is not enough to overcome Satan, but as a surrendered Christian, we have the power of Jesus in us. The very power that raised Jesus from the dead is alive in us. This is the power of the Holy Spirit.

We must learn to get to the place where we can say, even as Apostle Paul did, "It is no longer I that lives, but Christ lives through me."[18] Spending time with Jesus in worship, prayer and Bible reading will increase His power and Presence in your life. (We will learn practical ways to do this in *Workbook 3: Discover Growth*.)

In order for God to give you the power to change you must admit that on your own you are powerlessness and humble yourself before Him.[19]

> But he gives us more grace. That is why Scripture says: "God opposes the proud but shows favor to the humble." Submit yourselves, then, to God. Resist the devil, and he will flee from you. Come near to God and he will come near to you. Wash your hands, you sinners, and purify your hearts, you double-minded. Grieve, mourn and wail. Change your laughter to mourning and your joy to gloom. Humble yourselves before the Lord, and he will lift you up. — **James 4:6-10**

1. **Why is it hard to admit that you are powerless on your own?**

THE POWER OF THE HOLY SPIRIT

> For God is working in you, giving you the
> desire and the power to do what pleases him.
> — **Philippians 2:13 NLT**

Overcoming sin is not just *modification* of behavior; we must experience *transformation* of spirit and minds. We must be born again.

> Jesus answered and said to him, "Truly, truly, I
> say to you, unless one is born [again he cannot
> see the kingdom of God." —John 3:3 NASB

The Holy Spirit applies God's transforming power to your life. The Greek word for transform is where we get the English word *metamorphosis*.[20] (Think about the change process that a caterpillar goes through to become a butterfly.)

After we are born again, we must allow the Holy Spirit to reshape—transform—how we think, what we believe and how we act. As we have already learned, Christians relearn everything with Jesus in charge. This is what it means to truly say *Jesus is Lord!* (Romans 10:9-10).

The process of reshaping—relearning—is also called "renewing our minds."

> And do not be conformed to this world, but
> be transformed by the renewing of your mind,
> so that you may prove what the will of God is,
> that which is good and acceptable and perfect.
> —**Romans 12:2 NASB**

2. **What does it mean to be transformed by the Holy Spirit?**

The fire of God's Spirit is often referred to as the power of God to remove sin and impurities from us.

> I [John] baptize you with water for repentance.
> But after me comes one who is more powerful
> than I, whose sandals I am not worthy to carry.
> He will baptize you with the Holy Spirit and fire.
> — **Matthew 3:11**

Transformation comes through submitting to and cooperating with the Holy Spirit. While Scripture commands us to actively resist the devil, it is a mistake to assume change is based solely upon our efforts. The Holy Spirit is the Power that will transform you. (We will explore the transforming work of the Holy Spirit in more detail in *Workbook 3: Discover Growth*)

Encounters. Sometimes God's power will immediately bring healing or break a stronghold through an encounter with the Holy Spirit. You might have experienced freedom from a particular sin when you were saved or through another encounter with the Holy Spirit.

Process. Other times freedom comes through a process of leaning on Him as you daily surrender to His power. Many times, God uses a process to free us rather than a single encounter, because it teaches us to rely on Him. It teaches us to form new habits and thought processes. Often, lasting freedom comes through a combination of both encounter and process.

Whether you receive freedom immediately through a divine encounter or over a period of time through divine process, you must still learn to rely on God and resist Satan in order to live in

freedom. God can free you, but if you keep subjecting yourself to the input of the world, and keep adopting the patterns of the world's thinking, you will return to bondage.

Pray and ask God for immediate freedom. If it does not come, choose to obey God and learn to lean on His Power every day to overcome temptation. As you learn to grow in your relationship with God by engaging in the principles outlined in this workbook, as well as what you will learn in *Workbook 3: Discover Growth*, you will receive increasing strength to overcome Satan.

3. **Do you think it makes God any less powerful if He brings freedom in your life through a process rather than through an immediate experience? Explain:**

THE POWER OF THE WRITTEN WORD

The power of the written word of God to break strongholds in our life cannot be overstated. The Bible is like a sword that we use to fight our spiritual enemy—Satan.

> Take the helmet of salvation and the sword of
> the Spirit, which is the word of God.
> — **Ephesians 6:17**

> As we learned earlier in yesterday's lesson,
> Jesus overcame Satan through the word of God.

> Jesus answered, "It is written: 'Man shall not
> live on bread alone, but on every word that
> comes from the mouth of God.'"
> — **Matthew 4:4**

On *Day 10: Spiritual Maturity,* we learned that overcoming Satan causes us to spiritually mature. Notice that overcoming Satan is directly linked to the Word of God abiding in you.

> I have written to you, fathers, because you
> know Him who has been from the beginning.
> I have written to you, young men, because you
> are strong, and the word of God abides in you,
> and you have overcome the evil one.
> — **I John 2:14 NASB**

This concept is reinforced by the following Scriptures.

> How can a young man keep his way pure? By
> keeping it according to Your word.
> — **Psalm 119:9 NASB**

> I have hidden your word in my heart that
> I might not sin against you. — **Psalm 119:11**

Since sin is a result of lies we believe, the primary way to overcome the lies of Satan is through the truth of the Word of God. We learn truth by learning God's Word.

> Sanctify them in the truth; Your word is truth.
> — **John 17:17 NASB**

4. How does the Bible give us power to overcome Satan?

the personal responsibility factor

> Yes, each of us will give a personal account to God.
> — ROMANS 14:12 NLT

taking responsibility

Before change can happen in your life, you must take personal responsibility. When we say "take personal responsibility" we are not suggesting that change is all up to you. As we have already learned, your power and strength are no match for Satan. The power for change has to come from God. However, you have a part to play. Your responsibility is to *confess* your sin and then *cooperate* with the Holy Spirit's power and work in your life.

CONFESSION

To confess literally means to *agree or acknowledge*.[21] By confessing, you agree that you are guilty of sin and acknowledge that you must change. Before any change can be made, you have to see the need to change. Rather than confessing our need for change we often deny or make excuses for our behavior.

COMMON RESPONSES TO BEING CONFRONTED WITH SIN

Denial. This is refusing to admit that you are guilty. You either deny that you have committed the sin, or you deny that the behavior is actually a sin. A sin is a sin whether you believe it is or not. You may believe that denial will let you off the hook, but the relief you feel through denial is temporary. Your sin will destroy you.

Another form of denial is admitting that you engage in the sin, but refusing to acknowledge the extent of your engagement, it is easy to fool yourself into believing that you have sin "under control."

Dismiss Responsibility. It's also easy to blame others for our sin. If you are guilty of a sin, you must accept your responsibility in engaging in it. Don't blame others, your genes or your circumstances. Admit your part.

It is true that your past has contributed to who you are today. But who you become is up to you. In order to change, you must stop the blame game and take responsibility for your life.[22]

For example, you do not have your dad's temper—you have your temper. He may have taught you to act a certain way; however, you are responsible if you keep acting it out.

Other times, we dismiss responsibility for our actions because we feel "provoked" into responding a certain way. *"They asked for it,"* *"They made me angry,"* or *"They started it"* are examples of dismissing responsibility for our actions and blaming what we do on others.

Remember that you might not be able to control another person's actions; however, you can control how you respond to their actions.[23] If necessary, remove yourself from the situation altogether if it is causing you to respond in a sinful way.

Downplay it. We often downplay our sin. We use excuses such as, *"Boys will be boys,"* *"It's legal,"* and, *"At least I'm not as bad as..."* When God calls something wrong and says it leads to death, you must see it for what it is: destructive. Stop minimizing it, downplaying it, making excuses for it and taking it lightly. If God says that something is sin and leads to death, you must become serious about changing it.

> The wages of sin is death... — **Romans 6:23a**

Remember that God loves you enough to warn you about things that are destructive. Even if you do not want to agree with Him, you must learn to submit to His Lordship and realize that He knows best.

Divert Attention. People often try to divert attention from their sins by pointing out the sins of others—particularly by pointing out the sins of the person who is confronting the sin in their life. By diverting attention to someone else's problems, it temporarily gets the heat off of us.

It is common to divert attention by accusing the other person of judging you or not loving you if they suggest your behavior is sin. Although it is true that some people are critical and judgmental, you must realize that those who love you should talk to you if they believe that you are doing something destructive.

While the Bible tells us not to judge or condemn, there are direct orders for people in the church to teach believers right from wrong. This includes the command to restore (bring back) believers who are caught in sin.

> Brothers and sisters, if someone is caught in a sin, you who live by the Spirit should restore that person gently. But watch yourselves, or you also may be tempted. — **Galatians 6:1**

How can someone restore you to the right path if they are never allowed to tell you that you are sinning?

While it's true that others also sin, and someone may actually be sinning by arrogantly pointing out your faults, it does not change the fact that if you are guilty, you are guilty. Diverting attention does not erase your sin.

1. **Which of these ways have you used to deal with your sin?**

The only response that will break the hold of sin in your life is confession. Confession is taking personal responsibility for your actions and admitting that you need to change.

> If we confess our sins, he is faithful and just and will forgive us our sins and purify us from all unrighteousness. — 1 John 1:9

confession

After you learn what behaviors are sinful, you have to actually confess or admit to them before you can change them. Remember the common responses to being confronted with sin that we have learned:

- Deny

- Dismiss Responsibility

- Downplay

- Divert Attention

While these responses might give you temporary justification for your sin, the only response that will break the hold of sin in your life is confession.

Confession can be difficult for many different reasons. Many people were raised in families that never talked about problems. Issues were "swept under the rug." Often if matters were discussed, it was done so in anger or through manipulation.

Other times, we just don't want to deal with the "fallout" or pain associated with honesty. We fear that we will fail if we attempt to change or we fear the consequences of being honest. Understand, refusing to talk about an issue only delays or prolongs the suffering. It does not cause the pain to go away. You are as sick as your secrets. Your weaknesses lose power once they are brought into the light.[24]

> This is the verdict: Light has come into the world, but people loved darkness instead of light because their deeds were evil. Everyone who does evil hates the light, and will not come into the light for fear that their deeds will be

exposed. But whoever lives by the truth comes into the light, so that it may be seen plainly that what they have done has been done in the sight of God. — **John 3:19-21**

THE POWER OF CONFESSION

Confession to yourself causes you to step out of denial. Confessing to yourself that you have a problem is the first step to destroying its power over you.

> But if we were more discerning with regard to ourselves, we would not come under such judgment. — **1 Corinthians 11:31**

1. **Why is it difficult to admit we need to change?**

Confession to God brings forgiveness. Through confessing to God, we find forgiveness and cleansing from our sin. Even our guilt can be erased.

> If we confess our sins, he is faithful and just and will forgive us our sins and purify us from all unrighteousness. — **1 John 1:9**

2. **What, if anything, is keeping you from confessing your sins to God and asking for forgiveness?**

Confession to another person helps bring healing. Entering into an ongoing honest relationship with another believer is an essential part of overcoming Satan's work in your life. Confession and prayer are powerfully effective and bring healing from the damage that sin has done to you.

Should you confess your sins to everyone? No. However, Scripture teaches that confession and prayer with someone will help you to receive healing from the effects of your sin.[25] We will discuss this in more detail in *Section 5: The Partner Factor.*

> Therefore confess your sins to each other and
> pray for each other so that you may be healed.
> The prayer of a righteous person is powerful
> and effective. — **James 5:16**

Consider sharing the following with your accountability partner:

- Sins that typically tempt you. (This indicates the presence of a stronghold.)

- Sins you have recently committed.

- Bitterness, hurt or shame from sins that were committed against you.

If the fear of legal or other ramifications keeps your sin secret from others, consider the following possibilities:

- Talk to a minister or Christian counselor to protect your confidentiality. First ask the minister or counselor what they are required to report, and then decide how much you want to share.

- Consider using this as an opportunity to come completely clean and face whatever consequences are associated with your sin. If you make this decision, talk with your pastor and ask for support and help as you do so.

Note: If you are coming clean from past sins or crimes, contacting victims of your crimes or sins should be done so cautiously. Typically, it is advised not to contact them if doing so will cause more harm or pain.[26] We will learn more about this in *Workbook 4: Discover Relationships.*

3. **Why is it difficult to confess our faults to others?**

CAUTIONS WITH CONFESSING SIN

Don't allow sin to become your identity. Confessing sin does not mean to wear that sin as your identity. Your sin is not your identity. Your identity is a child of God.

For example, you are not an alcoholic, an addict, a liar, glutton or thief. You are a child of God who *struggles* with alcohol, addictions, lying, overeating or stealing. Remember, God is changing you from what you are to what He desires.[27]

If Jesus is your Lord and you have been born again, God sees you as His child.

> Yet to all who did receive him, to those who believed in his name, he gave the right to become children of God. — **John 1:12**

God sees you as a saint, not a sinner.

> …giving thanks to the Father, who has qualified us to share in the inheritance of the saints in Light. — **Colossians 1:12 NASB**

4. **How have you allowed yourself to be identified by your sin?**

Don't allow guilt to define you. The purpose of confession is to get sin out in the open and deal with it, not to remain in guilt and condemnation. Although it is true that you should seek to repair the damage your sin has caused as much as possible, it is not God's will for you to live under guilt.

> Therefore, there is now no condemnation for those who are in Christ Jesus. — **Romans 8:1**

5. **Pause and thank God for His gift of forgiveness to you and ask Him to remove your guilt as well.**

cooperating with the Holy Spirit

After you have confessed your sin to God, you must also *cooperate* with His power and work in your life.

COOPERATING WITH THE HOLY SPIRIT

> But he gives us more grace. That is why
> Scripture says: "God opposes the proud but
> shows favor to the humble." Submit yourselves,
> then, to God. Resist the devil, and he will flee
> from you. — **James 4:6-7**

This passage teaches that submission to God brings power. But it also teaches that overcoming Satan will take active *effort* on your part.[28] You are commanded to submit to God and resist the devil. In other words, you have to cooperate with God and push back against your fleshly desires.

> So I say, walk by the Spirit, and you will not
> gratify the desires of the flesh. — **Galatians 5:16**

As you walk by the Spirit and cooperate with His Spirit, you will fulfill God's desires rather than gratifying the desires of your old nature.

Notice the following passage tells us that God's divine Power has given us everything we need to live a Godly life as a spiritually reborn child of God; but then He commands us to add some things to our faith:

> His divine power has given us everything we
> need for a godly life through our knowledge
> of him who called us by his own glory and
> goodness. Through these he has given us his

very great and precious promises, so that
through them you may participate in the divine
nature, having escaped the corruption in the
world caused by evil desires. For this very
reason, make every effort to add to your faith
goodness; and to goodness, knowledge; and
to knowledge, self-control; and to self-control,
perseverance; and to perseverance, godliness;
and to godliness, mutual affection; and to
mutual affection, love. — **II Peter 1: 3-7**

The previous three passages teach us that God gives us what we need to overcome sin, but we must actually put forth effort and resist the devil, walk in the spirit, and add virtues to our faith. We have a responsibility in the change process: we must choose obedience.

Many people falsely believe that if God desires something to happen in their life then it will automatically happen, with or without their cooperation. But Scripture teaches that we actually have a great deal of authority to influence the outcomes of many things in the world.

Notice in the following Scripture passage that people were given the choice to choose death or life. By the tone of the Scripture, you can tell that God desired life for them, but they had to make the choice.

This day I call the heavens and the earth as
witnesses against you that I have set before
you life and death, blessings and curses. Now
choose life, so that you and your children
may live. — **Deuteronomy 30:19**

Remember, you can either cooperate with the Spirit and let Him change you or you can quench His transforming work in you and grieve Him.

Do not quench the Spirit. — **1 Thessalonians 5:19**

And do not grieve the Holy Spirit of God, with whom you were sealed for the day of redemption. — **Ephesians 4:30**

1. **What does it mean when we say that we have to cooperate with God's Spirit?**

2. **What do you think it means to quench or grieve the Holy Spirit's work in your life?**

notes

the partner factor

> "Though one may be overpowered, two can defend themselves.
>
> A cord of three strands is not quickly broken."
>
> **—ECCLESIASTES 4:12**

spiritual partners

But he gives us more grace. That is why Scripture says: "God opposes the proud but shows favor to the humble." Submit yourselves, then, to God. Resist the devil, and he will flee from you. — **James 4:6-7**

As we have already learned, this passage teaches that submission to God brings power. But it also teaches that overcoming Satan will take active resistance on your part. Resisting Satan and His schemes is more effective when you have partners to help.[29]

Two are better than one, because they have a good return for their labor: If either of them falls down, one can help the other up. But pity anyone who falls and has no one to help them up. Also, if two lie down together, they will keep warm. But how can one keep warm alone? Though one may be overpowered, two can defend themselves. A cord of three strands is not quickly broken. — **Ecclesiastes 4:9-12**

For lack of guidance a nation falls, but victory is won through many advisers. — **Proverbs 11:14**

THE VALUE OF SPIRITUAL PARTNERS

- They can help you see your "blind spots" and potential pitfalls.

- They can model a Godly lifestyle to you and help reinforce what God is teaching you.

- They can pray for you, support you and encourage you.

- They can help you be accountable for your actions.

> Listen to advice and accept discipline, and at
> the end you will be counted among the wise.
> — **Proverbs 19:20**

This is only possible if you are honest and allow your spiritual partner to speak the truth. When you are serious about overcoming Satan's work in your life, you stop worrying about being judged by others. You will be willing to ask mature Christians to point out your faults and help you get stronger. In *Workbook 4: Discover Relationships* we will further explore the benefits found in strong Christian relationships.

Other people can only assist your change. Other people cannot "fix" you or change you. Their job is to support your change. They cannot change you. The Power for change can only come through God. The decision for change can only come from you.

In other words, you do not have to walk your journey alone. But no one can walk it for you.

> So then, each of us will give an account of
> ourselves to God. — **Romans 14:12**

1. In what ways have you looked to other people to "fix" you or change you?

2. What does it mean to allow others to assist you with change? How is this different from looking to them to "fix'" you?

TIPS FOR CHOOSING PARTNERS

An accountability partnership should be considered prayerfully. Important factors to consider when choosing an accountability partner include:

Gender. Accountability partners should be the same gender. Spouses who are accountability partners for each other should also find other accountability partner(s) of the same gender.

Godliness. Your accountability partner should model a Godly life— a life that seeks to grow closer to God.

Trustworthiness. Your accountability partner should be someone you can trust to be reliable, consistent and honest.

Personal Accountability. Your accountability partner should have strong accountability in his or her own life. Someone who has gone through a similar discipleship process will understand their role better.

3. What are the benefits in each of these tips for choosing accountability partners?

4. What is keeping you from developing strong spiritual partners in your life?

5. How will you overcome this?

6. Who are possible spiritual partners for you?

accountability dangers to avoid

In *Workbook 4: Discover Relationships*, we will learn how to discover and live with God-honoring relationships in our lives. For the purpose of this study, let's look at a few factors that hinder us in developing healthy relationships with accountability partners.

Self-sufficiency. Choosing to isolate yourself from others is often motivated by the fear of being rejected or hurt. Suffering pain or disappointment in relationships makes keeping everyone at a distance seem safer than to risk getting hurt.

To move beyond the feeling of being alone, grasp the reality that God has always been with you. He has led you, helped you, picked you up. Even when you could not feel His presence, He was there.

> It was I who taught Ephraim to walk, taking them by the arms; but they did not realize it was I who healed them. I led them with cords of human kindness, with ties of love. To them I was like one who lifts a little child to the cheek, and I bent down to feed them. — **Hosea 11:3-4**

You may have felt deserted by God because He did not stop others from hurting you. But He was with you each moment.

> You keep track of all my sorrows. You have collected all my tears in your bottle. You have recorded each one in your book.
> — **Psalm 56:8 NLT**

We may never understand why God does not stop people from abusing their free will to harm others; but we do know He promises healing, and He promises that one day He will settle the score.

"But I will restore you to health and heal your wounds," declares the Lord…
— **Jeremiah 30:17a**

Do not take revenge, my dear friends, but leave room for God's wrath, for it is written: "It is mine to avenge; I will repay," says the Lord.
— **Romans 12:19**

1. **Has being hurt or the fear of being hurt caused you to withdraw from relationships? If yes, explain:**

Scripture teaches that people need you and that you need people.

> Two are better than one, because they have a good return for their labor: if either of them falls down, one can help the other up. But pity anyone who falls and has no one to help them up. Also, if two lie down together, they will keep warm. But how can one keep warm alone? Though one may be overpowered, two can defend themselves. A cord of three strands is not quickly broken. — **Ecclesiastes 4:9-12**

> Carry each other's burdens, and in this way you will fulfill the law of Christ.
> — **Galatians 6:2**

Remember, like a lion stalking prey, Satan waits for you to become isolated and alone, and then jumps in for the kill. Do not be ignorant of his tricks. Build strong relationships with safe people.

> Be alert and of sober mind. Your enemy the devil prowls around like a roaring lion looking for someone to devour. — **I Peter 5:8**

2. **Is it easy or hard for you to build relationships? Why?**

3. **In what ways has approaching life on your own left you weak and/or vulnerable?**

Codependency. Codependent means *having an excessive emotional or psychological reliance upon a partner.*[30] It is having one's sense of well-being tied to someone else's attention, approval and/or affection. A codependent relationship brings together two extremes: the *Damsel (or Dude) in Distress* and the *Rescuer.* The first is always in crisis and the second finds validation by rescuing the one in crisis.

When you are building healthy accountability relationships, you are not asking others to do for you what you should do for yourself and on the other hand, you are not trying to force others to change. You are helping and supporting each other through change. We will explore this in more depth in *Workbook 4: Discovering Relationships.*

Here is a simple illustration of how healthy relationships work:

- Imagine a solitary board standing upright by itself. How stable is it standing by itself? It does not take much pressure to knock it over. *This is the result of self-sufficiency.*

- Now imagine two boards leaning against each other at the top, like an upside-down V. They are dependent upon each other. If one falls, the other falls with it. *This is like a codependent relationship.*

- Lastly, imagine a framed wall. Several boards standing strong, connected to other boards and anchored to the floor. If one board falls it may weaken the wall, but the other boards will not necessarily fall with it. *This is companionship: linking your strengths to others' strengths.*

Godly accountability means you are able to give into the lives of others, as well as receive from others. When one is weak, the other is strong. Linked together, we are stronger than when we are apart.

> As iron sharpens iron, so one person sharpens another. — **Proverbs 27:17**

4. **Is it easier for you to give help or receive help? Why?**

5. **How does linking your strengths with other people's strengths, make you stronger?**

notes

the plan factor

Good planning and hard work lead to prosperity, but hasty shortcuts lead to poverty. — **PROVERBS 21:5 NLT**

the importance of a plan

There are many people who try to resist Satan but fail to learn about his tactics and develop a plan to defeat him. The Apostle Paul recognized Satan's attacks and instructed fellow believers in overcoming them. We can do the same.

> ...in order that Satan might not outwit us. For we are not unaware of his schemes.
> — **II Corinthians 2:11**

Remember that overcoming sin is a spiritual war for your life. Earthly armies do not go into battle without a plan, and neither should you. You must be intentional in waging war and have a strategy to demolish spiritual strongholds in your life.

> Good planning and hard work lead to prosperity, but hasty shortcuts lead to poverty.
> — **Proverbs 21:5 NLT**

WHAT DOES IT REALLY MEAN TO CHANGE?

Think about changing your clothes. When you change your clothes, you are not just taking off your old clothes; you are putting on other clothes. If you don't put on other clothes your change is incomplete (and that's a whole other story!)

Notice how the following passages of Scripture instruct us to "throw off" or "take off" old things, and then "put on" new things.

Throw off your old sinful nature and your former way of life, which is corrupted by lust and deception. Instead, let the Spirit renew your thoughts and attitudes. Put on your new nature, created to be like God—truly righteous and holy. — **Ephesians 4:22-24 NLT**

Do not lie to each other, since you have taken off your old self with its practices and have put on the new self, which is being renewed in knowledge in the image of its Creator. — **Colossians 3:9-10**

The night is almost gone; the day of salvation will soon be here. So remove your dark deeds like dirty clothes, and put on the shining armor of right living. — **Romans 13:12 NLT**

Turning away from sin is only half of the choice; you must also turn toward something new. It is not only about saying "no" to wrong things; it is learning to say "yes" to right things. It is "taking off" an old way of thinking to "put on" a new one.

There are things that you must stop doing. For your change to be complete, there are also new things you must start doing.

1. **Explain how failing to replace a behavior with something new is incomplete change.**

DEVELOPING A PLAN FOR CHANGE

A good plan to tear down strongholds will help you identify and replace the four parts of spiritual strongholds:

- Change the *action itself.*

- Change the *beliefs that motivate the action.*

- Change the *input that influences your beliefs about the action.*

- Change how you view your *results.*

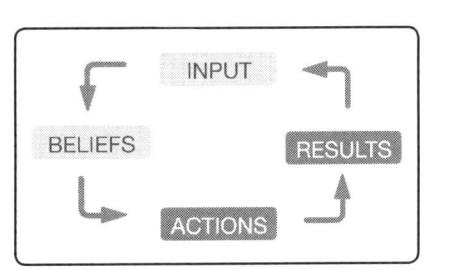

This section will address each of these areas of change.

identifying sinful actions

Sometimes it is difficult to discover a spiritual stronghold in your life because it is a protected or hidden belief. *The visible, sinful action that it produces is easier to recognize.* If you want to find hidden strongholds start with a visible, sinful action and work inward.

HOW TO IDENTIFY A SINFUL ACTION

Everyone has a different value system and opinions about what is right or wrong. Depending upon the culture in which you were raised, some things that seem normal and right to you are actually destructive and need to change.

> There is a way that appears to be right, but in the end it leads to death. — **Proverbs 16:25**

> The human heart is the most deceitful of all things, and desperately wicked. Who really knows how bad it is? — **Jeremiah 17:9 NLT**

As a Christian, you must go to God and find out what He says. You have submitted your life to Christ's Lordship, which means that you accept His standard for right and wrong.

Study the written Word of God. The Bible was given to us to show what God desires. As a Christian, God's Word—not people's opinions, your culture or your family's traditions—must constitute your moral compass.

> All Scripture is God-breathed and is useful for teaching, rebuking, correcting and training in righteousness, so that the servant of God may be thoroughly equipped for every good work.
> — **II Timothy 3:16-17**

Understanding the usefulness of Scripture does not mean that all Christians agree when it comes to defining sin. There is debate over interpretation and application of Old Testament laws, in addition to how some New Testament customs should be applied to life today. Even people who claim to believe in the "entire" Bible have passages that they do not live out. As we will learn in *Workbook 3: Discover Growth,* it is important to have a clear system of interpreting and applying all Scripture to your life.

What cannot be denied is that the New Testament clearly outlines sinful behavior—called acts, deeds, or works—of the flesh, which we must turn from. The warning is repeatedly clear that if we do not turn from these things, we will not inherit the kingdom of God.

> Now the deeds of the flesh are evident, which are: immorality, impurity, sensuality, idolatry, sorcery, enmities, strife, jealousy, outbursts of anger, disputes, dissensions, factions, envying, drunkenness, carousing, and things like these, of which I forewarn you, just as I have forewarned you, that those who practice such things will not inherit the kingdom of God.
> — **Galatians 5:19-21 NASB**

This list of sins, with a few more added to it, is repeated in other passages of Scripture: Ephesians 5:3-5, 1 Corinthians 6:9-10, Revelations 21:8, and Romans 1:29-32.

The *Personal Sin Inventory* in *Appendix 2,* will give you a complete list of these sins along with their definitions to help you identify which ones have been and which ones are currently active in your life.

Pray and ask the Holy Spirit. When you are open and honest before God, He will point out things in your life that need to change. You may know that something is wrong, but still justify or overlook it. Ask the Holy Spirit to point it out to you.

It is important to understand that God will not violate His Word and give you a "pass" on sin.

> Search me, God, and know my heart; test me
> and know my anxious thoughts. See if there is
> any offensive way in me, and lead me in the
> way everlasting. — **Psalm 139:23-24**

Ask a more mature Christian. Again, this is evidence of how God uses other people in your life. Others can see "blind spots" in your character that you can't. You should have someone in your life that you will allow to be honest with you about your behavior.

> As iron sharpens iron, so one person sharpens
> another. — **Proverbs 27:17**

1. What are the benefits of each of these three methods for recognizing sin in your life?

CAUTIONS WITH IDENTIFYING SIN

Deal with your own sin first. It is easy to recognize sins in other people's lives. But Jesus taught that you should look first at the sin in your own life. Each of us should recognize sin in ourselves and humbly ask Jesus to rescue us. When appropriate, you should warn and offer assistance to other believers who struggle with sin. However, your first priority is addressing the sin in your own life.

> Why do you look at the speck of sawdust in your brother's eye and pay no attention to the plank in your own eye? How can you say to your brother, "Let me take the speck out of your eye," when all the time there is a plank in your own eye? You hypocrite, first take the plank out of your own eye, and then you will see clearly to remove the speck from your brother's eye.
> — **Matthew 7:3-5**

2. **Why is it easy to recognize sins in other people's lives while ignoring our own?**

Don't elevate certain sins. It is easy to place sin in different categories and then feel better about yourself because you do not commit certain ones. This is dangerous because it causes you to ignore your own sin. This also causes you to hide your sin if you struggle with those that you have decided are worse.

While it is true that some sins have stronger societal implications (e.g., murder typically causes more harm than lying), all sin must be turned from, because it causes *you spiritual death.*

> …I warn you, as I did before, that those who live like this *[all the works of the flesh, not some of them]* will not inherit the kingdom of God.
> — **Galatians 5:21b** *(Brackets and Emphasis added)*

3. Why is it easy to elevate some sins while ignoring others?

Remember that before any change can be made, you have to see the need to change. To confess literally means *to agree*. When you confess sin, you are admitting you are guilty and need God's help.

ACTION STEP

Turn to *Appendix 2* and complete the *Personal Sin Inventory*. This will help you to identify and confess over 30 different sins that might be in your life. As you work through the Inventory, be completely honest. You can destroy it later.

*   Step out of **denial** and admit your sins to yourself (1 Corinthians 11:31).

*   Find **forgiveness** by confessing your sin to God (1 John 1:9).

*   Find **healing** from your sins by confessing and praying with another believer (James 5:16).

To download a printable copy of the *Personal Sin Inventory*, go to the *Additional Resources* page of **www.discoverdiscipleship.com**

changing sinful actions

Through the *Personal Sin Inventory,* we have identified and confessed sinful actions that we must stop doing.

True repentance is a clear decision to walk away from that sin. You should renounce sin through your words and actions. You can no longer keep holding on to the sin, no matter how comforting it is. You must also rid yourself of anything that could lead you back into sin—this can include relationships, locations, objects and influences.

Don't forget that walking away from sin is only half of the choice; you must also turn toward something new. It is not just about saying *no* to wrong things; it is learning to say *yes* to right things. It is *taking off* an old way of thinking and *putting on* a new one. This means if we are going to change our actions, there are some behaviors that we must stop doing, and new behaviors that we must start.

Jesus taught in Luke 11:24-26 that if you do not fill yourself with something new and good, the old destructive thing will return and be even worse. It is not just enough to simply stop doing something that you know is sin. You have to replace that behavior with something new that is also good and healthy and be filled with the Holy Spirit.

1. **Why is it important to not only stop the old behavior, but to replace it with something else?**

REPLACE OLD ACTIONS WITH NEW ACTIONS

After Apostle Paul listed several sinful acts of the flesh in Galatians 5:19-21, he then listed the type of behavior that God's Spirit brings into your life.

> But the fruit of the Spirit is love, joy, peace, patience, kindness, goodness, faithfulness, gentleness, self-control; against such things there is no law. — **Galatians 5:22-23 NASB**

2. **Carefully review Galatians 5:22-23 and think about the fruit that the Spirit of God will produce in your life. How do they differ from the sinful acts of the flesh?**

For a period of time, you will have to consciously choose new actions. Up to now, the sinful acts of the flesh have been normal behaviors for you. As you turn away from those, you must make a conscious choice to turn toward new actions and the fruit of God's Spirit in your life.

As God's input is increased in your life, He will produce new kinds of desires and behaviors in you. As with any behavior, the more you do it the stronger it will be. Repeated experience will form a new habit in your mind.

For example: Anger outbursts might have been normal for you, but the Holy Spirit's peace will cause you to act more calmly. Rather than acting out of anger, learn to respond in a way that is honest, but is influenced by self-control and peace. Sexual immorality might be normal for you but choose actions that are influenced by the self-control and true love of the Holy Spirit.

3. **Think about a sinful act of the flesh you struggle with. Describe a specific action that is influenced by the fruit of God's Spirit, that can replace that old, sinful action in your life.**

FILL THE TIME VOID

It is also important to remember that turning from sin will leave a void in your time. How will you replace that time? If you drink yourself to sleep each night, what will you do now? If you party every Friday night, what will you do then? If you view pornography or overeat when you are bored, how will you fill the time? Scripture teaches that we must shift our focus from what the world values (substitute identities) to heavenly things (God's purposes).

> Since, then, you have been raised with Christ, set your hearts on things above, where Christ is, seated at the right hand of God. Set your minds on things above, not on earthly things. For you died, and your life is now hidden with Christ in God. — **Colossians 3:1-3**

Consider the following ways to fill your time:

- Worship, prayer and Bible study.

- Building healthy relationships.

- Repairing damaged or neglected relationships.

- Serving your church and community.

- Healthy hobbies.

ACTION STEP

Turn to *Appendix 3: A Plan for Change,* and complete *Section 1.*

To download a printable copy of *A Plan for Change,* go to the *Additional Resources* page of **www.discoverdiscipleship.com**

A CAUTION

It is very important that you are honest about the sin in your own life as you begin to work on your *Plan for Change.* Many people will skim over the *Personal Sin Inventory* and make light of sins they struggle with.

Once again, remember the danger of denying or downplaying sin. Be honest with yourself and with God and select an area of sin to begin addressing. Ask the Holy Spirit to shine His light in your life and point out any sins that might be hidden from your sight. Also, don't forget to ask other mature Christians that know you, if they see an area you should focus on. It's time to identify and lay sin aside. Notice this instruction from Scripture.

> Therefore, since we have so great a cloud of witnesses surrounding us, let us also lay aside every encumbrance and the sin which so easily entangles us, and let us run with endurance the race that is set before us,
> **—Hebrews 12:1 NASB**

As you begin developing *A Personal Plan for Change,* identify the sin that easily entangles *you.*

the power of underlying beliefs

In order to break a spiritual stronghold in your life, it helps to understand the conscious and unconscious beliefs that you have about it. It is hard to *change* the way you think if you do not *understand* the way you think. Satan is cunning, so you have to be smart concerning his tricks.

> ...in order that Satan might not outwit us.
> For we are not unaware of his schemes.
> — **II Corinthians 2:11**

Trying to change a behavior without addressing underlying beliefs is like trying change the course of a boat while it is set on autopilot. The moment you release tension off the wheel, it reverts to the "set" way it was going. If you attempt to stop a visible behavior (the seen sin) without understanding and replacing your belief about it, change may be very difficult or even impossible to maintain. This happens because your beliefs are automatically producing your behavior.

Remember, we are often not conscious of when we formed beliefs or that we even have them. (Remember the doorknob example?) However, if you are going to change a behavior, you must identify and change your belief about the behavior.[31]

All sin is based on false beliefs. When you sin, you act on a lie. You believe that your core need (for security, worth or fulfillment) can be found in something in the world (substitute identities). You believe this lie because you have spent a lifetime receiving and accepting worldly input.

Here's the tricky part. Most of us are not aware of the lies we believe, lies about life. Many people continue to remain bound to these old ways of thinking and acting, even after believing in Christ. Lasting change does not happen in their life because they do not identify the false beliefs they have formed. If you do not identify these underlying factors and confront the lie, your effort to change your sinful behavior will be short-lived.

> Don't copy the behavior and customs of this world, but *let God transform you into a new person by changing the way you think. Then you will learn to know God's will for you,* which is good and pleasing and perfect.
> — **Romans 12:2 NLT** *(Emphasis added)*

Failure to address motivating beliefs is why people will quit one sin, such as alcoholism, only to replace it with another addictive behavior, such as gambling. Underlying beliefs and motives will keep producing different sins as long as core desires are sought from false sources—sources other than God.

Changing behavior is difficult. When you replace underlying thoughts and motives, it gets easier. Your new thoughts and beliefs will produce new behaviors.

> Do not be deceived: God cannot be mocked. A man reaps what he sows. Whoever sows to please their flesh, from the flesh will reap destruction; whoever sows to please the Spirit, from the Spirit will reap eternal life. Let us not become weary in doing good, for at the proper time we will reap a harvest if we do not give up.
> — **Galatians 6:7-9**

You may find that as you begin to address the underlying factors to one or two spiritual strongholds in your life, others will crumble. The same patterns of thinking often produce several different visible sins. As you plant new seeds—new influences in your life—you will reap the harvest of a changed life in several areas.

1. Why is it important to identify your false beliefs and confront the lies that motivate your sin?

DAY 25

changing your beliefs

On *Day 11: How Spiritual Strongholds Form,* you read examples of Spiritual Strongholds that three individuals needed to overcome. This lesson built upon what you began in *Workbook 1: Discover Identity,* when you identified *substitute identities* that give the illusion of providing your core needs for security, worth and fulfillment. These core desires can only be fulfilled in God. Trying to fulfill them apart from Him leads to sinful acts of the flesh.

Let's review the examples from *Day 11: How Spiritual Strongholds Form.* Let's look at the underlying lies these individuals believe, and compare those lies to God's Truth:

For the young woman, searching for worth through affection led to sexual immorality.

> The lie she believes: *I believe affection gives me worth.*
>
> To overcome the sin of sexual immorality, she must recognize the lie and choose to believe the truth: *True worth can only be found in God.*

The first man sought fulfillment through abilities and accomplishments, which led him to be competitive and jealous.

> The lie he believes: *I believe my abilities and accomplishments give me fulfillment.*
>
> To overcome the sins of competitiveness and jealousy, he must recognize the lie and choose to believe the truth: *True fulfillment can only be found in God.*

The second man's search for security through power led him to manipulation, deception and anger.

> The lie he believes: *I believe power gives me security.*

> To overcome the sins of manipulation, deception and anger, he must recognize the lie and choose to believe the truth: *True security can only be found in God.*

IDENTIFY THE FALSE BELIEF

Until you discover whatever the lie is that you believe about your behavior, changing your actions will be short-lived. You can attend church and go through religious motions, but until you change fundamental beliefs that you have concerning your security, worth and fulfillment, you will not overcome the spiritual strongholds Satan has formed in your life.

In other words, you must *stop* believing the lies that culture has taught you and believe the truth found in God's Word.

For example, the sins of pride and lying are often motivated by the false belief that your worth lies in getting attention or approval from people.

The basis of this stronghold can be stated as:

> Searching for *worth* through *attention* has led to *pride and lying.*

REPLACE FALSE BELIEFS WITH THE TRUTH

In the previous example, the underlying lie can be stated as:

> I believe *attention* gives me *worth.*

The truth is:

> *I am a child of God, made in His image. My security, worth and fulfillment comes only through living in my identity as His child.*

Remember that the biggest battle you will fight with Satan is in your mind. You have to intentionally reject thoughts that produce sin and replace them with the truth of God's Word.

> For though we live in the world, we do not wage war as the world does. The weapons we fight with are not the weapons of the world. On the contrary, they have divine power to demolish strongholds. We demolish arguments and every pretension that sets itself up against the knowledge of God, and we take captive every thought to make it obedient to Christ.
> — **II Corinthians 10:3-5**

Practically speaking, this means every time you have a jealous thought you must recognize it, reject it and instead think about the truth found in God's Word: *I am a child of God. His love is enough for me. Lasting value is not found in the attention I receive from others.*

Every time you have a lustful thought you must recognize it, reject it and instead think about the truth from God's Word: *I am a child of God. I am to see others as Christ sees them, not as sexual objects. Lasting fulfillment does not come through sexual gratification.*

Every time you have an angry thought you recognize it, reject it and instead think about the truth from God's Word. *I am a child of God. I will respond in a way that is honest, yet reflects the character of Christ. Lasting security does not come through power or being in control.*

You must do this with every thought that produces sin in your life. This will not be easy at first, but over a period of time this will reshape your beliefs and your life.

ACTION STEP

Turn *to Appendix 3: A Plan for Change* and complete *Section 2.*

identifying initial trigger points

It can be helpful to understand how, when and why a stronghold began in your life. What was the initial trigger? There's nothing you can do to change the trigger point. However, identifying and understanding it can shed a lot of light into why it has become so strong in your life. These trigger points often continue to speak to us years later, providing constant reinforcing input that strengthen and protect spiritual strongholds.

Jesus can bring healing to this area of your life as you begin to understand it, confess it and ask for help and healing.

Identifying the initial trigger point can help provide a *reason* for some of our behaviors. However, it is not to be used as an *excuse* for continuing the behavior.

INITIAL TRIGGER POINTS

Trauma: The trigger point to a stronghold in your life might have been a traumatic experience such as abuse, neglect, betrayal, or the death of a loved one. Traumatic experiences can significantly alter our view of the world and cause us to do anything we feel necessary to cope, survive or feel normal. This often triggers substance abuse as well as other self-destructive or self-indulging behaviors.

1. **List ways in which trauma has impacted your life.**

Rejection: Being rejected by people or the fear of being rejected can lead us to try to overcompensate or do things to earn love. Being raised poor can often cause people to become too attached to possessions. Being put down by others will often cause people to become preoccupied with proving their value through several of these substitutes. Neglect by a parent or spouse can cause you to validate yourself through accomplishments.

2. **List ways in which rejection has caused you to feel the need to "prove" yourself.**

Shame/self-hate: We often suffer from the shame of other people's actions toward us. Being berated, abused and belittled can cause to feel shame and then overcompensate to be loved. Often the shame that comes from sexual abuse can cause us to seek validation and love and can alter the way we view relationships and affection.

The shame of our past mistakes can also cause us to feel it's useless to try to change. We take on the identity of our sin and keep living it out and developing new strongholds.

3. **List ways in which shame or self-hatred has driven you to seek validation or move further into sin.**

Underlying emotional/psychological factors: While this issue is quite complex and cannot be fully explored in a couple of paragraphs, it should at least be acknowledged; like all other parts of our body, our minds can experience disease/disorders.

Sometimes a tendency to engage in certain sins is motivated by an attempt to seek temporary relief to emotional diseases/disorders such as anxiety and depression. We should pray and seek healing from emotional disorders. If healing doesn't immediately come, it is wiser to seek the help of Christian mental health providers, than it is to revert to sinful, destructive behaviors.

4. **Do you struggle with any emotional/pshchological disorders that might contribute to your struggle with sin?**

Modeling: As previously learned, the trigger point could have been simply seeing it modeled as a way of life or having it offered to you.

5. **What are some strongholds that you developed by having them modeled to you?**

Remember, no matter the trigger point, freedom and healing can be found through Jesus.

> So if the Son makes you free, you will be free indeed. — **John 8:36 NASB**

changing your input

It is important for you to understand what parts of your environment continue to reinforce spiritual strongholds in your life. Your environment and culture have shaped most of your value system and beliefs.

The word *culture* is from the Latin word for *a cultivated area.*[32] You can think of the culture that you grew up in as your garden. You have consciously and unconsciously let it influence most of your beliefs and actions. Because of this, something that is sinful and destructive may seem normal. It seems normal because everyone you know does it or believes it is morally acceptable.

> There is a way that appears to be right, but in the end it leads to death. — **Proverbs 16:25**

IDENTIFY NEGATIVE INPUT

The following things shape you:

The people you are around the most. Christ has called you to be an influence to others in the world. However, you should carefully guard who *influences you* with their behavior and advice. Make a conscious effort to choose your friends.

> The righteous choose their friends carefully, but the way of the wicked leads them astray.
> — **Proverbs 12:26**
>
> Do not be misled: "Bad company corrupts good character." — **1 Corinthians 15:33**

Walk with the wise and become wise, for
a companion of fools suffers harm.
— **Proverbs 13:20**

What you read, watch and listen to. Subtle and not-so-subtle examples that come to you through media consciously and unconsciously influence your beliefs and values. Be aware of what you feed your mind.

I will not look with approval on anything that is
vile. I hate what faithless people do; I will have
no part in it. — **Psalms 101:3**

What you think and talk about. Your thoughts and conversations constantly reinforce your beliefs—so guard them carefully.

How you "talk" about yourself and your circumstances to yourself in your mind counts as well. Negative self-talk has the same result as repeating lies to yourself continuously—it reinforces your spiritual strongholds.

May the *words of my mouth* and the *meditation
of my heart* be pleasing to you, O LORD, my
rock and my redeemer.
— **Psalms 19:14 NLT** *(Emphasis added)*

REPLACE NEGATIVE INPUT WITH GODLY INPUT

It has been said that insanity is doing the same thing over and over again and expecting different results. Your results in life are directly linked to your input and influences.

- If you want different results, you must do something different

- To do something different, you have to think different

- To think different, you have to change your *input*

Do not be deceived: God cannot be mocked.
A man reaps what he sows. Whoever sows
to please their flesh, from the flesh will reap

destruction; whoever sows to please the Spirit,
from the Spirit will reap eternal life.
— **Galatians 6:7-8**

The most powerful change you can make in your input is continuing to grow in your relationship with God. As you learn how
to build a stronger relationship with God in *Workbook 3: Discover
Growth*, the strength of God in you will make you stronger.

**Replace the people that you are around who are not good
influences.** You should actively seek ways to build new relationships with other believers who model, support and reinforce the
changes you are making.

> Flee the evil desires of youth and pursue
> righteousness, faith, love and peace, *along with
> those who call on the Lord out of a pure heart.*
> — **II Timothy 2:22** (*Emphasis added*)

Remember the value of spending time with God as you replace the
people who influence you. As you spend time in God's Presence
in worship and prayer, He will reform your heart and mind. As
you spend more time in God's Presence, you will find that you
will desire more of Him and less of sin.

> Come near to God and he will come near to
> you. — **James 4:8a**

> So I say, walk by the Spirit, and you will not
> gratify the desires of the flesh. — **Galatians 5:16**

Replace what you read, watch and listen to. Remember the
value of the steady input of God's Word when you begin to work
on changing this area of input. Memorizing and thinking about
Scripture will destroy Satan's work in your mind and life. The
input of God's Word will deconstruct your old ways of thinking
and replace them with new ways.

> I have hidden your word in my heart that I
> might not sin against you.
> — **Psalm 119:11**

Identify and begin memorizing key verses that teach the truth about *substitute identities* and the works of the flesh that you struggle against. See *Appendix 1: Substitute Identities and Scriptures* for the list of *substitute identities* and helpful Scripture.

Change what you think and talk about. Scripture tells us that we should guard our hearts, and it instructs us about the types of things that we should think about.

> Finally, brothers and sisters, whatever is true, whatever is noble, whatever is right, whatever is pure, whatever is lovely, whatever is admirable—if anything is excellent or praiseworthy—think about such things.
> — **Philippians 4:8**

> Above all else, guard your heart, for everything you do flows from it. — **Proverbs 4:23**

CONSIDER THE FOLLOWING CHANGES:

- Whom do I need to end a relationship with? Whom do I need to begin a relationship with?

- Whom do I need to spend less time with? Whom do I need to spend more time with? (This includes God and other believers.)

- What do I need to stop reading, watching or listening to? What new things do I need to start reading, watching and listening to? (This includes Scripture.)

- What do I need to stop thinking and talking about? What new thoughts and conversations do I need to start having?

ACTION STEP
Turn to *Appendix 3: A Plan for Change* and complete *Section 3*.

changing your focus

The Bible teaches that sin leads to death (Romans 6:23). Sin might give us the illusion of meeting our core needs, but it will ultimately kill us. There are two factors that distort the reality of the results of our sin: short-term benefits and reinforcing lies.

SHORT-TERM BENEFITS VS. LONG TERM REWARDS

Identify the short-term benefits of the sin. You continue to do things even if they are harmful to you because they give you short-term benefits. They may make you feel good now, but the pleasure cannot last. Short-term benefits are things you may want, but they are not what you truly need.

Replace your focus on short-term benefits with a focus on long-term rewards. Rather than simply focusing on immediate gratification, think about the rewards you will receive by not doing harmful things.

> [Moses] chose to be mistreated along with the people of God rather than to enjoy the fleeting pleasures of sin. He regarded disgrace for the sake of Christ as of greater value than the treasures of Egypt, because he was looking ahead to his reward. — **Hebrews 11:25-26**

REINFORCING LIES VS. THE TRUTH

Identify the reinforcing lies you tell yourself about this behavior. It is easy to tell yourself lies to make yourself feel that there will not be long-term consequences.

Examples of reinforcing lies:

- One time won't matter…

- I'm not really hurting anyone…

- I deserve this...

- Everyone else is doing it so it must not be that bad...

- It's not illegal…

- At least I'm not as bad as_____.

Replace reinforcing lies with the truth about your actions. In order to have lasting change, your motive for changing should be an acknowledgement of the pain your actions cause. It is not enough to change because you are "growing up," got caught, feel guilty or have had your fun. The Bible teaches that only Godly sorrow leads to true change.

> Godly sorrow brings repentance that leads to salvation and leaves no regret, but worldly sorrow brings death. — **II Corinthians 7:10**

> Come near to God and he will come near to you. Wash your hands, you sinners, and purify your hearts, you double-minded. Grieve, mourn and wail. Change your laughter to mourning and your joy to gloom. Humble yourselves before the Lord, and he will lift you up. — **James 4:8-10**

The truth is that our sinful actions always cause pain. To remind yourself of the truth about sin, ask yourself the following:

- How does this action hurt me?

- How does this action hurt others?

- How does this action hurt God?

Understanding the truth about sin will lead to Godly sorrow—which leads to change.

> **ACTION STEP**
>
> Go to *Appendix 3: A Plan for Change* and complete *Section 4.*

be prepared for temptation

The last area of change we will look at is temptation. Although we cannot change what tempts us, we can learn to be prepared for it.

IDENTIFY YOUR TEMPTATION TRIGGERS

Be aware of when you are most vulnerable to temptation. You might think that Satan blindly trips you up, but there are usually indicators when you are getting ready to fall. These warning signs may not be sin, but they are indicators of when you are vulnerable.[33]

The best time to reach out for help is *before* you are in the crisis. However, most people wait until they are in the middle of a crisis situation before they reach out for help. Learn to identify what *leads* to the sin crisis and then you can be better prepared for it.

- What emotions make you more vulnerable? (e.g. stress, depression, anxiety, exhaustion, happiness)

- What people make you more vulnerable?

- What places make you more vulnerable?

- What times of the year (e.g. holidays, anniversary of a death) make you more vulnerable?

- What things or objects make you more vulnerable?

1. **Why is it better to reach out for help when you feel tempted—before you are in a crisis?**

REPLACE TEMPTATION WITH PREPARATION

Once you begin to understand when you are most vulnerable to temptation triggers, you must prepare for them. If at all possible, completely avoid tempting situations.

> Stay away from every kind of evil.
> — **1 Thessalonians 5:22 NLT**

> Run from anything that stimulates youthful lusts. Instead, pursue righteous living, faithfulness, love, and peace. Enjoy the companionship of those who call on the Lord with pure hearts. — **II Timothy 2:22 NLT**

Because it is not always possible to avoid every tempting situation, it is important to have a plan in place before you get into a vulnerable situation.

Think of it like this: How do you keep from wrecking on icy roads? First, avoid driving on them. But if you have no other choice, drive slowly and carefully.

You might think that this rule does not apply to you, that you can be around tempting situations without your decisions being affected. Consider the wisdom of this ancient proverb:

> Can a man scoop fire into his lap without his clothes being burned? —**Proverbs 6:27**

The following Scripture implies that there is a path that *leads* to temptation. Learn to recognize it and avoid it. Have a backup plan in place if you cannot.

> ...and lead us not into temptation, but deliver us from the evil one. — **Matthew 6:13**

The following verse declares that God will show you a way out of temptation. But, it is up to you to take it.

If you think you are standing strong, be careful not to fall. The temptations in your life are no different from what others experience. And God is faithful. He will not allow the temptation to be more than you can stand. When you are tempted, he will *show you a way out so that you can endure.* — **1 Corinthians 10:12-13 NLT** *(Emphasis added)*

Remember the power factor. Call on the power of God during these vulnerable times. Jesus taught that prayer helps you avoid temptation. Remember that every tempting situation you go through is an opportunity to declare once again that Jesus is your Lord. Ask for His authority and power in that moment. If He is your Lord, you will not live according to your desires. You will live according to His will.

> For I can do everything through Christ, who gives me strength. — **Philippians 4:13 NLT**

Remember the partner factor. Go to God first, but do not underestimate the value of calling on a partner to pray with you and for you. The following verse explains how a partner can help you overcome tempting situations.

> Though one may be overpowered, two can defend themselves. A cord of three strands is not quickly broken. — **Ecclesiastes 4:12**

A plan to involve your partner for prayer can be as simple as saying, "If I send you a text to pray for me, it means that I am really struggling to resist the urge to _____ at that moment, *so pray for me!* Don't just call me or worry about me, pray for me! If I send you two texts to pray, please call me and *pray with me!*"

Accountability Questions. Once we identify what makes us vulnerable, we should give our partners permission to regularly ask us how we are doing in these areas. Constructing a list of questions for your partner to randomly ask you will help you stay accountable for your actions.

WHEN PREPARING FOR TEMPTATION, ASK YOURSELF THE FOLLOWING

- What situations do I need to avoid?

- If I can't avoid the situation, how will I specifically involve God's Power to overcome temptation?

- If I can't avoid the situation, how will I specifically involve my partners to overcome temptation?

- What specific accountability questions should my partner ask me?

2. Do you think it will benefit you to think through and be prepared for what tempts you? Why or why not?

ACTION STEP

Go to *Appendix 3: A Plan for Change* and complete *Section 5*.

To download a printable copy of A *Plan for Change,* go to the *Additional Resources* page of **www.discoverdiscipleship.com**

DAY 30

following through with change

Understand that change will not happen automatically. You have to be intentional about replacing old behavior with new habits.[34]

> … train yourself to be godly. "Physical training is good, but training for godliness is much better, promising benefits in this life and in the life to come." — **1 Timothy 4:7b-8 NLT**

Start somewhere! It has been said that a journey of a thousand miles begins with a single step. What is the *first step* that you need to take toward your goal? Doing *something* toward your goal will often give you the motivation to do the next thing. You may downplay the significance of a single step because it is small, but it is one step further than you were before.

For example: Five minutes of exercise is better than none. It might not be the 30 minutes a day goal that you desire to meet, but it is a start and is more than you were doing.

> Do not despise these small beginnings, for the Lord rejoices to see the work begin…
> — **Zechariah 4:10a NLT**

Do the *next* right thing. How do you finish a journey of a thousand miles? One step at a time. As you begin to make changes in your life, remember that it will take time. You did not get into trouble overnight. You will not get out of it overnight either.

If you think about having to make every change you need to all at once, it will seem impossible. You will get discouraged and quit. Learn to focus on the next right thing. Take one step at a time.

For example: You may know that you need to go for detox and rehab. That might seem like an impossible goal. Simply begin by finding a number to call. Do not think about when or how you will make the call, just find the number. After you find the number, your next right thing is to figure out how and when to make the call. After you make the call, focus on what the next step will be.

> Therefore do not worry about tomorrow, for tomorrow will worry about itself. Each day has enough trouble of its own. — **Matthew 6:34**

Expect opposition. Paul would not have described overcoming sin as a war if it were easy (Romans 7:23).

Expect opposition within yourself. If you have operated from a certain belief system for most of your life, it will feel awkward when you start to change. If you have believed a lie to be the truth, the truth may initially seem like a lie. Changing your influence and your input will change this perspective.

Expect opposition from others. Some people will discourage you because they are concerned about you and do not understand the changes you are making. Have honest discussions with them about why you are changing and listen to their concerns. However, if your changes are positive, do not let them influence you away from them.

Some people will discourage you because your changes make them feel uncomfortable. They may stand to lose something if you change, or your change may remind them of their own need to change. You must learn to ignore these people. Remember to build a strong positive support system and stay focused on moving forward.

Expect spiritual opposition. Last but not least, do not forget that you have a real spiritual enemy who seeks your destruction. Scripture would not have instructed you to resist the Devil (James 4:7) if you were not going to be opposed by him.

> For our struggle is not against flesh and blood,
> but against the rulers, against the authorities,
> against the powers of this dark world and
> against the spiritual forces of evil in the
> heavenly realms. — **Ephesians 6:12**

Stay faithful. Again, change will not happen overnight. You have spent a lifetime thinking and acting certain ways. Changing these patterns will take time. It is often very hard to stay faithful if you do not see immediate results. But when you make right choices, over a period of time, you will receive a harvest of a changed life.

> Let us not become weary in doing good, for at
> the proper time we will reap a harvest if we do
> not give up. — **Galatians 6:9**

You will not immediately resolve all of your issues, but if you work faithfully at them you will receive the harvest of a changed life. The importance of repetition over a long period of time cannot be overstated. Daily engaging in Scripture and in prayer, and regularly involving yourself in conversations with other Christians will form new thoughts. Over time, this will transform your mind and life.

Who you are today is the result of seeds that you and others planted in your mind yesterday. If you want a different life tomorrow, you have to plant new seeds, new thoughts, today.

Stay focused on the "why." Making changes is not pleasant. But the end result is worth it.

For example: When you begin strength training you feel pain because you are tearing muscle tissue. After a few days, the pain leaves and your muscle is stronger.

Remind yourself of why you are changing. This includes reminding yourself of the consequences of destructive behavior as well as the rewards of a changed life.

No discipline seems pleasant at the time,
but painful. Later on, however, it produces a
harvest of righteousness and peace for those
who have been trained by it. — **Hebrews 12:11**

Let us throw off everything that hinders and
the sin that so easily entangles. And let us run
with perseverance the race marked out for
us, fixing our eyes on Jesus, the pioneer and
perfecter of faith. For the joy set before him he
endured the cross, scorning its shame, and sat
down at the right hand of the throne of God.
— **Hebrews 12:1b-2**

Celebrate small successes. Learn to celebrate where you have
come from and the progress that you have made. If you have
an all-or-nothing mentality it will be hard to acknowledge your
progress if you are not 100 percent changed.

Learn to recognize and celebrate even the small changes.
This will help you realize how far you've come and will
motivate you to keep pressing forward. But do not become
comfortable in that place. Keep moving forward.

But thanks be to God! He gives us the victory
through our Lord Jesus Christ. Therefore,
my dear brothers and sisters, stand firm. Let
nothing move you. Always give yourselves
fully to the work of the Lord, because you know
that your labor in the Lord is not in vain.
— **1 Corinthians 15:57-58**

When you fall, get up and start again. A failure is only a
real failure if you stay down. Learn from it, get up and keep
moving forward.

For though the righteous fall seven times,
they rise again, but the wicked stumble when
calamity strikes. — **Proverbs 24:16**

what's next?

Congratulations on making it to the end of this workbook! You have gained some valuable tools, skills and practices to help you live in Freedom.

In the next workbook, *Workbook 3: Discover Growth*, you will learn how to develop skills that will help you grow in your relationship with God.

You are on an exciting journey of discovering and growing in your identity as a child of God. Keep pushing forward!

> Brothers and sisters, I do not consider myself yet to have taken hold of it. But one thing I do: Forgetting what is behind and straining toward what is ahead, I press on toward the goal to win the prize for which God has called me heavenward in Christ Jesus.
> — **Philippians 3:13-14**

NOTE: This workbook is the second in a series of a six-workbook study entitled Discover Discipleship. Each workbook focuses on a different area of growth in the life of a disciple of Jesus.

If you have not yet completed *Workbook 1: Discover Identity*, it is recommended that you complete it next, then move on to the rest of the study. Go to **www.discoverdiscipleship.com** for ordering information.

notes

WORKBOOK 2:

freedom checkpoint

Before you move on to *Workbook 3: Discover Growth*, take a few minutes to evaluate how you are applying the principles learned in this workbook:

1. Do you have a spiritual accountability partner that is part of your church? If yes, who?

2. Have you completed *A Personal Sin Inventory* and discussed it with an accountability partner? Have you talked through this with God? If yes, when?

3. Have you developed a *Plan for Change* with your
    accountability partner?

4. When was the last time you reviewed your *Plan for
    Change* with your accountability partner? When was
    the last time you reviewed your plan with God?

notes

appendices

APPENDIX 1

substitute identities & scriptures

ACCOMPLISHMENTS

I am defined by what I can do or by what I know.

Even youths grow tired and weary, and young men stumble and fall; but those who hope in the LORD will renew their strength. They will soar on wings like eagles; they will run and not grow weary, they will walk and not be faint.

—Isaiah 40:30

But whatever was to my profit I now consider loss for the sake of Christ. Yes, everything else is worthless when compared with the infinite value of knowing Christ Jesus my Lord. For his sake I have discarded everything else, counting it all as garbage, so that I could gain Christ.

—Philippians 3:7-8

Whatever you do, do your work heartily, as for the Lord rather than for men.

—Colossians 3:23 NASB

ABILITIES

I am defined by a skill or ability that I have.

You may say to yourself, "My power and the strength of my hands have produced this wealth for me." But remember the LORD your God, for it is he who gives you the ability to produce wealth, and so confirms his covenant, which he swore to your ancestors, as it is today.

—Deuteronomy 8:17-18

For by the grace given me I say to every one of you: Do not think of yourself more highly than you ought, but rather think of yourself with sober judgment, in accordance with the faith God has distributed to each of you.
—**Romans 12:3**

Therefore, as the Scriptures say, "If you want to boast, boast only about the LORD."
—**1 Corinthians 1:31**

POSSESSIONS

I am defined by what I own.

Then he said to them, "Watch out! Be on your guard against all kinds of greed; a man's life does not consist in the abundance of his possessions." —**Luke 12:15**

Keep your lives free from the love of money and be content with what you have, because God has said, "Never will I leave you; never will I forsake you." —**Hebrews 13:5**

No one can serve two masters. Either he will hate the one and love the other, or he will be devoted to the one and despise the other. You cannot serve both God and Money.
—**Matthew 6:24**

Therefore I tell you, do not worry about your life, what you will eat or drink; or about your body, what you will wear. Is not life more important than food, and the body more important than clothes? —**Matthew 6:25**

APPEARANCE

I am defined by how I look.

Charm is deceptive, and beauty is fleeting; but a woman who fears the LORD is to be praised. —**Proverbs 31:30**

For women who claim to be devoted to God should make themselves attractive by the good things they do. —**1 Timothy 2:10 NLT**

APPROVAL

I am defined by who accepts me.

I'm not interested in crowd approval. And do you know why? Because I know you and your crowds. I know that love, especially God's love, is not on your working agenda. —**John 5:41-42 The Message**

Peter and the other apostles replied: "We must obey God rather than men! —**Acts 5:29**

Am I now trying to win the approval of human beings, or of God? Or am I trying to please people? If I were still trying to please people, I would not be a servant of Christ. —**Galatians 1:10**

On the contrary, we speak as men approved by God to be entrusted with the gospel. We are not trying to please men but God, who tests our hearts. —**1 Thessalonians 2:4**

We were not looking for praise from people, not from you or anyone else, even though as apostles of Christ we could have asserted our authority. —**1 Thessalonians 2:6**

Blessed are you when people insult you, persecute you and falsely say all kinds of evil against you because of me. Rejoice and be glad, because great is your reward in heaven, for in the same way they persecuted the prophets who were before you. —**Matthew 5:11-12**

AFFECTION

I am defined by who loves me.

...all things (including you) have been created through him (Jesus) and for him (Jesus). —**Colossians 1:16b**

The Lord appeared to us in the past, saying: "I have loved you with an everlasting love; I have drawn you with unfailing kindness. —**Jeremiah 31:3**

For I am convinced that neither death nor life, neither angels nor demons, neither the present nor the future, nor any powers, neither height nor depth, nor anything else in all creation, will be able to separate us from the love of God that is in Christ Jesus our Lord. —**Romans 8:38-39**

ATTENTION

I am defined by being noticed for positive or negative behavior, or by getting sympathy from others.

> How can you believe since you accept glory from one another but do not seek the glory that comes from the only God? —**John 5:44**

> Do nothing out of selfish ambition or vain conceit. Rather, in humility value others above yourselves. —**Phillipians 2:3**

> Be careful not to practice your righteousness in front of others to be seen by them. If you do, you will have no reward from your Father in heaven. —**Matthew 6:1**

POWER

I am defined by being in control.

> Son of man, say to the ruler of Tyre, "This is what the Sovereign LORD says: In the pride of your heart you say, "I am a god; I sit on the throne of a god in the heart of the seas.' But you are a man and not a god, though you think you are as wise as a god." —**Ezekiel 28:2**

> Trust in the LORD with all your heart and lean not on your own understanding; in all your ways submit to him, and he will make your paths straight. —**Proverbs 3:5-6**

> Look to the LORD and his strength; seek his face always. —**1 Chronicles 16:11**

> "Not by might nor by power but by my Spirit" says the Lord God Almighty. —**Zechariah 4:6**

There is no one holy like the LORD; there is no one besides you; there is no Rock like our God.

—**1 Samuel 2:2**

APPETITIES

I am defined by my desires. These can be natural desires such as those of food or sex, or acquired desires such as those for drugs and alcohol.

Appetite for food

"My food," said Jesus, "is to do the will of him who sent me and to finish his work."

—**John 4:34**

I know what it is to be in need, and I know what it is to have plenty. I have learned the secret of being content in any and every situation, whether well fed or hungry, whether living in plenty or in want. I can do everything through him who gives me strength.

—**Philippians 4:12-13**

Their destiny is destruction, their god is their stomach, and their glory is in their shame. Their mind is on earthly things. —**Philippians 3:19**

Sexual appetite

"...How then could I do such a wicked thing and sin against God?" (Joseph's response to sexual temptation.) —**Genesis 39:9b**

Flee from sexual immorality. All other sins a person commits are outside the body, but whoever sins sexually, sins against their own body. Do you not know that your bodies are temples of the Holy Spirit, who is in you, whom

you have received from God? You are not your own; you were bought at a price. Therefore honor God with your bodies.
—1 Corinthians 6:18-20

Appetite for alcohol or other drugs.

Do not get drunk on wine, which leads to debauchery. Instead, be filled with the Spirit.
—Ephesians 5:18

Wine is a mocker and beer a brawler; whoever is led astray by them is not wise.
—Proverbs 20:1

PLEASURE

I am defined by being comfortable and feeling good.

But he will pour out his anger and wrath on those who live for themselves, who refuse to obey the truth and instead live lives of wickedness. —Romans 2:8

And I'll say to myself, "You have plenty of grain laid up for many years. Take life easy; eat, drink and be merry." But God said to him, "You fool! This very night your life will be demanded from you. Then who will get what you have prepared for yourself?"
—Luke 12:19-20

a personal sin inventory

If we confess our sins, he
is faithful and just and will
forgive us our sins and purify
us from all unrighteousness.
—1 John 1:9

DETERMINING SIN

Everyone has a different value system and opinions about what's right or wrong. Some things that seem normal and right to you because of the culture in which you were raised could actually be sinful and destructive. These things need to change.

> There is a way that appears to be right, but in the end it leads to death. — **Proverbs 16:25**

As a Christian, you must go to God and find out what He says. You've submitted your life to Christ's Lordship, which means you accept His standard for right and wrong. The Bible was given to us to show what God desires. As a Christian, God's Word—not people's opinions, your culture or your family's traditions—must act as your moral compass.

> All Scripture is God-breathed and is useful for teaching, rebuking, correcting and training in righteousness, so that the servant of God may be thoroughly equipped for every good work. — **II Timothy 3:16-17**

Understanding the usefulness of Scripture doesn't mean that all Christians agree when it comes to defining sin. There is debate over interpretation and application of Old Testament laws, in addition to how some New Testament customs should be applied to life today. Even people who claim to believe in the "entire" Bible have passages they don't live out. It's important to have a clear system of interpreting and applying Scripture to your life. (We will learn a system for Biblical interpretation in *Workbook 3: Discover Growth.*)

What cannot be denied is that the New Testament clearly outlines sinful behavior—called acts, deeds, or works—of the flesh, that we must turn from. The warning is repeatedly clear that if we do not turn from these things, we will not inherit the kingdom of God. Remaining in sin indicates we haven't.

Now the deeds of the flesh are evident, which are: immorality, impurity, sensuality, idolatry, sorcery, enmities, strife, jealousy, outbursts of anger, disputes, dissensions, factions, envying, drunkenness, carousing, and things like these, of which I forewarn you, just as I have forewarned you, that those who practice such things will not inherit the kingdom of God.
— **Galatians 5:19-21 NASB**

This list of sins, with a few more added, is repeated in other passages of Scripture:

But immorality or any impurity or greed must not even be named among you, as is proper among saints; and there must be no filthiness and silly talk, or coarse jesting, which are not fitting, but rather giving of thanks. For this you know with certainty, that no immoral or impure person or covetous man, who is an idolater, has an inheritance in the kingdom of Christ and God. — **Ephesians 5:3-5 NASB**

Put to death, therefore, whatever belongs to your earthly nature: sexual immorality, impurity, lust, evil desires and greed, which is idolatry. — **Colossians 3:5**

Or do you not know that the unrighteous will not inherit the kingdom of God? Do not be deceived; neither fornicators, nor idolaters, nor adulterers, nor effeminate, nor homosexuals, nor thieves, nor the covetous, nor drunkards, nor revilers, nor swindlers, will inherit the kingdom of God.
— **1 Corinthians 6:9-10 NASB**

But for the cowardly and unbelieving and abominable and murderers and immoral persons and sorcerers and idolaters and all liars, their part will be in the lake that burns with fire and brimstone, which is the second death." — **Revelations 21:8 NASB**

being filled with all unrighteousness, wickedness, greed, evil; full of envy, murder, strife, deceit, malice; they are gossips, slanderers, haters of God, insolent, arrogant, boastful, inventors of evil, disobedient to parents, without understanding, untrustworthy, unloving, unmerciful; and although they know the ordinance of God, that those who practice such things are worthy of death, they not only do the same, but also give hearty approval to those who practice them.
— **Romans 1:29-32 NASB**

These sinful acts of the flesh described in the New Testament, are built on the moral code of the Old Testament. God's moral code- how one treats God and others- wasn't done away with in the New Covenant that came through Christ, it was actually expanded.

While the Old Covenant between God and Israel focused mainly on external behaviors, the New Covenant God makes with us through Christ highlights the importance of our hearts and motives behind our sin. This is why Jesus would say things like, "You have heard it said 'Do not murder.' But I say to you, "Do not hate.'" Murder is a seen, physical sin; hate is an unseen sin that motivates the visible sin. As we identify the sinful acts of the flesh, you'll notice that both visible and unseen sins are included.

A note on the process used to develop this Inventory.

- If a sin appears in more than one passage of Scripture, it's only listed once.

- Sins are identified by the specific Greek words used.[35]

- Some of the sins are from the same Greek word, but translators chose different names while translating it into English. This is usually noted, and the sin is only listed once, by the original Greek word, not multiple times as different sins.

- English words used are from the translations of the passages above. The English word is not as important as the Greek word and its definition.

- Your definition of an English word could be different from its original meaning. Words often change meaning as they are used in a culture. This is why we go back and examine the Greek definitions, which more accurately indicate the intended meaning.

- Sins with very similar definitions are listed as one sin; the different English names and Greek words are noted.

- Sins are listed in categories to make it easier to work through this *Inventory*. The categories do not determine the severity of the sins. Don't get hung up on the category label. The individual sins listed are what's important.

NOTE FOR SPIRITUAL PARTNERS: If you're acting as a spiritual partner, assisting others through this process, take time to reengage with the *Personal Sin Inventory* and reevaluate your life as the participants work through the *Inventory*. Sin has a way of creeping back in. Schedule time with your mentors and partners and talk back through newly identified struggles. As the participant talks to you, share from your own life and experiences as you feel comfortable. Allow the participant plenty of opportunity to talk.

GUIDELINES FOR USING THIS INVENTORY

1. Take your time as you go through the sins. Underline or circle parts of the definitions that apply to you.

2. Admit and explain how you are, or were, guilty of any listed sin. You don't have to go into every instance; just give a general summary. This helps you step out of denial and be honest with yourself.

3. Use the checkpoint at the end of each Category Section to review the sins in that category and identify how your sin has hurt God, yourself and others; and how others' sins have hurt you.

4. Confess these sins to God and receive His forgiveness. Ask God to help you to forgive others.

5. Talk through your sins with a partner you trust. How much you share depends on you, and the level of trust you have with your partner. If the fear of legal or other ramifications keeps your sin secret from others, consider the following possibilities:

   - Talk to a minister or Christian counselor to protect your confidentiality. First ask the minister or counselor what they are required to report, and then decide how much you want to share.

   - Consider using this as an opportunity to come completely clean and face whatever consequences are associated with your crime. If you make this decision, talk with your pastor and ask for support and help as you do so (Refer back to the suggestions on *Day 17: Confession.*)

6. Make note of any sin that you are still struggling with.

7. As you review this *Inventory* with a partner, stop and talk at the checkpoints. Pray with each other before moving on to a new section.

   - Thank God for His forgiveness.

   - Declare complete deliverance from these sins and strongholds, in the name of Jesus.

   - Pray that God will bring healing from the effects of sin.

SECTION I: SINS OF UNBELIEF AND FALSE WORSHIP

Sins of unbelief and false worship involve false or misplaced worship. They include refusing to believe in God or Christ, rebellion against God, or renouncing your belief due to hardship.

1. HATRED OF GOD

(theostyges): Refusing to show respect or reverence for God.

Scripture Reference: Romans 1:30

- Outright rejection of belief in God and/or expressing hostility about belief in God.

- Showing no respect for God or expressing hostility toward God despite belief in God.

Have you ever committed the sin of *Hatred of God*? If yes, explain:

2. REJECTING SPIRITUAL UNDERSTANDING

(asynetos): Having no mind for salvation.

Scripture Reference: Romans 1:31

- Rejecting the revelation of God given to you internally by the Holy Spirit.

- Refusing to hear or understand about the person of Jesus or the basic message of salvation through Him (the Gospel).

NOTE: This does not refer to not understanding parts of Scripture, but rather to refusing to hear or understand the message of Who God or Jesus is.

Have you ever committed the sin of *Rejecting Spiritual Understanding?* If yes, explain:

3. UNBELIEF

(apistos): Understanding the truth of the Gospel but then rejecting Jesus' Lordship.

Scripture Reference: Revelations 21:8

- Understanding the message of the person of Jesus and salvation through Him, but rejecting Him, unlike rejecting spiritual understanding, which is refusal to understand.

- Refusal to believe in or accept Jesus' Lordship (Jesus' rightful, perfect, and loving leadership over one's life).

NOTE: Unbelief does not necessarily refer to whether or not you believe God will answer yes to a prayer you prayed. It refers to lack of belief in Jesus as Lord.

Have you ever committed the sin of *Unbelief?* If yes, explain:

4. SPIRITUAL COWARDICE

(deios): Caving in to fear and/or pressure and turning away from God.

Scripture Reference: Revelations 21:8

- Denying faith at the threat of financial ruin, physical harm or death.

- Being ashamed of Jesus in front of others for fear of rejection. Jesus declared that if we are ashamed of Him or His words before men, He would be ashamed of us when He returns (Luke 9:26).

Have you ever committed the sin of *Spiritual Cowardice?* If yes, explain:

5. SORCERY

(pharmakeia/pharmakos) also translated witchcraft: The use of drugs, evil spirits, magic, or spells.

Scripture References: Galatians 5:20, Revelation 21:8

- Using drugs to achieve a pseudo-spiritual experience. This is somewhat different from using drugs to be intoxicated, which is another sin.

- Worship of nature, false gods and/or spirits.

- Attempting to manipulate the natural and spiritual world for some kind of gain.

Have you ever committed the sin of *Sorcery/Witchcraft*. If yes, explain:

6. IDOLATRY

(eidololatria/eidololatres): The worship of, or reverence for any god other than the triune God of Scripture.

Scripture References: Galatians 5:20, 1 Corinthians 6:9, Ephesians 5:5, Revelation 21:8

- Participation in religions that worship idols, false gods, Satan, demons and/or other spirits.

- Worship of nature.

- Denial of supernatural entities and accepting science, reason or self as the ultimate authority.

- Worship of self. This includes placing your will and desires over the will and desires of God.

- Worship of others. This includes placing the will, opinion and desires of someone else, over the will, opinion and desires of God.

- Allowing anything to consume your time and turn you away from a God-ordered life. This can include hobbies, recreation, jobs possessions or relationships.

Have you ever committed the sin of *Idolatry?* If yes, explain:

7. GREED/COVETOUSNESS

(pleonexia/pleonektes): Excessively desiring more than your share.

Scripture References: Romans 1:29; Ephesians 5:3,5; Colossians 3:5

Why is *Greed/Covetousness* listed as a sin of unbelief and false worship? Colossians 3:5 declares *greed is idolatry:*

> Put to death, therefore, whatever belongs
> to your earthly nature: sexual immorality,
> impurity, lust, evil desires and greed, which is
> idolatry. —**Colossians 3:5**

- Excessive desire for more wealth or possessions.

- Keeping far more than you need to be Biblically responsible to reasonably prepare for the future, without the willingness to give to those in need.

- Placing material objects in competition with God. Anything can become an idol to us. Greed and covetousness–the desire for more and more–turn things of this world into false gods, even if there's not an "official" religion built around it.

- Prioritizing fulfillment of appetites. Philippians 3:19 teaches that people's bellies and appetites have become their gods.

- Gluttony, which is overindulgence: greed expressed as consuming excessively more than you need or more than your share.

The base, sinful motive behind greed, covetousness and gluttony is the desire for or consumption of *more* material things. Identifying greed in your life can be tricky. Most people don't want to admit that they're greedy. Here are some questions to consider to identify greed:

- Do material objects demand a lot of your time?

- Are you frequently dissatisfied with what you have and desire more?

- Do you work more than you should, solely to increase your wealth or possessions beyond what you need?

- Do you stockpile wealth or goods purely for pleasure or a sense of security, without a willingness to give them away to meet another's need?

- Do you overindulge any of your appetites?

- Do you consume or buy things to the point of excess?

Have you ever committed the sin of *Greed/Covetousness*? If yes, explain:

SINS OF UNBELIEF AND FALSE WORSHIP CHECKPOINT

Pause and review the sins from this section. As you answer the questions, specifically identify the sins you are referring to.

1. In what ways have *you hurt God* by participating in any of these sins of Unbelief and False Worship? List and explain:

2. In what ways have *you hurt yourself* by participating in any of these sins of Unbelief and False Worship? List and explain:

3. In what ways you have *you hurt others* by participating in any of these sins of Unbelief and False Worship? List and explain:

4. In what ways have *you been hurt by someone* participating in any of these sins of Unbelief and False Worship? List and explain:

5. Stop and talk and pray with your spiritual partner, using the Guidelines found at the beginning of this Inventory.

SECTION II: SINS OF DECEPTION

Sins of deception are sins that involve breaking trust and/or misleading others. This begins with the subtler sin of untrustworthiness and deceit and continues to more blatant sins such as lying and theft.

8. UNTRUSTWORTHINESS

(asynthetos): Not following through on commitments.

Scripture Reference: Romans 1:31

- Breaking promises.

- Neglecting obligations or duties.

NOTE: Untrustworthiness is a base level sin that can lead to more lying and deception. Jesus taught that people should be able to depend on what we say. Your word should be your bond (Matthew 5:36-37).

Have you ever committed the sin of *Untrustworthiness*? If yes, explain:

9. LYING

(pseudes): Intentionally speaking something that is not true.

Scripture Reference: Revelations 21:8

- Falsely accusing others.

- Speaking *anything* that is untrue, even if it isn't a false accusation.

- Speaking untruth about your actions to gain an advantage or to avoid consequences or trouble.

- Speaking untruth about someone else's actions to gain an advantage or to avoid consequences or trouble.

- Exaggerating the truth and boasting.

Have you ever committed the sin of *Lying?* If yes, explain:

10. DECEIT

(dolos): Seeking to entrap others by misleading them.

Scripture Reference: Romans 1:29

- Lying with the intent to manipulate.

- Leaving out pertinent details to gain an advantage or to avoid consequences or trouble.

- Manipulating truth versus the straightforward untruth of lying.

Have you ever committed the sin of *Deceit?* If yes, explain:

11. THEFT

(kleptes, klepto): Taking what does not belong to you.

Scripture Reference: 1 Corinthians 6:10

- Intentionally taking things from other people.

- Subtler theft such as robbing your employer or others of time and receiving payment for it.

- Borrowing and refusing to return.

Have you ever committed the sin of *Theft?* If yes, explain:

12. SWINDLING

(harpax) also translated extortion: Tricking someone out of something that belongs to them.

Scripture Reference: 1 Corinthians 6:10

- Tricking or deceiving others to get what belongs to them.

- Threatening someone with some type of physical, financial, personal or psychological harm to get what you want.

- Using violence to rob.

Have you ever committed the sin of *Swindling?* If yes, explain:

SINS OF DECEPTION CHECKPOINT

Pause and review the sins from this section. As you answer the questions, specifically identify the sins you are referring to.

1. In what ways have *you hurt God* by participating in any of these Sins of Deception? List and explain:

2. In what ways have *you hurt yourself* by participating in any of these Sins of Deception?   List and explain:

3. In what ways you have *you hurt others* by participating in any of these Sins of Deception? List and explain:

4. In what ways have *you been hurt by someone* participating in any of these Sins of Deception? List and explain:

5. Stop and talk and pray with your spiritual partner, using the Guidelines found at the beginning of this Inventory.

SECTION III: **SINS OF PRIDE AND DIVISION**

Sins of pride and division are focused on pride and feeling superior to others. These begin with sins of personal arrogance and progress to sins that separate us from people with whom we disagree.

13. ARROGANCE

(hyperephanos) also translated pride: Exalting one's self.

Scripture Reference: Romans 1:30

*   Preoccupation with self – your wants, needs, desires, position, image, opinions, feelings, etc.

*   Feeling superior to others, in any way.

*   Exalting yourself over God

NOTE: Since sin results from believing that your way is better than God's way, all sin can be traced back to pride. Scripture teaches that pride leads to destruction (Proverbs 16:18) and that God opposes the proud but gives grace to the humble (James 4:6). Satan's sin was pride. He thought he was better than God (Isaiah 14:12-17).

Have you ever committed the sin of *Arrogance/Pride*? If yes, explain:

14. BOASTING

(alazon): Pretending to be something you think is bigger or better than you are.

Scripture Reference: Romans 1:30

- Bragging.

- Constantly talking about yourself, who you are and what you can do.

NOTE: Boasting is rooted in the sin of pride.

Have you ever committed the sin of *Boasting?* If yes, explain:

15. DISOBEDIENCE

(apeithes) also translated rebellious: Refusing to comply with rules or standards, or purposely disregarding expectations.

Scripture Reference: Romans 1:30

- Resistance to God and God-ordered authority; God-ordered authority refers to the authority God has placed in the family, church and government.

- Thinking of yourself above the direction of God-ordered authority.

- Constant defiance—even defiance in your heart and thoughts—to those in authority; this indicates a rebellious heart.

- Rebellion.

Biblical guidelines for obedience:

- Children are to obey their parents and others in authority over their lives and parents are to protect their children and not provoke them to anger (Ephesians 6:1, 1 Peter 2:13).

- Husbands and wives are to honor and submit to each other (Ephesians 5:33).

- The church is to obey and honor its leaders and leaders are to serve the church. (Hebrews 13:17).

- Citizens are to obey and pray for their government and government is to punish wrongdoers. (Romans 13:1-5, 1 Peter 2:13-14).

NOTE: Scripture teaches that we can disobey authority when they order us to sin (Acts 5:29)

Have you ever committed the sin of *Disobedience/Rebellion*? If yes, explain:

16. ENVY/JEALOUSY

(phthonos/zelos): Envy and jealousy are from two different Greek words that have very similar meanings: Wanting what others have or wanting to outdo others, even to the point of anger or malice.

Scripture References: Galatians 5:20-21, Romans 1:29

- Displeasure over someone else's perceived good fortune or success.

- Contentious rivalry, which is meaner than healthy rivalry.

- Lowering others to set up one's self.

- Corrupted zeal; the Greek word for jealousy is zelos which means zeal–a strong desire. This can even lead to pursuing a right cause through wrong means.

- Feeling upset or negative emotions when someone else gets attention, receives a compliment, accomplishes something or has something you want.

Have you ever committed the sin of *Envy/Jealousy?* If yes, explain:

17. ENMITY

(echthra) also translated hatred: Refusing to get along with someone over a real or perceived disagreement or difference.

Scripture Reference: Galatians 5:20

- Hostility or bickering between individuals or groups.

- Refusal to forgive.

- Bitterness, which Scripture teaches us to get rid of (Ephesians 4:32).

Enmity/hatred can be difficult to determine. Hatred seems a strong word and we're often reluctant to say we hate someone. The following questions will help you determine if enmity/hatred is in your heart:

- Do you get defensive, hostile and/or angry over people of another group, ethnicity, culture or political party?

- Do you feel wronged by a group or individual?

- Do you live in conflict – in action or thought – with a person/group that offends or has offended you in some way?

- Do you struggle to move past a real hurt and live in conflict – in action or thought – with the person/group who hurt you?

- Do you repeatedly share offenses committed against you?

- Do you share negative information about a person/group who hurt or offended you?

- Do you attempt to get others to see a person/group in the same negative way you do?

- Does anger or another negative emotion rise up in you at the mention of a particular person/group? Or when you see them?

Answering yes to any of these can indicate the presence of enmity/hatred in your heart.

Have you ever committed the sin of *Enmity/Hatred?* If yes, explain:

18. FACTIONS/DISSENSION

(hairesis/dichostasia): Factions and dissensions are from two different Greek words with similar definitions: conflict between groups over differences in opinions or goals.

Scripture Reference: Galatians 5:20

To understand factions/dissension, think of the ways we divide over religious beliefs, ethnicity, and political or national allegiance.

- Feeling you and your group are the only ones right.

- A divisive, combative attitude, particularly with other Christians; this Scripture reference more specifically address relations within the church and how we treat other believers.

- Moving from conflict to separation from those who disagree with you over matters that are not essential to Christian belief. The key factor is someone who has a critical attitude that is consistently seeking to prove others wrong and themselves as right—thus superior.   This is, as other sins are, rooted in the core sin of pride.

- Separating from the world, rather than seeking common ground so that the Gospel can be shared.

NOTE: This does not mean that truth is relative, and everyone is right. Holding certain beliefs are essential for being a Christian. But so much division between Christians occurs over personal styles, preferences and interpretations of secondary matters, not essential truths. Factions/Dissensions primarily refers to maintaining a segregated, contentious attitude toward those with whom you disagree over secondary issues, thereby destroying peace, causing hostility, and limiting the spread of the Gospel.

Have you ever committed the sin of *Factions/Dissensions?* If yes, explain:

19. STRIFE/DISCORD

(eris/eritheia) also translated selfish ambition: Wanting to start arguments or provoke controversy, usually to get what you want.

Scripture References: Galatians 5:20; Romans 1:29

- Having a contentious, argumentative or combative attitude, rather than an orientation toward solving problems. This sin is often accompanied by factions.

- Being motivated by hatred or bitterness (Proverbs 10:12).

- Refusal to follow Matthew 18:15-17 instructions to talk through personal or church conflict and use mediators and church leaders to facilitate resolution when necessary.

Have you ever committed the sin of *Strife/Discord/Selfish Ambition?* If yes, explain:

SINS OF PRIDE AND DIVISION CHECKPOINT

Pause and review the sins from this section. As you answer the questions, specifically identify the sins you are referring to.

1. In what ways have *you hurt God* by participating in any of these sins of Pride and Division? List and explain:

2. In what ways have *you hurt yourself* by participating in any of these sins of Pride and Division? List and explain:

3. In what ways you have *you hurt others* by participating in any of these sins of Pride and Division? List and explain:

4. In what ways have *you been hurt by someone* participating in any of these sins of Pride and Division? List and explain:

5. Stop and talk and pray with your spiritual partner, using the Guidelines found at the beginning of this Inventory.

SECTION IV: **SINS OF DIRECT HARM**

While most sins can harm others, these intentionally target harming a person's character, dignity or life. This category progresses from unmerciful / unloving attitudes, to berating, shaming, and slandering others to murder.

20. BEING UNLOVING/UNMERCIFUL

(astorgos/aneleemon): Being Unloving/Unmerciful comes from two different Greek words with similar meaning: lacking affection for those you should care about.

Scripture Reference: Romans 1:31

- Treating others' needs as less valid or important than your own.

- Disregard for others' feelings.

- Not caring about the effect your actions could have on others.

- Refusing to make allowances for others' weaknesses.

- Harshly judging others by their actions, while rationalizing your behavior by your intentions.

Have you ever committed the sin of being *Unloving/ Unmerciful?* If yes, explain:

21. SLANDER

(katalalos): Saying untrue negative things about someone.

Scripture Reference: Romans 1:30

- Intentionally spreading lies about someone.

- Repeating negative things about people, without verifying the truth, often because you want them to be guilty. For example: speaking negatively about people who have wronged you, disagree with you, or those of a different political party or ethnicity, based on your opinion.

Have you ever committed the sin of *Slander?* If yes, explain:

22. GOSSIP

(psithyristes): Talking about others in an unhelpful way.

Scripture Reference: Romans 1:29

- Repeating what you know or believe is the truth about someone, or think could be true of them, but in an unhelpful way.

- Repeatedly sharing with others when we feel someone has wronged us, though Scripture teaches we should talk directly to the person/people involved or talk to someone who can help mediate the disagreement (Matthew 18:15-17).

- Pointing out to others when you think someone is sinning, disregarding the Scriptural approach to have a conversation directly with the person and seek to restore them (Galatians 6:1-2).

If you're not part of a problem, nor part of its solution, you should probably not discuss it with others. If you're concerned about a person's actions, talk *to* them, not *about* them. If you are sharing the problem with others, the goal should be for Biblical intervention and restoration of the person.

NOTE: Many believe that repeating the truth is not gossip. Slander is intentionally lying about someone and gossip is spreading negative information about others that is or could be true. Both are character assassinations and are sin.

Have you ever committed the sin of *Gossip?* If yes, explain:

23. REVILING/INSOLENCE

(loidoros,loidoreo/ hybristes): Reviling and insolence are from different Greek words that have similar meanings: Saying harsh things, or assaulting others verbally. Using insulting, mean-spirited words to humiliate.

Scripture Reference: 1 Corinthians 6:10; Romans 1:30

- Insulting, shaming or mistreating someone, usually because you think you are better than they are.

- Wanting to humiliate someone in response to a perceived or real wrong.

- Allowing pride to cause you to insult or mistreat others.

- Bullying.

Have you ever committed the sin of *Reviling/Insolence?* If yes, explain:

24. ANGER OUTBURSTS

(thymos) also translated fits of rage: Showing intense, uncontrolled anger over a real or perceived wrong.

Scripture Reference: Galatians 5:20

- Losing your temper.

- Throwing fits when things don't go your way.

- Yelling at others when angry.

- Threatening or plotting revenge.

- Holding on to anger.

NOTE: Anger is a natural emotion, but Scripture teaches that if we do not let go of it quickly, it will become sin (Ephesians 4:26-27).

Have you ever committed the sin of *Anger Outbursts/Fits of Rage?* If yes, explain:

25. MALICE/INVENTING EVIL

(kakos/kakoetheia): The desire to come up with ways to do wrong or cause trouble.

Scripture Reference: Romans 1:29-30, Colossians 3:5

- Wanting to damage the reputation of a person or group.

- Wanting to hurt or harm someone physically, emotionally, financially, etc.

- Thinking of ways to cause mischief.

- Coming up with ways to deceive, harm, or injure others.

- Plotting ways to commit crime.

Have you ever committed the sin of *Malice/Inventing Evil?* If yes, explain:

26. MURDER

(phonos, phoneus): The deliberate, wrongful taking of a human life.

Scripture References: Romans 1:29, Revelations 21:8

Murder can be extended to mean the deliberate ending of unborn human life through abortion. In the case of abortion, it is often shame that keeps someone in silence. Remember that confession breaks the power and shame of sin.

Have you ever committed the sin of *Murder*? If yes, explain:

SINS OF DIRECT HARM CHECKPOINT

Pause and review the sins from this section. As you answer the questions, specifically identify the sins you are referring to.

1. In what ways have *you hurt God* by participating in any of these Sins of Direct Harm? List and explain:

2. In what ways have *you hurt yourself* by participating in any of these Sins of Direct Harm? List and explain:

3. In what ways you have *you hurt others* by participating in any of these Sins of Direct Harm? List and explain:

4. In what ways have *you been hurt by someone* participating in any of these Sins of Direct Harm? List and explain:

5. Stop and talk and pray with your spiritual partner, using the Guidelines found at the beginning of this Inventory.

SECTION V: **SEXUAL SINS**

God's design in Genesis and reaffirmed throughout Scripture in the Old and New Testaments, is one man and one woman united in a life-long covenant relationship we call marriage. Sexual expression outside of this context is sexual sin. Sexual sins range from lustful thoughts, to "dirty" language, and on to physical sexual acts.

27. IMPURITY/LUST

(akatharsia/akathartos/pathos): Impurity and lust come from different Greek words with similar meaning: Being sexually or morally unclean. Living a lustful, sinfully sexual lifestyle, in thought and/or action.

Scripture References: Galatians 5:19, Ephesians 5:3, Colossians 3:5

- Having an "unbridled" lustful thought life.

- Allowing your passions and desires to control you; this is the literal definition of lust.

- Looking at others (with the exception of a spouse) with sexual desire in your mind (according to Jesus in Matthew 5:28).

- Viewing pornography, committing voyeurism and indulging sexual urges through erotic literature, novels, movies, media or other means.

NOTE: Jesus taught that lust was the same as adultery, affirming Gods' heightened moral code in the New Testament. A sinful act is not the only wrong; actively desiring to sin is itself sin. While we can't stop a thought or desire from entering our mind, we can and should choose not to dwell on it.

Have you ever committed the sin of *Impurity/lust?* If yes, explain:

28. SENSUALITY

(aselgeia) Also translated debauchery and lasciviousness:
Being driven by senses and passions.

Scripture Reference: Galatians 5:19

- Outward displays of lust or lewdness, which include leering or making suggestive comments or actions.

- Willfully trying to arouse lust or desire in someone that is not your spouse, through provocative actions, insinuations, flirting or even how you dress. (Some refer to this as impurity; for purposes of this Inventory, we include it under sensuality. Both are sin.)

- Eliciting attention through your sexuality, from someone you are not married to.

- Immodesty; though it can be difficult to determine what's modest, each of us knows if we're trying to get sexual attention through dress or actions. Allow mature, Godly people to guide you concerning possible immodesty in your dress and actions. Don't use the truth that other people are responsible for their own thoughts and actions as an excuse to disregard Biblical responsibility to be modest.

NOTE: No one has the right to harass or rape someone who is sensual or provocative in dress and/or actions. But each of us is responsible to not exploit our own sensuality.

Have you ever committed the sin of *Sensuality/Debauchery/Lasciviousness*? If yes, explain:

29. COARSE/OBSCENE/FOOLISH LANGUAGE

(eutrapelia/ aischrotes/ morologia). **Ephesians 5:4 uses these
three different Greek words to refer to sinful language. These
sins include dirty, "coarse" joking as well as filthy/obscene and
foolish language.**

Scripture Reference: Ephesians 5:4

- Failure to respect the dignity and value of others in the area of sex: objectification.

- Using a word considered obscene or coarse by the culture in which you are speaking or writing. Language is important because it reveals the condition of our heart (Luke 6:45).

- Thinking and speaking in ways that deny God's ordained order for sexuality.

NOTE: Scripture does not provide a list of words that are sinful, but the guidelines in this passage should direct our language.

**Have you ever committed the sin of *Coarse/Obscene/
Foolish Language?* If yes, explain:**

30. ADULTERY

(moichos): **Engaging in sexual or intimate activity with someone
else's spouse.**

Scripture Reference: 1 Corinthians 6:9

- Having sex with someone else's spouse, even if you are single. Two single people having sex when they are unmarried is fornication, another sin.

- Having sex with someone other than your spouse if you are married.

- Engaging in emotionally intimate relationships with someone other than your spouse.

Have you ever committed the sin of *Adultery?* If yes, explain:

31. HOMOSEXUALITY

(malakos/arsenokoites): Same-gender sexual activity.

Scripture Reference: 1 Corinthians 6:9

- *Arsenokoites* refers to homosexuality in general.

- *Malakos* (translated "the effeminate") refers specifically to the passive sexual partner in a homosexual relationship. This includes a prostitute.

- Any use of one's body in homosexual activity.

NOTE: There is a difference between being attracted to the same sex and actively engaging in homosexual behavior. Everyone has sinful desires. Engaging in homosexual acts or entertaining homosexual, lustful thoughts, moves the attraction to expressed sin.

Have you ever committed the sin of *Homosexuality* or do you struggle with same sex attraction? If yes, explain:

32. FORNICATION/IMMORALITY

(porneia/pornos/pornois): Fornication/immorality is a general term for all types of sexual sin.

Scripture References: 1 Corinthians 6:9; Galatians 5:19; Ephesians 5:3,5; Colossians 3:5; Revelation 21:8

This general term for sexual sin covers all sexual activity outside of the covenant of a marriage between one man and one woman. Many of these sexual sins have already been discussed.

Fornication/immorality covers sexual intercourse with:

- someone else's spouse (adultery)

- someone to whom you are not married (fornication)

- someone of the same gender (homosexuality, lesbianism)

- close relatives (incest)

- animals (bestiality)

NOTE: Individuals who have been raped or molested are NOT guilty of committing a sexual sin when the abuse happened. If this has happened to you, it is the offender who is guilty of sexual sin.

While this a very sensitive subject, and you might be uncomfortable talking about it, shame can be lifted, and inner healing can begin, when trauma is brought to light. Explicit details and names of offenders do not necessarily have to be shared as this can increase the trauma or create a "backlash" that you are not ready to deal with.

If you are uncomfortable speaking about this with your Bible study partners, consider talking with a Pastor, church leader or Christian therapist.

If you are currently experiencing sexual abuse, you have a right to get help to end it.

Have you ever committed the sin of *Fornication/Immorality*? If yes, explain:

SEXUAL SINS CHECKPOINT

Pause and review the sins from this section. As you answer the questions, specifically identify the sins you are referring to.

1. In what ways have *you hurt God* by participating in any of these Sexual Sins? List and explain:

2. In what ways have *you hurt yourself* by participating in any of these Sexual Sins? List and explain:

3. In what ways you have *you hurt others* by participating in any of these Sexual Sins? List and explain:

4. In what ways have *you been hurt by someone* participating in any of these Sexual Sins? List and explain:

5. Stop and talk and pray with your spiritual partner, using the Guidelines found at the beginning of this Inventory.

SECTION VI: **SINS OF INTOXICATION**

33. DRUNKENNESS/INTOXICATION

(methe, methysos): To be drunk or intoxicated.

Scripture References: 1 Corinthians 6:10, Galatians 5:21

- Seeking satisfaction in drinking alcohol or using drugs or other intoxicating substances.

- Being under the influence of alcohol or other intoxicating substances, instead of the influence of the Holy Spirit (Ephesians 5:18).

NOTE: Many Christians defend their right to drink without getting drunk. Scripture is very clear that intoxicating substances are deceptive and destructive (Proverbs 20:1). In other words, you think you have control of the intoxicating substance, but it can end up controlling and destroying you, often before you realize it.

In light of this, we should examine our hearts to determine why we justify or defend our right to drink or use intoxicating substances. A strong desire to justify the use of an intoxicating substance could indicate that it has control over your life.

Have you ever committed the sin of *Drunkenness/ Intoxication?* If yes, explain:

34. CAROUSING

(komos) also translated orgies: Literally translated it means drinking parties, particularly those that go late into the night and/or involve moving from place to place.

Scripture Reference: Galatians 5:21

- Involvement in wild drinking or drug parties and groups.

- Group intoxication and the other sins that go along with it.

- Sexual parties.

- Causing trouble as part of a group of people.

Have you ever committed the sin of *Carousing?* If yes, explain:

SINS OF INTOXICATION CHECKPOINT

Pause and review the sins from this section. As you answer the questions, specifically identify the sins you are referring to.

1. In what ways have *you hurt God* by participating in any of these Sins of Intoxication? List and explain:

2. In what ways have y*ou hurt yourself* by participating in any of these Sins of Intoxication? List and explain:

3   In what ways you have *you hurt others* by participating in any of these Sins of Intoxication? List and explain:

4   In what ways have *you been hurt by someone* participating in any of these Sins of Intoxication? List and explain:

5. Stop and talk and pray with your spiritual partner, using the Guidelines found at the beginning of this Inventory.

SECTION VII: **UNRIGHTEOUSNESS**

Following are several words used in Scripture to describe all sin. All sin is turning from God, wanting something outside of God's will or breaking God's laws. As you read over these final sins and descriptions, think through any time you have broken God's laws. Identify any other sin in your life that you have not yet mentioned.

UNRIGHTEOUSNESS

(adikia, adikos) also translated iniquity: To be not right, either with man's understanding of what is right or God's standard of holiness. Violating justice or breaking God's laws.

Scripture References: Romans 1:29, 1 Corinthians 6:9

WICKEDNESS/EVIL

(poneria/kakia): Although these are two different Greek words, they are very similar in meaning: having evil purposes or desires, which means doing and wanting things outside God's will.

Scripture Reference: Romans 1:29

Evil is destructive. It alters, distorts, corrupts, misrepresents, misuses, misapplies, twists, degrades. It intends harm or other types of wrong.

ABOMINATION

(bdelysso): To turn yourself away from God and what is good. To take something good and pollute it.

Scripture Reference: Revelations 21:8

What other sins are present in your life that you have failed to mention in this Inventory?

Go to the *Additional Resources* page of **www.discoverdiscipleship. com** to download a printable version of *A Personal Sin Inventory.*

notes

a plan for change

Good planning and hard work lead to prosperity, but hasty shortcuts lead to poverty. —**Proverbs 21:5 NLT**

My Name:

My Spiritual Partners:

1: CHANGE MY ACTIONS

IDENTIFY THE SINFUL ACT OF THE FLESH

Which sinful act of the flesh am I addressing with this plan?

Refer to the *Personal Sin Inventory.*

REPLACE THE SINFUL ACT OF THE FLESH

Which of the fruit of the Spirit will help me overcome this sinful action?

But the fruit of the Spirit is love, joy, peace, patience, kindness, goodness, faithfulness, gentleness, self-control; against such things there is no law. Galatians 5:22-23 NASB

How will I fill the void that turning from this sin leaves?

When I would normally _____ (sinful act of the flesh), I will:

2: CHANGE MY BELIEFS

Searching for _____

                            (security, worth or fulfillment)

through _____

                          (substitute identity)

has led to _____

                        (sinful act of the flesh)

What was the entry point of this stronghold in my life?

CONFRONT THE LIE

The **lie** I believe: _____

                          (substitute identity)

gives me _____

                        (security, worth or fulfillment)

REPLACE FALSE BELIEFS WITH THE TRUTH

I will choose to believe **the truth:** I am a child of God made in His image. My security, worth and fulfillment is only found though living in my identity as His child.

3: CHANGE MY INPUT

IDENTIFY NEGATIVE INFLUENCE

I need to **stop** watching, reading and listening to:

I need to **stop** (or limit) spending time with:

I need to **stop** thinking and talking about:

REPLACE NEGATIVE INFLUENCE WITH GODLY INFLUENCE

I need to **start** watching, reading and listening to:

I need to **start** spending time with:

I need to **start** thinking and talking about:

Make sure to include key verses that address the Sinful Act of the Flesh and the Substitute Identity that fuels it. Refer to *Appendix 1.*

4: CHANGE HOW I SEE MY RESULTS

CHANGE MY FOCUS FROM SHORT-TERM BENEFITS TO LONG TERM REWARDS

What short-term benefits am I getting through this sin?

What long-term rewards should I focus on?

CHANGE MY FOCUS FROM REINFORCING LIES TO THE REAL TRUTH ABOUT SIN

What reinforcing lies do I tell myself about this sin?

Examples: One time won't matter; I'm not really hurting anyone; I deserve this; everyone else is doing it so it must not be that bad; it's not illegal; at least I'm not as bad as_____.

What is the real truth about this sin?

How does this sin hurt God?

How does this sin hurt me?

How does this sin hurt others?

5: BE PREPARED FOR TEMPTATION

TEMPTATION TRIGGERS

Who makes me more vulnerable?

When am I more vulnerable?

Where am I more vulnerable?

What things or objects make me vulnerable?

What emotions make me vulnerable?

TEMPTATION PREPARATION

Go back and write how you can avoid each temptation trigger that makes you vulnerable.

List what you will do when you cannot avoid any of these triggers.

If I can't avoid the situation, how will I specifically involve *God's Power* to decrease temptation?

If I can't avoid the situation, how will I specifically involve my Partners to decrease temptation?

List some specific accountability questions your partner should ask you.

> ...in order that Satan might not outwit us.
> For we are not unaware of his schemes.
> **—II Corinthians 2:11**

To download a printable copy of *A Plan for Change,* go to the *Additional Resources* page of **www.discoverdiscipleship.com**

ENDNOTES

[1] This is adapted from the Westminster Shorter Catechism, developed in 1646-1647. A catechism is a summary of Christian doctrines, taught in question and answer format. Refer to: http://www.shortercatechism.com/resources/wsc/wsc_001.html

[2] https://www.blueletterbible.org/lang/lexicon/lexicon.cfm?Strongs=G3340&t=KJV

[3] This list of *Incomplete Beliefs* was inspired by: The Wesley Center Online. "The Sermons of John Wesley – Sermon 1: Salvation by Faith." wesley.nnu.edu. http://wesley.nnu.edu/john-wesley/the-sermons-of-john-wesley-1872-edition/sermon-1-salvation-by-faith

[4] Francis Chan and Mark Beuving. *Multiply: Disciples Making Disciples.* Colorado Springs, CO: David C. Cook. 2012. Pg. 16-17.

[5] https://www.wordreference.com/definition/-ian

[6] https://www.blueletterbible.org/lang/lexicon/lexicon.cfm?Strongs=G40&t=KJV

[7] https://www.blueletterbible.org/lang/lexicon/lexicon.cfm?Strongs=G5485&t=KJV

[8] Neighbour, Ralph. *The Arrival Kit: A Guide for Your Journey in the Kingdom of God.* Houston, TX: TOUCH Publications. Pg. 16

[9] Neighbour. Pg. 14-19

[10] This idea is based on a psychological therapeutic model know as Behavioral Cognitive Therapy. The concepts are similar to what Apostle Paul taught in Romans 2; however, there are some differences. For a comparison, reference: https://biblical-counseling.com/resources/acbc-essays/cbt-therapist-us/

[11] Warren, Rick. *Preaching For Life Change Conference.* Pastors.com

[12] This list of substitute identities was developed over time. It was initially inspired by concepts presented in: Breen, Mike. "An Obituary for the American Church." Verge. http://www.vergenetwork.org/2012/02/02/obituary-for-the-american-church-mike-breen/

[13] https://www.blueletterbible.org/lang/lexicon/lexicon.cfm?Strongs=G1939&t=KJV

[14] Romans 12:2

[15] Breen, Mike. "An Obituary for the American Church." Verge. http://www.vergenetwork.org/2012/02/02/obituary-for-the-american-church-mike-breen/

[16] Matthew 4:4

17 Matthew 4:3

18 Galatians 2:20

19 Baker, John and Richard D. Warren. *Life's Healing Choices: Freedom from Your Hurts, Hang-ups, and Habits.* New York, NY: Howard Books, 2007. Pg. 20-22.

20 https://www.blueletterbible.org/lang/lexicon/lexicon.cfm?Strongs=G3339&t=KJV

21 Oxford Dictionaries Online: https://en.oxforddictionaries.com/definition/confess

22 Baker and Warren. Pg. 7

23 Baker, John. *Celebrate Recovery Updated Leader's Guide.* Grand Rapids, MI.: Zondervan. 1998. Pg. 12

24 Baker. Pg. 58-60.

25 Baker and Warren. Pg. 110-112

26 Baker. Principle 6

27 Baker and Warren. Pg.123

28 Warren, Rick. *The Purpose Driven Life: What on Earth Am I Here for?* Grand Rapids, MI: Zondervan, 2007. Pg. 218-220.

29 Baker and Warren. Pg. 110-112

30 Oxford Dictionaries Online: https://en.oxforddictionaries.com/definition/co-dependent

31 Warren. Pg. 181

32 Oxford Dictionaries Online: https://en.oxforddictionaries.com/definition/culture

33 Warren. Pg. 206

34 Several of the principles in this lesson were inspired by: Cloud, Henry. *9 Things You Simply Must Do To Succeed in Love and Life: A Psychologist Probes the Mysteries of Why Some Lives Really Work and Others Don't.* Nashville, TN: Integrity Pub., 2004.

35 Greek Dictionaries, Lexicons and Concordances available at www.blueletterbible.com were used in researching the original Greek words and definitions from these Scriptures.

Workbook 2: Freedom Checkpoint—Icon made by Roundicons from Flaticon is licensed by Creative Commons BY 3.0

Discover Discipleship Course

1. IDENTITY

2. FREEDOM

3. GROWTH

4. RELATIONSHIPS

5. MISSION

6. ALIGNMENT

For purchasing information and bulk discounts
go to discoverdiscipleship.com

Plug into learning at

MicrosoftPressStore.com

The Microsoft Press Store by Pearson offers:

- Free U.S. shipping

- Buy an eBook, get three formats – Includes PDF, EPUB, and MOBI to use with your computer, tablet, and mobile devices

- Print & eBook Best Value Packs

- eBook Deal of the Week – Save up to 50% on featured title

- Newsletter – Be the first to hear about new releases, announcements, special offers, and more

- Register your book – Find companion files, errata, and product updates, plus receive a special coupon* to save on your next purchase

 Pearson

Hear about it first.

Since 1984, Microsoft Press has helped IT professionals, developers, and home office users advance their technical skills and knowledge with books and learning resources.

Sign up today to deliver exclusive offers directly to your inbox.

- New products and announcements

- Free sample chapters

- Special promotions and discounts

- ... and more!

MicrosoftPressStore.com/newsletters

 Pearson